DECISIONS AT STONES RIVER

BOOKS BY MATT SPRUILL

The U. S. Army War College Guide to the Battle of Chickamauga

Storming the Heights: A Guide to the Battle of Chattanooga

Echoes of Thunder: A Guide to the Seven Days Battles
with Matt Spruill IV

Winter Lightning: A Guide to the Battle of Stones River
Second Edition, with Lee Spruill

*Summer Thunder: A Battlefield Guide to
the Artillery at Gettysburg*

*Decisions at Gettysburg: The Nineteen Critical Decisions
That Define the Gettysburg Campaign*

Summer Lightning: A Battlefield Guide to the Second Battle of Manassas
with Matt Spruill IV

DECISIONS
AT STONES RIVER

The Sixteen Critical Decisions
That Defined the Battle

Matt Spruill and Lee Spruill

Maps by Tim Kissel

COMMAND DECISIONS
IN AMERICA'S CIVIL WAR

The University of Tennessee Press / Knoxville

Names: Spruill, Matt, author. | Spruill, Lee.
Title: Decisions at Stones River: the sixteen critical decisions that defined
the battle / Matt Spruill and Lee Spruill; maps by Tim Kissel.
Description: First edition. | Knoxville: The University of Tennessee Press, 2018. |
Series: Command decisions in America's Civil War | Includes bibliographical
references and index. | Description based on print version record and CIP data
provided by publisher; resource not viewed.
Identifiers: LCCN 2017027913 (print) | LCCN 2017029765 (ebook) |
ISBN 9781621903796 (pdf) | ISBN 9781621903857 (Kindle) |
ISBN 9781621903789 (pbk.)
Subjects: LCSH: Stones River, Battle of, Murfreesboro, Tenn., 1862–1863. |
Command of troops—Case studies.
Classification: LCC E474.77 (ebook) | LCC E474.77.S679 2018 (print) |
DDC 973.7/33—dc23
LC record available at https://lccn.loc.gov/2017027913

*To our companions and partners
in all things, our wives,*

Kathy and Nicole

CONTENTS

ILLUSTRATIONS

Photographs

Maps

Diagrams

PREFACE

Our increased interest with the Battle of Stones River began when we were researching and writing *Winter Lightning: A Guide to the Battle of Stones River*. After several years of work we began to ask, "Now that we know what happened, why did it happen?" Were any actions or decisions so important that they influenced everything from that point on? Over time, we began to develop a list of decisions of such magnitude that had they not been made, the events at Stones River would have unfolded differently. These were critical decisions.

The chart on the next page shows the "Decisions Hierarchy." At the bottom are various "Decisions," above those is a lesser number of "Important Decisions," and at the top are a very few "Critical Decisions."

The criterion for a critical decision is that it is a decision of such magnitude that it shaped not only the events immediately following, but also the campaign or battle thereafter. Without these critical decisions, or in the event of other decisions the sequence of events for Stones River would have been significantly different.

The Battle of Stones River did not happen as a result of random chance. Events occurred as they did because of the decisions made at all levels of command on both sides. Some decisions were the normal ones that were made during any campaign or battle. Others were more important. A limited number of critical decisions shaped the way the campaign and battle unfolded.

It is important that you, the reader, understand the concept of a critical decision. Without this awareness, this book will appear to be only a short,

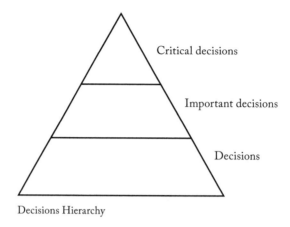

Decisions Hierarchy

selected narrative history of Stones River. Yet this book is not that. It is a work that explores the development of the battle and campaign and focuses on the *why* instead of the *what*.

Critical decisions will cover the entire spectrum of war: strategy, operations, tactics, organization, logistics, and personnel. Of the Stones River critical decisions four were operational, ten were tactical, and two were organizational. Some of the tactical decisions appeared to be minor but had far-reaching consequences upon the battle. Had the sixteen critical decisions not been made, the character of the battle and the decisions that followed would have been different. The difference would have been so great as to change the sequence and course of events of the Battle of Stones River.

Sixteen critical decisions for the Battle of Stones River are grouped into three specific time periods:

> Before the Battle
> > Confederate Army Reorganized
> > Bragg Loses a Division
> > Bragg Orders the Cavalry to Raid
> > Rosecrans Moves South
> > Bragg Decides to Concentrate at Murfreesboro
> > Harker is Recalled
>
> The Armies Collide—Wednesday, December 31, 1862
> > Bragg Decides to Attack Rosecrans's Right Flank
> > Bragg Fails to Significantly Weight the Main Attack
> > Rosecrans Cancels His Attack

The critical decisions were chosen based on our military background and education, experience on the ground at Stones River, and extensive reading of primary and secondary sources. Depending on their training and background, other historians might choose different decisions and interpret important events in different ways. However, we firmly believe that this book enumerates the sixteen critical decisions of the campaign and the battle.

This is not to say that alternate choices would have made Maj. Gen. William S. Rosecrans the vanquished and Gen. Braxton Bragg the victor. Though it might have happened that way, such speculation is beyond the scope of this book. We leave it to the reader to decide if the result would have been different. However, the sequence of events leading to the outcome would have been different, and the orientation of the opposing forces may have been different. The battle could have lasted for two days or four days rather than three. And it may have occurred away from Murfreesboro rather than in close proximity to the town.

The possibility of chance or luck cannot be ruled out. These factors can make an apparently good decision produce a bad result. Likewise, what initially appears to be a bad decision can sometimes produce a positive result. While our bias occasionally appears, we have attempted to refrain from identifying decisions as good or bad. Instead, we have concentrated on the consequences of each decision and discussed how it affected the campaign or battle.

This is not another history covering all events and decisions of the Battle of Stones River. Instead, out of the hundreds of decisions made at all levels of command, this work discusses the sixteen that had the greatest impact on the battle. It is not our purpose to offer a brand-new interpretive history of the battle, but rather to lay out some basic facts and present a relatively clear outline of a complex situation. Without neglecting important details, this account is designed to present the reader with a coherent and manageable blueprint as to why the battle developed and followed the course that it did.

We propose that once you know what happened the next question is, why did it happen? Asking that question and using the critical decision methodology will provide the reader a new look at the Battle of Stones River. The discussion of each critical decision is presented generally in the following format: the situation, the options available to the decision-maker, the decision made, the results/outcome of the decision, and other possible outcomes had another decision been chosen. This methodology can also be applied to any other campaign or battle in any war.

As you read you will notice that the Union and the Confederacy used similar, but often different, methods to identify units. Therefore, some explanatory comments are appropriate. Both sides used the same method to identify units at the company, battalion, and regimental level. Companies were identified by a letter—e.g., A Company. Regiments and battalions were usually identified by a number—e.g., Fifty-ninth (or 59th) Illinois, Eighth (or 8th) Tennessee. Above regimental level, both sides diverged in how units were identified.

The official designations of Union brigades, divisions, and corps were numeric and begin with a capital letter. Examples include First Brigade, First Division, Right Wing or Col. P. Sidney Post's First Brigade, Brig. Gen. Jefferson C. Davis's First Division, Maj. Gen. Alexander McD. McCook's Right Wing (later a corps). When referring to a brigade or division belonging to or commanded by an individual, lowercase letters are used. For example, Post's brigade, Davis's division, or McCook's wing.

Early in the war the Confederacy used a numbering and a name system for unit designations. As the war progressed, the numbering system was used less and the name system was most commonly used. The official designations of Confederate brigades, divisions, and corps were the commanders' names followed by Brigades, Divisions, or Corps. For example, Donelson's Brigade, Cheatham's Division, or Polk's Corps.

The Confederate system can sometimes be confusing. The unit officially designated Smith's Brigade at Stones River had earlier been commanded by Brig. Gen. Preston Smith—hence its official designation. At Stones River it was commanded by Col. Alfred J. Vaughan, but it was not called Vaughan's Brigade as the designation was officially Smith's Brigade. Lowercase letters are used when referring to a brigade, division, or corps belonging to or commanded by an individual. Examples include Brig. Gen. Daniel S. Donelson's brigade, Maj. Gen. Benjamin F. Cheatham's division, or Lieut. Gen. Leonidas Polk's corps. As with anything pertaining to the Civil War, there are always exceptions.

There is value in being in close proximity to the place where a decision was made or carried out. You have the opportunity to view the terrain and the tactical situation as the decision-maker did. This in itself provides valuable insights. In some cases this is not feasible—for instance, if you are at Stones River and a decision was made in Nashville or somewhere else away from the battlefield. However, most of the critical decisions were made and carried out at or near Stones River/Murfreesboro. We have included an appendix with a battlefield driving tour that will place you on the ground near where critical decisions were made or carried out. Excerpts from the *Official Records* are included in the tour. Today, some words are spelled differently than they were in 1863—for example, *entrenchments* rather than *intrenchments*. We have left the spelling and grammar as it appears in the original documents.

This brief guide has the specific, practical purpose of helping a reasonably well-informed reader get through the battle *on the ground* and gain further insights into the battle and the effects of the critical decisions. The interpretive elements are designed to support the parts of the book that are more like a traditional guidebook.

We hope this book with its battlefield guide appendix will form a foundation for further reading, study, and reflection on the Battle at Stones River.

ACKNOWLEDGMENTS

We wish to thank Dr. Timothy Smith and Ranger Jim Lewis, who also read our first book on Stones River, *Winter Lightning*, for reading this manuscript and providing many valuable comments and suggestions. We are especially indebted to living historian Frank Wood, who portrays John Mendenhall—chief of artillery for the Left Wing, Army of the Cumberland—for valuable assistance in researching that officer.

Thanks also to Scot Danforth, director of University of Tennessee Press, and his exceptional team who have guided and supported us through the publication and marketing process. Among them are Thomas Wells, Stephanie Thompson, Jon Boggs, and Tom Post; again, we extend our deepest thanks. A big thanks to Betsy Crowder for the excellent copy editing and refining of this book.

As always, our wives and best friends, Kathy and Nicole, provided constant support and encouragement as this work developed from concept to book.

Matt Spruill
Littleton, Colorado

Lee Spruill
Red Oak, Texas

INTRODUCTION

The Civil War year of 1862 began as one of promise for the Union. In the Eastern and Western Theaters, Union forces were poised to strike deadly blows into and against the Confederacy.

In the East, a division-size force under Union Brig. Gen. Ambrose E. Burnside landed inside the North Carolina Outer Banks and secured a lodgment from which future operations into eastern North Carolina and southeastern Virginia could be conducted. In March the revitalized and reorganized Army of the Potomac, under the command of Maj. Gen. George B. McClellan, used sea power to conduct a turning movement against the Confederate army in northern Virginia, landing on the Peninsula. McClellan then began a campaign up the Peninsula to capture the Confederate capital of Richmond. Although movement was not as rapid as planned, by the middle of June McClelland's army was on the eastern outskirts of Richmond. It appeared that it was only a matter of time before the city, a major manufacturing center, would fall into Union hands.[1]

In the far West, a small Confederate army under the command of Brig. Gen. Henry H. Sibley marched from west Texas into New Mexico and then north toward Colorado. Repelled by a Union force at Glorieta Pass, near Santa Fe, in late March, Sibley retreated back to Texas. This expedition ended the Confederacy's only serious attempt to expand its borders on the southwest frontier.[2]

In southwest Missouri Confederate hopes of adding that state to the eleven that had previously seceded were checked at the Battle of Wilson's Creek (August 10, 1861) and the Battle of Pea Ridge (March 7–8, 1862).[3]

In the Western Theater Union armies and naval forces gained early and decisive victories. Middle Tennessee was opened, and the Confederate defensive line from the mountains west to the Mississippi River was broken. Fort Henry on the Tennessee River was captured on February 6. Ten days later, Brig. Gen. Ulysses S. Grant captured Fort Donelson on the Cumberland River. These developments were followed by Grant's early April victory at Shiloh and the Union navy's April 25 capture of New Orleans, the Confederacy's largest city.[4]

By late summer the euphoria from these victories was gone as Confederate armies went on the offensive and diminished early Union victories. In the last summer months of 1862 the Confederacy was riding the crest of a wave that could fulfill Southerners' dream of independence.

In Virginia Gen. Robert E. Lee, newly appointed to command the Confederate army around Richmond (which he renamed the Army of Northern Virginia), unleashed a turning movement against McClellan. During the Seven Days Battles (June 25 to July 1), Lee drove McClellan away from Richmond and eventually caused his army to depart the Peninsula. Lee's subsequent brilliant campaign of maneuver transferred the center of conflict to northern Virginia. At the Second Battle of Manassas (Bull Run) he soundly defeated Union Maj. Gen. John Pope's Army of Virginia.[5]

Capitalizing on this success, Lee's army began crossing the Potomac River into Maryland on September 4. Once his line of communication to the Shenandoah Valley and Virginia was secured, Lee planned to advance into Pennsylvania by way of the Cumberland Valley. One of Lee's objectives was to influence the 1862 US congressional elections in favor of politicians more sympathetic to the Confederacy and opposed to the war.[6]

On September 17, thirteen days after beginning the invasion, Lee's army fought the Army of the Potomac near Antietam Creek. This was the bloodiest day in American history. Although the Battle of Antietam was a tactical draw, Lee elected to end his campaign; his army recrossed the Potomac River and returned to Virginia. Lee finished the year with the dramatic defeat of the Army of the Potomac, now commanded by Maj. Gen. Ambrose E. Burnside, at Fredericksburg, Virginia, in mid-December.[7]

In the West the bright earlier Union successes began to dim. Grant commenced his offensive to capture Vicksburg, Mississippi, and open the Mississippi River in the first week of November. After suffering reverses at Holly Springs and Chickasaw Bluffs in December, Grant terminated his initial operations and developed new avenues of approach.[8]

In late summer a two-pronged Confederate offense was launched into Kentucky. Maj. Gen. Edmund Kirby Smith led his Army of Kentucky north from Knoxville, Tennessee, and reached Lexington, Kentucky, on September 1. Gen. Braxton Bragg's Army of the Mississippi joined this campaign on August 28, traveling to Kentucky from Chattanooga, Tennessee. Bragg's army reached Bardstown, Kentucky, on September 23.[9]

Strong Confederate forces in Kentucky could have significant adverse consequences for the Union. Maintaining an army or armies on the Ohio River would bring the South three major strategic advantages. First, Kentucky would become part of the Confederacy, if not through secession, then through occupation. This development would open access to considerable amounts of food, livestock, and horses. Secondly, a Confederate Kentucky would provide a strategic buffer on Tennessee's northern border and protect the critically important "Heartland" (more on this later). Thirdly, Confederate forces on the Ohio River would be able to interdict a vital river transportation route between the eastern and western Union. However, before these advantages could be realized, Union and Confederate armies fought the Battle of Perryville on October 8, 1862.

Maj. Gen. Don Carlos Buell's Army of the Ohio followed Bragg into Kentucky, slipped around him, and reached Louisville on September 29. On October 1, Buell's army departed Louisville to locate and attack the Confederate forces. In the meantime, Bragg had ordered his army and Kirby Smith's army to concentrate in the Harrodsburg-Perryville area. As Buell approached Perryville, Bragg seized the initiative and attacked on October 8, even though his force was not concentrated. Buell's mismanagement of the battle prevented him from gaining a significant victory, and some parts of the North considered the episode a Union defeat. However, Bragg's and Smith's armies retreated back to Tennessee and eventually took up positions south of Nashville.[10]

Historian Thomas L. Connelly named the area of Tennessee, north-central Alabama, north-central Georgia, and north-east Mississippi "the Heartland." The region's northern boundary was a 400-mile line that went east from Columbus, Kentucky, to Bristol, Tennessee. The 365-mile eastern boundary reached south from Bristol, Tennessee, to Macon, Georgia. The southern boundary extended 210 miles west from Macon to Selma, Alabama, then continued on for 195 miles to Jackson, Mississippi. The western boundary reached 345 miles north from Jackson to Columbus. This 150,000-square-mile area was the Confederacy's geographical, logistical, and communicational Heartland.[11]

Within the Heartland were ironworks, munitions factories, gun powder mills, copper mines, other production facilities, and raw materials necessary to sustain the war effort. The area's fertile farmland provided significant quantities of food, livestock, horses, and mules.[12]

Railroads crossed the area and connected the Confederacy east to west and the western Confederacy north to south. There were three major rail junctions where north-to-south and east-to-west railroads intersected: Corinth, Mississippi; Atlanta, Georgia; and Chattanooga, Tennessee. At Grand Junction, Tennessee; Jackson, Mississippi; and Meridian, Mississippi there were secondary rail junctions. These railroads provided a capability to shift troop units laterally and served as lines of supply and communication for invading and defending armies.[13]

Important rivers flowed throughout the Heartland. On its western edge was the Mississippi River. Within were the Tennessee, Cumberland, Alabama, Chattahoochee, and Coosa Rivers. These rivers provided a means to move a large amount of troops and supplies. The Tennessee and Cumberland were direct avenues of approach into the Heartland.[14]

The loss of all or part of this area would deprive the Confederacy of a vast source of material, livestock, and food. In addition, such a loss would split the South in two and have a devastating effect on Southern morale.

The key strategic objective within the Heartland was Atlanta, Georgia. Located 254 miles south of Nashville, Atlanta was one of the Confederacy's most important population centers. This Deep South city was a major junction point with railroad lines radiating to the four points of the compass. In addition, it was a vital manufacturing and supply center, providing clothing, food, and weapons to the armies of the Confederacy. The capture of this strategic objective would cut all east-west rail communications across the Confederacy, split the Heartland in two, and critically reduce, or even halt, production and gathering of many valuable war-sustaining resources.[15]

The most direct, and practical, avenue of approach for a Union army invading the Heartland to capture Atlanta would be along the Nashville-Chattanooga-Atlanta axis. Chattanooga, an interim strategic objective, was a vital supply base for any army advancing into northern Georgia. It was also a major east-west railroad center; its capture would cut communications with Virginia and the upper Heartland. A Union army in northern Middle Tennessee using Nashville as a forward supply base would have two options for an advance to Chattanooga. The first was the Nashville-Murfreesboro-Tullahoma-Stevenson-Chattanooga axis. This 133-mile avenue of approach was the most direct route, and the Nashville-Chattanooga Railroad provided a supply and communications link to the Nashville base. The second option was the Knoxville-Chattanooga axis. Before the advance could be attempted, however, the army would have to move from Kentucky through the Cumberland Gap and into Eastern Tennessee. Although providing the relief to a loyal Union population that Lincoln wanted, it was the most difficult avenue of approach for a

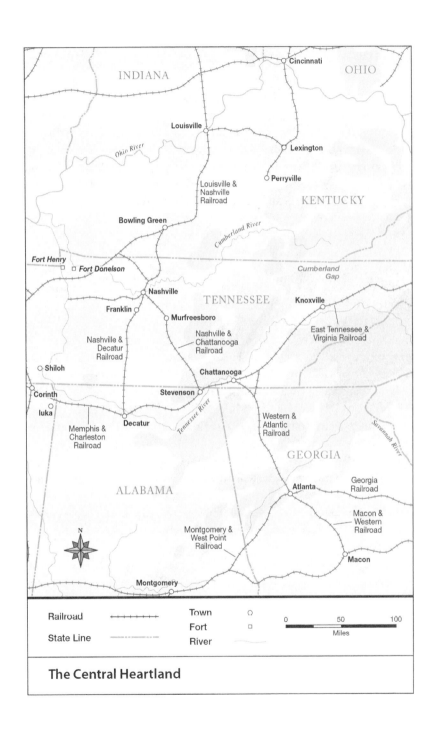

INDIANA

OHIO

Cincinnati

Louisville

Lexington

Louisville &
Nashville
Railroad

Perryville

KENTUCKY

Ohio River

Bowling Green

Cumberland River

Fort Henry

Fort Donelson

Cumberland
Gap

Nashville

TENNESSEE

Knoxville

Franklin

Murfreesboro

East Tennessee &
Virginia Railroad

Nashville &
Decatur
Railroad

Nashville &
Chattanooga
Railroad

Shiloh

Chattanooga

Corinth

Stevenson

Tennessee River

Iuka

Decatur

Memphis &
Charleston
Railroad

Western &
Atlantic
Railroad

Savannah River

GEORGIA

ALABAMA

Georgia
Railroad

Atlanta

Macon &
Western
Railroad

N

Montgomery &
West Point
Railroad

Macon

Montgomery

Railroad	+++++++	Town	○	0	50	100
State Line	- - - - -	Fort	□		Miles	
		River				

The Central Heartland

large force. The logical decision for any Union army commander was the more direct avenue of approach to Chattanooga. Using Chattanooga as a forward supply base, an incursion of 119 miles into northern Georgia would lead to the strategic objective of Atlanta.[16]

As the year drew to a close, Bragg's newly named Army of the Tennessee and what would shortly become the Union Army of the Cumberland, previously the Army of the Ohio, now under the command of Maj. Gen. William S. Rosecrans, fought a bloody battle along Stones River from December 31, 1862, to January 2, 1863. Although hard-pressed at first, Rosecrans would eventually win the Battle of Stones River. Bragg would retreat farther south toward Chattanooga. Coming at the end of a series of Union defeats, this victory would give Lincoln and the Northern population a bright ray of hope during a fall and winter of Confederate victories.

The Confederate army at Stones River came into existence in the spring of 1862 as the Army of the Mississippi. Gen. Albert S. Johnston concentrated Confederate forces at Corinth, Mississippi, for an attack on Grant's army at Shiloh (Pittsburg Landing). Johnston was killed at Shiloh, and his deputy, Gen. P. G. T. Beauregard, took command and ordered the army back to Corinth. Shortly thereafter, Gen. Braxton Bragg replaced Beauregard as the army commander. In mid-July, Bragg began transferring his army to Chattanooga. From Chattanooga, in conjunction with Maj. Gen. Kirby Smith's Army of Kentucky, he began offensive maneuvering, which became an invasion of Kentucky ending at Perryville. After the Battle of Perryville, Bragg and Smith retreated from Kentucky to Middle Tennessee. On November 20, Smith's army was absorbed into Bragg's, which was renamed the Army of Tennessee. Bragg brought 37,712 soldiers to Stones River.[17]

The Union army that came to Stones River was the Army of the Cumberland. It was constituted on November 15, 1861, under the command of Maj. Gen. Don Carlos Buell as the Army of the Ohio. Under Buell's command the army fought at Shiloh, pursued Bragg and Smith into Kentucky, and fought in the Battle of Perryville.[18]

Major General Rosecrans replaced Buell on October 30, and the army was renamed the Fourteenth Corps, with three wings: Left, Center, and Right. Unofficial practice was to call it the Army of the Cumberland, and seven days after the Battle of Stones River this became the army's official title. Throughout this book we have used this name for Rosecrans's force. Rosecrans had 43,400 soldiers at Stones River.[19]

Normally, Civil War armies ceased major operations during the winter months. Unfavorable road conditions made it difficult, if not impossible, to move ammunition, supply wagons, and artillery. Even marching large formations of soldiers was a challenge. Bragg was preparing to place his army in winter quarters and thought that Rosecrans was doing the same at Nashville. When Rosecrans marched his army south out of Nashville, he caught Bragg by surprise.[20]

The marching and fighting occurred in the most adverse weather conditions of any Civil War battle. When the Army of the Cumberland marched from Nashville on December 26, it was moving in a cold rain. From that day until the end of the battle, and during all but one day of Bragg's retreat, weather conditions included early morning cold mist or fog, rain that sometimes turned to sleet, and nighttime temperatures close to or at the freezing mark. Under these circumstances, roads became quagmires of mud during the day and froze over at night.[21]

The three-day Battle of Stones River that began on New Year's Eve 1862 involved multiple maneuvers. This complex engagement was the eighth most costly of the Civil War. Stones River began a twenty-two-month odyssey that took the Army of the Cumberland and the Army of Tennessee from north Tennessee through Middle Tennessee to Chickamauga and Chattanooga and eventually to Atlanta, Georgia. During this period, vital territory and resources were captured by the Union. The South's capability for making and sustaining war was drastically reduced, almost to the point of nonexistence. These developments all commenced with the Union success at Stones River.[22]

CHAPTER 1

BEFORE THE BATTLE

If you have bypassed the preface, please return there and read the definition of a critical decision to fully understand the presentations in this book.

Six critical decisions were made before the armies joined in battle at Stones River. These choices about organization and maneuvers set the stage and created the conditions that brought Maj. Gen. William S. Rosecrans's Army of the Cumberland and Gen. Braxton Bragg's Army of Tennessee to fight a decisive battle. This encounter would initiate the Union penetration into the center of the Heartland.

Confederate Army Reorganized

Situation

The invasion of Kentucky was conducted by two separate Confederate armies, Maj. Gen. Edmund Kirby Smith's Army of Kentucky and Gen. Braxton Bragg's Army of the Mississippi. Smith's army was composed of twelve infantry brigades organized into four divisions, three cavalry brigades, and fourteen artillery batteries attached to the infantry brigades. Smith's strength was approximately 23,000 men. Bragg's army was composed of twelve infantry brigades, organized into three divisions, two cavalry brigades, and twelve artillery batteries attached to the infantry brigades. Bragg commanded approximately 27,000 men.[1]

After the Battle of Perryville on October 8, 1862, Bragg's and Smith's armies began maneuvering away from Maj. Gen. Don Carlos Buell's Union Army of the Ohio. By October 13, the Armies of Kentucky and the Mississippi had begun to retreat from Kentucky back to Tennessee. Their route took them southeast through the Cumberland Gap into Eastern Tennessee, south to Knoxville, and then southwest to Chattanooga. From Chattanooga the Confederate forces moved northwest into Middle Tennessee with advance elements at Murfreesboro. Occupying positions in Middle Tennessee allowed troops to gather food and forage in the Stones, Duck, and Elk River Valleys. It also positioned Confederate forces to block any Union advance from Nashville to Chattanooga along the route of the Nashville and Chattanooga Railroad.[2]

The operations in Kentucky had shown the weakness in having two separate armies, with neither commander having overall command, operating in close proximity to each other. If combined, these two forces would have had an approximate strength of 50,000 soldiers, sufficient for a possible Confederate victory at Perryville. In addition, such a force maneuvering in a coordinated fashion in central Kentucky would have presented Union commanders with a more powerful threat than two uncoordinated and separate forces. This absence of unity of command was allowed to exist while both armies were in Kentucky and through October and into November when they returned to Tennessee.

The situation now facing the Confederate government, particularly Jefferson Davis, was whether to keep the armies separate or combine them into one unit. Leaving two armies near one another in Tennessee would continue a fragmented force structure that would hinder, or even prevent, the full use of Confederate forces in the state. Although Davis might hope for future cooperation and/or coordination between the two commanders, past experience indicated this probably would not happen. In a letter dated November 3, 1862, Bragg pointed out this problem to Gen. Samuel Cooper, the Confederate adjutant general: "The force I shall be enabled to carry to Middle Tennessee from the Army of the Mississippi will be inadequate. Having been unable to see Lieutenant-General Smith, I cannot say how far he will co-operate with me, but I submit whether movements involving so much should be left to the uncertainty of two officers agreeing in their views, however much the Government may confide in them or they in each other."[3]

Options

Two options were available to President Davis. He could allow both armies to be independent commands, or he could combine the two units into one.

Option 1

Davis could choose to leave Bragg's and Smith's forces distinct from one another and hope that the commanders would develop some form of effective collaboration. Past events suggested that effective coordination and cooperation between the two commanders was unlikely. This decision would leave two armies of less-than-optimal strength operating in proximity to each other, and it would do nothing to unify command.

Option 2

The two armies could be combined into one under the command of the senior of the two commanders. The other officer could be placed in a subordinate role or transferred to a new assignment away from the army. This decision would create a force of sufficient strength to confront the Union army taking position at Nashville. In addition, a unified command would be established over Confederate field forces in central Tennessee.

Decision

Davis chose the second of the two options. On November 20, 1862, Bragg issued General Order 151 combining his Army of the Mississippi and Smith's Army of Kentucky into the Army of Tennessee, a name the army would keep for the remainder of the war. This order also commenced the deployment of the entire army into Middle Tennessee.[4]

President Jefferson Davis, CSA.
National Archives.

Results/Impact

The Army of Tennessee was organized into three corps named after their commanders: Polk's, Hardee's and Smith's. In the initial organization Lieut. Gen. Leonidas Polk's corps was composed of three infantry divisions, Maj. Gen. Benjamin F. Cheatham's of four brigades, Maj. Gen. Jones M. Withers's of four brigades, and Maj. Gen. John C. Breckinridge's of three brigades. Lieut. Gen. William J. Hardee's corps consisted of two divisions, Maj. Gen. Simon B. Buckner's of four brigades, and Brig. Gen. James Patton Anderson's of four brigades. Lieut. Gen. (promoted from October 9, 1862) Edmund Kirby Smith's corps consisted of two divisions, Maj. Gen. Carter L. Stevenson's of three brigades, and Maj. Gen. John P. McCown's of three brigades.[5]

In mid-December one of Bragg's divisions was sent to Mississippi to reinforce Lieut. Gen. John C. Pemberton (more on this later). The loss of this division precipitated further army reorganization. At its completion the Army of Tennessee had the organizational and command structure with which it would fight at Stones River.[6]

Maj. Gen. Carter L. Stevenson's division of Smith's two division corps was selected to go to Pemberton. This left only one division in the corps, and Kirby Smith, now a lieutenant general, requested to be reassigned. This was done with Smith returning to East Tennessee and then going on to the Trans-Mississippi Department. Smith's Corps ceased to exist when the re-

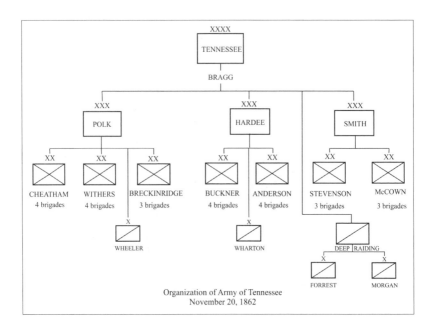

Organization of Army of Tennessee
November 20, 1862

maining division, Maj. Gen. John P. McCown's, was assigned to Hardee's Corps. In addition, Brig. Gen. James Patton Anderson's division was broken up and the brigades, and in some instances the individual regiments, were reassigned throughout the army.[7]

In its reorganized form the Army of Tennessee was composed of two infantry corps. Polk's Corps now contained two divisions rather than three, as Breckinridge's Division was reassigned to Hardee's Corps. Polk's two divisions were Cheatham's and Withers's. Cheatham's Division kept the four brigades that it previously had. Withers's Division also maintained a four-brigade strength, but one of its brigades had gone to Breckinridge's Division while Jones's Brigade from Anderson's Division, now under the command of Brig. Gen. James Patton Anderson, and some individual regiments replaced it. Hardee's Corps increased in size from two to three divisions when Breckinridge's Division was assigned from Polk's Corps. Breckinridge's Division increased in size from three to five brigades. Hanson's, Palmer's and Walker's (now Preston's) Brigades remained with the division. In addition, Adams's Brigade from Anderson's old division was assigned to Breckinridge, and Jackson's Brigade from Withers's Division was temporarily attached. Buckner left his division and was replaced by Maj. Gen. Patrick R. Cleburne, while Brig. Gen. Lucius E. Polk assumed command of Cleburne's old brigade. McCown's Division from Smith's Corps was transferred to Hardee.

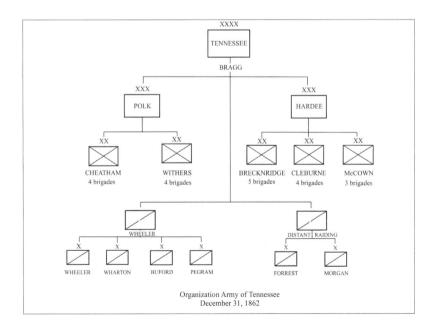

Organization Army of Tennessee
December 31, 1862

McCown brought two of his original three brigades and received Rains's Brigade from Stevenson's Division before it was transferred farther west.[8]

There was no major reorganization of the artillery. Both armies had followed the concept of placing an artillery battery with each infantry brigade; this practice was continued.

Although there had been some discussion on replacing Bragg, Davis decided that he would remain in Tennessee and, as the senior ranking officer, command the Army of Tennessee. A class of 1837 US Military Academy graduate, Bragg was forty-five years old during the Battle of Stones River. Prior to the Civil War he had fought against the Seminoles and in the Mexican War. In 1856 he resigned his commission and became a planter in Louisiana. Bragg joined the Confederate army as a brigadier general in March 1861. He was promoted to major general in September 1861 and to general in April 1862. After the Battle of Shiloh, Bragg replaced P. G. T. Beauregard as commander of the Army of the Mississippi, and he led that unit's invasion of Kentucky in the late summer. After the Battle of Perryville, Bragg ordered his army to retreat back to Tennessee, where in November he was placed in command of the newly formed Army of Tennessee. After his defeat at Chattanooga, Bragg was relieved at his own request and became a military advisor to Jefferson Davis. Toward the end of the war he served in North Carolina. After the war Bragg lived in Alabama and in Galveston, Texas, where he died in 1876.[9]

General Braxton Bragg, CSA, Commanding Army of Tennessee. Library of Congress.

Lieutenant General Leonidas Polk, CSA,
commanding corps. Library of Congress.

Bragg had Lieut. Gens. Leonidas Polk and William J. Hardee to command the two corps. Polk, fifty-six years old when the Battle of Stones River occurred, was a graduate of the US Military Academy's class of 1827. Upon graduation he resigned his commission, entered the Episcopal ministry, and eventually became the missionary bishop of the Southwest and the bishop of Louisiana. Upon the war's outbreak, Polk joined the Confederate army as a major general and was promoted to lieutenant general in October 1862. In September 1861 he precipitated a political crisis when his troops occupied neutral Columbus, Kentucky. Polk was a corps commander at Shiloh and Perryville. After Stones River he led a corps at Chickamauga and was relieved by Bragg, but he rejoined the army as a corps commander at the beginning of the Atlanta Campaign. Polk was killed on June 14, 1864, by artillery fire at Pine Mountain near Marietta, Georgia. Though he was brave and his troops respected and liked him, Polk's tactical ability left much to be desired. He was also the chief architect of opposition to Bragg's authority within the army, helping to create a sense of distrust and contention in the senior leadership.[10]

Hardee, who was forty-seven years old when he fought in the Battle of Stones River, graduated from the US Military Academy in 1838. He saw service in the Mexican-American War, studied at the French cavalry school, served on the frontier, served as commandant of cadets at West Point, and

Lieutenant General William J. Hardee, CSA,
commanding corps. Library of Congress.

updated US Army tactics when he wrote *Rifle and Light Infantry Tactics*. When Hardee's home state of Georgia seceded from the Union he resigned his commission, and in June 1861 he was appointed a brigadier general in the Confederate army. He was promoted to major general in October 1861 and then to lieutenant general in October 1862. Hardee fought at the Battles of Shiloh and Perryville. After Stones River he left the Army of Tennessee, but he rejoined it as a corps commander in late 1863 for the battles at Chattanooga and the Atlanta Campaign. In the last months of the war he served in Georgia, South Carolina, and North Carolina. Hardee was a planter in Alabama after the war, and he died in 1873. The more tactically proficient of the two corps commanders, Hardee became a harsh critic of Bragg and helped fuel the constant bickering among the senior leadership of their army.[11]

Having reorganized his infantry with its attached artillery, Bragg proceeded to reorganize his cavalry. Prior to invading Kentucky, Bragg had grouped his cavalry into brigades and assigned them to each infantry corps. Kirby Smith had done the same in his army. When the two armies combined, Bragg organized his cavalry to accomplish two separate functions. One cavalry organization was to remain with the army and perform the traditional roles of reconnaissance, guard missions, economy-of-force missions, and close-in raiding. The other cavalry organization was to conduct raiding operations deep in the enemy's rear areas. To accomplish the traditional missions Bragg formed two brigades under the command of Brig. Gen. Joseph Wheeler and Col. John Wharton. These brigades were attached to Polk's and Hardee's corps. To carry out the deep raiding missions Bragg formed two brigades under Brig. Gen. Nathan B. Forrest and Col. John H. Morgan. These two units remained under direct army command and control and were sent out to attack supply and communication lines deep in the Union rear areas.[12]

In the December reorganization of his army Bragg further reorganized his cavalry. Forrest's and Morgan's brigades were still under army command and control for deep raiding operations. Wheeler's and Wharton's Brigades were removed from the infantry corps, and two small brigades under Brig. Gens. Abraham Buford and John Pegram were added to them. All four of these brigades were placed under the command of Brig. Gen. Joseph Wheeler, a newly selected chief of cavalry.[13]

Joseph Wheeler was twenty-six at the time of the Battle of Stones River. An 1859 graduate of the US Military Academy, he resigned his commission in April 1861 to serve the Confederacy. He then fought at Shiloh as an infantry colonel and transferred to the cavalry. Wheeler was the chief of cavalry for the Army of the Mississippi during Bragg's invasion of Kentucky. Promoted to brigadier general in October 1862, he became the chief of cavalry of the newly created Army of Tennessee and commanded at Stones River. Promoted to major general in January 1863, Wheeler continued with the cavalry in the

Brigadier General Joseph Wheeler, CSA, commanding cavalry. Library of Congress.

Chickamauga, Chattanooga, and Atlanta Campaigns and during Sherman's March to the Sea. After the war he was elected to Congress for eight terms, and he served as a major general of US Volunteers in the Spanish-American War. Wheeler died in 1906.[14]

The combining of Bragg's Army of the Mississippi and Kirby Smith's Army of Kentucky into the Army of Tennessee resulted in an army that was capable of deploying and potentially defending Middle Tennessee and the Nashville-Chattanooga-Atlanta avenue of approach into the Confederacy. This avenue of approach went deep into Southern territory and was of major strategic value. The continuation of two separate armies, even with the improbable hope that the commanders would work together and combine forces at a critically threatened location, was unacceptable from the beginning. Not only did this arrangement violate the principle of unity of command, but it also ensured that the individual armies would have insufficient strength to confront Union advances into their areas of operations.

The combining of both armies under one commander created the capability to position a stronger Confederate force astride the Union's primary avenue of advance. This would at least provide the potential for any Union movement to be halted before it penetrated deep into strategically vital Middle Tennessee. Had the Army of Tennessee not been created from the two smaller armies, there would have been insufficient combat power to challenge a Union advance south from Nashville. Under this condition, if Bragg had remained at Murfreesboro he would have risked having his army either destroyed or rendered combat ineffective by a much stronger Union army. A more practical scenario was that upon commencement of the Union advance, Bragg would have been forced to retreat south and await reinforcements. In this scenario there would have been no Battle of Stones River.

The final organization of the Army of Tennessee before the Battle of Stones River was to have far-reaching consequences. The army's organization determined how Bragg developed his plan of attack, scheme of maneuver, and allocation of combat power. These decisions flowed from the organizational decision and had a further effect on how the battle was fought. Having created this army and positioned it to protect a strategic avenue of approach, the Confederate government proceeded to weaken it by permanently detaching one division and sending it farther west. This was the next critical decision.

Bragg Loses a Division

Beginning with this critical decision you will find one of those connecting threads that runs throughout any battle or campaign. This decision is directly linked to Bragg's critical decision on the allocation of combat power for his December 31 attack. The connection continues on to Rosecrans's critical decision to shift units from his left to his right. Throughout this book you will find other connecting threads that will directly join critical decisions.

Situation

Soon after the combining of Bragg's and Smith's armies into the Army of Tennessee, events occurred that caused a reduction of Bragg's new three-corps army and resulted in the reorganization into a two-corps army. Two hundred and twenty-five miles southwest of Murfreesboro, Maj. Gen. Ulysses S. Grant's Army of the Tennessee commenced offensive operations into Mississippi with the objective of capturing Vicksburg and giving the Union control of the Mississippi River. Union victories at Iuka (September 19) and Corinth (October 3 and 4) gave Grant control of the east-west Memphis-Charleston Railroad, the Mobile and Ohio Railroad north of Corinth, and supply depots on the Tennessee and Mississippi Rivers. Using these supply depots and the connecting railroads, he established a large forward supply depot at Holly Springs, just south of the Tennessee-Mississippi state boundary. With this supply base and the Memphis depot, Grant devised a two-pronged converging maneuver to capture Vicksburg.[15]

Grant planned for a force under his command to proceed south along the Mississippi Central Railroad to Grenada and Jackson and then turn west and move directly on Vicksburg. At the same time, a second force under Maj. Gen. William T. Sherman would proceed south paralleling the Mississippi River. Sherman and his men would use the river and secondary waterways to attack Vicksburg from the north.[16]

To counter the Union threat against Vicksburg, Lieut. Gen. John C. Pemberton was ordered from South Carolina to Mississippi to command the Department of Mississippi and Eastern Louisiana, which included Vicksburg. Confronted by Grant's advance, Pemberton ordered his forces in north-central Mississippi to retreat fifteen miles south and establish new positions along the Tallahatchie River. As he retreated, Pemberton called for reinforcements.[17]

Lieut. Gen. Theophilus H. Holmes's Trans-Mississippi Department, which bordered the west bank of the Mississippi River, was the obvious source of reinforcements for Pemberton. Due to personality clashes, petty arguments, miscommunications, and poorly written orders, Holmes did not send any troops east across the river to support Pemberton. To solve this problem, Davis began to seriously consider sending a division from Bragg's army to Vicksburg.[18]

Options

Davis had two options. He could do nothing and rely upon cavalry raids to destroy Grant's supply base and supply lines, thereby forcing Grant to cancel his offensive and fall back. Additionally, Davis could order Bragg to send troops to Pemberton at Vicksburg.

Option 1

Bragg already had Forrest's Brigade conducting a raid against Union supply lines in Western Tennessee. Morgan's Brigade was preparing to raid Union supply lines in Kentucky. In addition, it was known that Maj. Gen. Earl Van Dorn with a large cavalry force was raiding Grant's rear area and approaching the Union supply base at Holly Springs. Davis could defer sending troops to Pemberton until the raids were complete to see if they had the desired effect.

Option 2

Davis could order Bragg to detach a division-size force from his army and send it to Pemberton. Doing so would seriously weaken Bragg's army at the same time that Rosecrans's army was near Nashville.

Decision

When Bragg and Gen. Joseph Johnston, the department commander, were informed of Davis's intentions to reduce the Army of Tennessee by one division they pointed out that Grant's offensive operations could be stopped by cavalry raids on his supply lines and supply depots. Johnston and Bragg estimated that Maj. Gen. William S. Rosecrans's Union army had 65,000 troops at Nashville and another 35,000 positioned along the railroad from Nashville to Louisville for a total strength of 100,000. Neither these figures, indicating Bragg was outnumbered, nor that the cavalry raid was already in progress convinced Davis to change his mind. On December 15, he ordered Bragg to send Carter. L. Stevenson's division to Mississippi. On December 18 the lead element of Stevenson's Division departed Murfreesboro by rail.[19]

Stevenson's Division had originally been part of Kirby Smith's Army of Kentucky. Once Bragg's and Smith's armies were combined to form the Army of Tennessee, Stevenson's troops became one of the two divisions of Smith's Corps. Prior to departing for Mississippi, Stevenson lost one of his brigades (Brig. Gen. James E. Rains's) when it was assigned to McCown's Division. In return he had received a brigade (Brig. Gen. Edward D. Tracy's) from McCown. Additionally, Col. Alexander W. Reynolds's brigade from East Tennessee was assigned to Stevenson.[20]

Result/Impact

Stevenson's Division passed along the rail route from Murfreesboro to Vicksburg, via Chattanooga, Atlanta, Mobile, Meridian, and Jackson. This route was eight hundred miles long. It required eight different railroads, several of which had different rail gages, and it involved unloading from railcars and reloading on different cars at numerous transfer points. Although the lead brigade of his division arrived in Vicksburg on December 29, it took three weeks from the time the first units left Murfreesboro until the entire division was assembled at Vicksburg.[21]

While this rail movement was underway, Brig. Gen. Nathan Bedford Forrest's cavalry brigade, which had departed on December 11 to raid into West Tennessee, struck Grant's supply line. Forrest destroyed supply depots, sixty miles of railroad track, and bridges that Grant depended upon. In addition, on December 20 a Confederate cavalry force under Maj. Gen. Earl Van Dorn attacked Grant's forward supply depot at Holly Springs. Vast amounts of supplies that Grant needed to sustain his movement into central Mississippi were destroyed. Faced with an unsustainable logistical situation, Grant had no choice but to terminate his movement south and withdraw back to Grand Junction, Tennessee. Then on December 29, Sherman's force was repulsed at the Battle of Chickasaw Bayou and forced to retreat.[22]

Davis's decision to send reinforcements from Bragg to Pemberton reduced the Army of Tennessee 7,500 to 10,000 men. As Bragg had predicted, the destruction of Grant's supply lines and bases halted his offensive into Mississippi to capture Vicksburg. In addition, Sherman's force had been defeated north of Vicksburg by the available Confederate forces, which included only Brig. Gen. Seth M. Barton's brigade of Stevenson's Division. These two events took place while the other brigades of Stevenson's Division were in transit. Stevenson's Division was of no immediate use to Pemberton, and it deprived Bragg of a significant maneuver force that he desperately needed to execute his attack plan at Stones River. These concepts will be further developed in the discussion of another critical decision.[23]

Another consequence of the departure of Stevenson's Division was a second reorganization of the Army of Tennessee. Stevenson's departure left Smith's Corps with only one division, McCown's. This division was transferred to Hardee's Corps. At the same time, Breckinridge's Division was transferred from Polk's Corps to Hardee's, and Anderson's Division was broken up and distributed throughout the army. This reorganization resulted in the Army of Tennessee having two infantry corps, Polk's and Hardee's, containing two divisions and three divisions respectively. A detailed discussion of this reorganization appears earlier in the chapter. In addition, Maj.

Gen. William S. Rosecrans, commander of the Army of the Cumberland, received information on the transfer of Stevenson's Division. This report influenced his decision to begin offensive operations south from Nashville in late December.[24]

The varied consequences of Davis's decision to reinforce Pemberton at Bragg's expense would come together on December 31, 1862, and affect Bragg's concept of operations, scheme of maneuver, and allocation of combat power. As a result, he had limited options to potentially capitalize on success as the battle progressed. The critical decisions regarding reorganization and loss of a division combined to have a major effect on how the battle would be fought. From these two decisions came others that greatly influenced the action.

Alternate Decision/Scenario

If Jefferson Davis had accepted Bragg's and Johnston's recommendations and not sent a division from Bragg's army to Pemberton, the events that followed could have resulted in several different scenarios altering the course of history.

Foremost among these situations would have been the army's organization and the way in which Bragg probably would have allocated combat power for his December 31 attack. The Army of Tennessee could have remained a three-corps army with two divisions in each corps. Even after Kirby Smith's transfer to the Trans-Mississippi, his corps could have been given to another officer. Alternately, his two divisions could have been assigned individually to Polk's and Hardee's Corps. In any event, Bragg's army would have had six infantry divisions for his attack.

Assuming that Bragg would have developed the same concept of operation and scheme of maneuver that he actually used on December 31, his allocation of combat power would have been significantly influenced. With three corps, Bragg could have assigned one corps to make the supporting attack and protect the army's right. The other two corps (four divisions) could have been assigned to the main attack—the envelopment of Rosecrans's right. These two corps could have been deployed one behind the other or beside each other, thus allocating sufficient combat power for the main attack to handle unforeseen situations.

If the divisions of Kirby Smith's old corps had been assigned to Hardee and Polk, the army would have two corps with three divisions each. Bragg would have been able to allocate three divisions in the main attack: one on the first line, followed by another in the second line (as was actually done), and then a third division following as a reserve, two divisions in the supporting attack, and one division protecting the army's right flank.

Either one of these allocations would have provided the strength necessary for the main attack to handle contingencies and maintain momentum. Maintaining momentum would increase the possibility of capturing and holding the Nashville Pike (Rosecrans's line of supply and communication) in the Army of the Cumberland's rear area, thereby cutting troops off from supplies and reinforcements in Nashville.

Following chapters contain more information on these events. As you read on, you will see a thread of actions and decisions beginning with Davis's critical decision and continuing through the fighting on December 31.

Bragg Orders the Cavalry to Raid

Situation

In December, with his and Smith's armies combined, reorganized as the Army of Tennessee, and positioned in Middle Tennessee, Bragg made a critical decision that would alter the strength of his cavalry and army and limit his capabilities in the battle at the end of the month.

When the two armies were combined, Bragg regrouped the cavalry into four brigades, later expanded to six. Four of these brigades were to operate in direct support of the army. The other two were to conduct distant raiding operations on Union supply and communication lines or operate in the vicinity of the army. The two brigades designated for raiding were commanded by Brig. Gen. Nathan B. Forrest, who commanded four cavalry regiments and two cavalry battalions, and the newly promoted Brig. Gen. John H. Morgan, who commanded nine cavalry regiments. Forrest and Morgan had a total of 5,600 soldiers.[25]

Options

In December Bragg had three options for the employment of his distant raiding cavalry. He could order these soldiers into north-central Tennessee and south-central Kentucky, send them on raids deeper into the Union rear areas in Tennessee and Kentucky, or keep them in close proximity to the army as a contingency.

Option 1

If ordered to raid in south-central Kentucky, Forrest and Morgan would be operating against Rosecrans's direct rail supply line that went from Louisville, Kentucky, to Nashville. Such operations could have an adverse impact on Rosecrans's ability to prepare his army for an immediate offensive operation south from Nashville. These two cavalry forces would also be placed where they could gain information as to whether the Union army was going into winter quarters or beginning a late-season campaign. If Rosecrans was to move south against Bragg, Forrest and Morgan might be able to place their brigades in positions where they could operate against Rosecrans's supply line from Nashville to his army.

Option 2

If Bragg sent Forrest and Morgan on raids deep into Union rear areas, they would be able to operate against railroads that supplied several Union armies. Such attacks would have a greater effect on the Union war effort than the previous option. However, both raiding brigades would be at extended distances from the army and would not be in position to provide assistance or intelligence if Rosecrans moved south from Nashville.

Option 3

There was also the option of doing nothing. This would keep both brigades in close proximity to the army, where they could be used for close-in raiding and reconnaissance if Rosecrans was to begin an operation. However, this option would allow several Union railroad supply lines to operate unhindered.

Decision

Bragg's army was going into winter quarters in December, and he assumed that Rosecrans was doing the same. If both armies were in winter quarters, the time for active campaigning would be over until the spring. With this fact in mind, Bragg ordered Forrest and Morgan to conduct cavalry raids against supply lines deep in the Union rear area.[26]

Result/Impact

The first raiding force to depart was Forrest's Brigade. His target was the Mobile and Ohio Railroad, which ran through Western Tennessee and was a major supply line for Grant's army as it moved towards Vicksburg. Bragg thought that if Forrest could destroy enough of this railroad, it would greatly impede Grant's offensive operations through Mississippi. Bragg was correct![27]

Nathan Bedford Forrest is considered by many to be the premier cavalry commander of the Civil War. He was forty years old when he enlisted as a private in the Seventh Tennessee Cavalry. In October 1861 he was promoted to lieutenant colonel, and he subsequently participated in the defense of Fort Donelson. Promoted to colonel, Forrest then fought at Shiloh. In June he

Brigadier General Nathan B. Forrest, CSA, commanding cavalry brigade. Library of Congress.

was made commander of a cavalry brigade, and in a July raid he captured the Union garrison and supplies at Murfreesboro. Forrest was then promoted to brigadier general. He led the raid against Grant's supply line and fought in the Chickamauga Campaign. Promoted to major general in December 1863, Forrest had an independent cavalry command in north Mississippi and West Tennessee. He successfully operated in these areas until he rejoined the Army of Tennessee for Hood's 1864 Tennessee Campaign. In February 1865 he was promoted to lieutenant general, and he operated in Alabama until April of that year. Forrest worked as a planter and railroad president after the war and died in 1877.[28]

Forrest left Columbia, Tennessee, on December 11. He crossed the Tennessee River at Clifton on December 15 and captured Lexington, Tennessee, two days later. Moving on, he intersected the Mobile and Ohio Railroad north of Jackson. From this point he raided north along the railroad for forty-two miles, destroying tracks and bridges, passing through Humbolt, Trenton, and Rutherford, and reaching Union City. On Christmas Day Forrest departed Union City, marching southeast. On New Year's Eve he fought pursuing Union forces at Parker's Crossroads, moved on to Lexington, recrossed the Tennessee River on January 2, and returned to Columbia. [29]

The second raid Bragg ordered targeted Rosecrans's supply line from Louisville, Kentucky, south to Nashville. Specific objectives were the Louisville

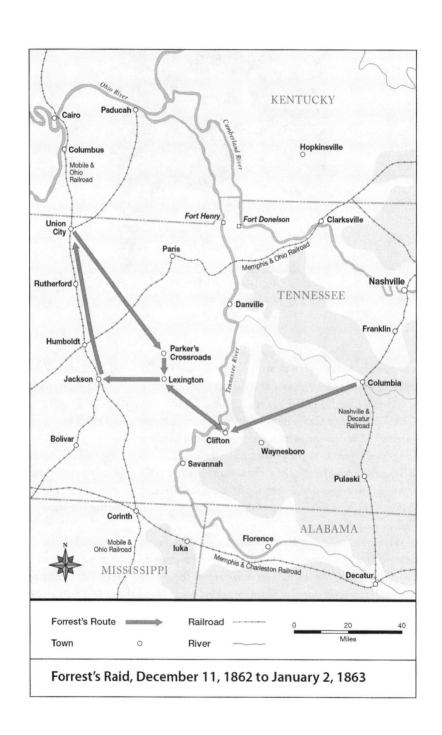

Cairo

Paducah

Ohio River

KENTUCKY

Columbus

Mobile &
Ohio
Railroad

Hopkinsville

Cumberland River

Union
City

Fort Henry

Fort Donelson

Clarksville

Paris

Memphis & Ohio Railroad

Rutherford

Nashville

Danville

TENNESSEE

Franklin

Humboldt

Parker's
Crossroads

Tennessee River

Jackson

Lexington

Columbia

Nashville &
Decatur
Railroad

Bolivar

Clifton

Waynesboro

Savannah

Pulaski

Corinth

ALABAMA

Mobile &
Ohio Railroad

Iuka

Florence

Memphis & Charleston Railroad

N

MISSISSIPPI

Decatur

Forrest's Route

Railroad

0   20   40

Town

River

Miles

Forrest's Raid, December 11, 1862 to January 2, 1863

Brigadier General John H. Morgan,
CSA, commanding cavalry brigade.
Library of Congress.

and Nashville Railroad and any supply caches on or near that route. Commanded by Brig. Gen. John Hunt Morgan, this cavalry raid consisted of 3,100 troopers and seven pieces of artillery that traveled 275 miles through northern Tennessee and middle Kentucky in two weeks.[30]

Born in 1825, Morgan attended Transylvania College and fought in the Mexican War. He organized the Lexington Rifles in 1857, and when war broke out he led them to Bowling Green, where they joined with Confederate forces. Morgan was promoted to brigadier general in December 1862. In 1862 and 1863 he conducted several raids against Union supply lines and depots in Tennessee, Kentucky, Indiana, and Ohio. Captured in 1863, he escaped and rejoined Confederate forces. Morgan was placed in command of the Department of Southwestern Virginia in April 1864. He was killed on September 4 of that year while en route to attack Union forces near Knoxville.[31]

Departing Alexandria, Tennessee, on December 22, Morgan crossed the Cumberland River and was in the vicinity of Glasgow, Kentucky, on December 24. Continuing north, Morgan crossed the Green River and intersected the Louisville and Nashville Railroad north of Munfordville. From that point the raiders proceeded north along the railroad for fifty-three miles, intermittently destroying track and bridges. They passed through Upton on December 26, Elizabethtown on December 27, and Bardstown on December 28, with part of the force going on to Shepherdsville, the northernmost point of the raid. At this point Morgan turned his command southeast and marched to Springfield on December 30. Turning south, he reached Columbia on

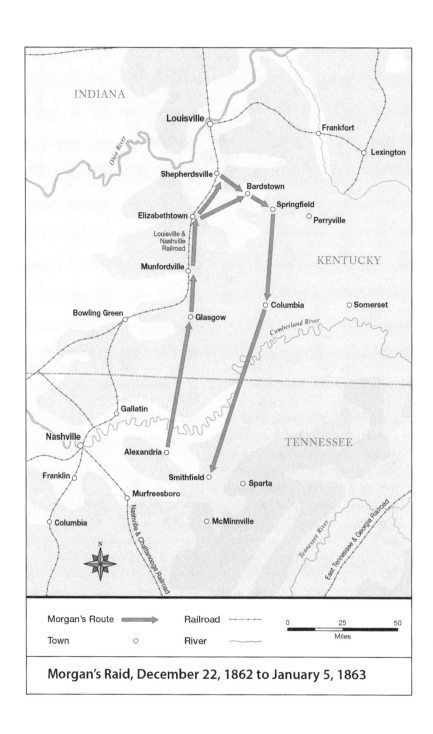

Morgan's Raid, December 22, 1862 to January 5, 1863

INDIANA

Louisville

Frankfort

Lexington

Ohio River

Shepherdsville

Bardstown

Springfield

Perryville

Elizabethtown

Louisville &
Nashville
Railroad

KENTUCKY

Munfordville

Columbia

Somerset

Bowling Green

Glasgow

Cumberland River

Gallatin

Nashville

TENNESSEE

Alexandria

Smithfield

Sparta

Franklin

Murfreesboro

McMinnville

Columbia

Tennessee River

East Tennessee & Georgia Railroad

Nashville & Chattanooga Railroad

N

Morgan's Route

Railroad

0   25   50
Miles

Town   ○

River

January 1, recrossed the Cumberland River, and arrived back in Confederate-controlled territory at Smithville, Tennessee, on January 5.[32]

At the tactical level both Forrest's and Morgan's raids were unqualified successes. The raids destroyed miles of track and many bridges on the key railroads that supplied two major Union armies. Moreover, the raiders captured or destroyed significant quantities of supplies and equipment.

At the operational level the results were different. In conjunction with Maj. Gen. Earl Van Dorn's raid, Forrest had an impact on the operational situation. On December 20 Van Dorn attacked, captured, and demolished Grant's forward supply depot at Holly Springs, Mississippi. Van Dorn destroyed the supplies Grant needed to support the part of his army maneuvering through north-central Mississippi to capture Vicksburg. Forrest's damage to the Mobile and Ohio Railroad prevented the ruined supplies from being replaced in a timely manner. The synergistic effect of Forrest's and Van Dorn's raids forced Grant to terminate the movement through central Mississippi and eventually order his army to retreat north to be supplied. Morgan's raid, on the other hand, did not have a decisive effect on Rosecrans's Army of the Cumberland.[33]

After Rosecrans took command of the Army of the Cumberland, one of his priorities was the repair of the Louisville and Nashville Railroad. This was accomplished in late November. Shortly thereafter, a steady stream of supplies and equipment began arriving at Nashville. One of Rosecrans's prerequisites for commencing an offensive was stockpiling sufficient supplies and equipment at Nashville to sustain his army if the railroad to Louisville was interrupted. Even though Morgan's raid was tactically successful, it was too late. Rosecrans had accumulated enough supplies to prevent just such an occurrence from deterring his operations.[34]

The missions (roles) of cavalry are reconnaissance, security, and economy of force operations. It is that way today, and so it was in 1862. Reconnaissance operations gain information about the enemy and the terrain. Security operations prevent the enemy from gaining information about the friendly force (sometimes called counterreconnaissance) and prevent the friendly force from being surprised by an enemy force. Security operations are of three types: guard missions, screen missions, and covering force operations. A guard mission is preformed close to the friendly main body and is characterized as advance guard, rear guard, or flank guard, depending on the cavalry's deployment in relationship to the main body. A cavalry force conducting a guard mission will fight to protect the main body or delay to gain the main body time to deploy on favorable terrain in preparation to attack or defend. During defensive operations cavalry will delay the advancing enemy to gain information on the size and composition of the force, thwart enemy reconnaissance, and conceal the location of the defensive position. The screen mission replaces the guard mission when the cavalry has insufficient force or must cover a very large front or flank. The screen mission is an observation-and-report type of operation. Covering force missions are the same as guard missions, only the cavalry force operates out of supporting distance of the force it protects/ guards. An economy of force operation is any tactical operation where a cavalry unit is used so that other combat forces can be deployed to a different location. For example, a cavalry force may hold a section of a defensive line to allow the infantry units that were there to be moved into a different position to add more weight to a main attack. The raid can be considered an economy of force mission.[35]

Bragg used part of his cavalry in an economy of force mission when he ordered Forrest and Morgan to raid Union supply lines. However, the two raids, placed some 5,600 cavalrymen at such a distance from Bragg's army as to be unable to assist in the battle along Stones River.

Alternate Decision and Scenario

A case can be made that Van Dorn's raid and the transfer of Stevenson's Division to Pemberton may have stalled, if not stopped, Grant's initial maneuvering toward Vicksburg. And the operation by Morgan's force had no effect on the battle between Bragg and Rosecrans. If this is so, then it might have been more effective for Bragg to keep Forrest's and Morgan's forces in close proximity to the rest of his army. Then the troops could have been deployed to support of the Army of Tennessee at the Battle of Stones River.

On December 31 Bragg commenced the battle, gaining the initiative by attacking first. He planned an envelopment of Rosecrans's right flank, and for this attack to be successful he needed to weight his left wing with as much combat power as he could muster. Part of Bragg's available cavalry supported the envelopment (guard mission). Part conducted a raid on Rosecrans's supply line from Nashville (economy of force mission). And a small brigade covered Bragg's right flank (guard mission). A full infantry division remained on the right in case there was a Union counterattack in that area.

On December 30 Brig. Gen. Joseph Wheeler's cavalry brigade departed for a thirty-six-hour raid against Rosecrans's supply line from Nashville to his army's rear area. If either Forrest's or Morgan's brigade had been available to Bragg, it could have been assigned this mission. That would have provided an additional cavalry force and freed Wheeler's brigade for deployment in a different mission.

With additional cavalry, several tactical options would have been available. First, the cavalry supporting the envelopment of Rosecrans's right (guard mission) could have been reinforced in order to defeat the Union cavalry protecting Rosecrans's flank. This arrangement would have placed a significant force in the right rear of the Union army. As a result, the turnpike and supply line from Nashville could have been interdicted and held by a significant-size force, thus isolating Rosecrans's army. Secondly, a stronger cavalry force could have been positioned on Bragg's right (guard and economy of force missions), thereby allowing an additional infantry division to be committed to the envelopment. Bragg was already short one division when Stevenson's was sent to Vicksburg. Extra infantry may have made up for Stevenson's absence and provided enough combat power for the envelopment to be a success.

Either of these options could have changed the subsequent course and events of the battle. But they were not available, as Forrest was in West Tennessee and Morgan was in Kentucky when the Battle of Stones River was fought.

Rosecrans Moves South

Situation

After the Battle of Perryville, Bragg broke contact with the Union army and moved east. With the decision to depart Kentucky, he then turned south and marched back into Eastern Tennessee. Bragg's and Kirby Smith's routes took them through the Cumberland Gap and on to Knoxville. From that city Confederate forces moved to Middle Tennessee and deployed in the vicinity of Murfreesboro.[36]

Maj. Gen. Don Carlos Buell's Army of the Ohio followed the retreating Confederates as far as the Crab Orchard–Mount Vernon area. But on October 17 the pursuit of Bragg's and Kirby Smith's forces was terminated.[37]

For some time prior, President Abraham Lincoln's political objective was the liberation of East Tennessee. Even though Buell had stopped his pursuit, Lincoln believed that Buell's army was now in a position to achieve this goal.[38]

Buell looked at the tactical situation and considered a move into East Tennessee fraught with danger and insurmountable obstacles. The difficult terrain and the lack of good roads would not only hamper forward movement but also prevent the establishment of a functioning supply line. These problems would be aggravated with the coming of winter. As retreating Confederates moved through the mountainous region they consumed what little subsistence was available. In addition, as Bragg's and Smith's soldiers retreated they came closer to and eventually reached the railroad from Knoxville, a sustainable supply line. On the other hand, Buell would be moving deeper into an area that would make it extremely difficult, if not impossible, to establish a supply line capable of supporting his army.[39]

In an October 17 message to Maj. Gen. Henry W. Halleck, the general-in-chief, Buell informed the administration that he was preparing to turn his army away from East Tennessee and march to Nashville. Halleck immediately informed Buell that it was President Lincoln's order that his army enter East Tennessee. Buell replied on October 20 that he could not comply with the president's order as he lacked sufficient troops, supplies, and supply routes. Buell also believed that a move into East Tennessee would leave Nashville exposed to capture if Confederate forces moved into Middle Tennessee. In fact, Bragg entered the region in November. Two days later, Halleck reiterated Lincoln's command for Buell to occupy East Tennessee. Buell failed to follow the orders and continued to march his army toward Nashville. On October 24 Halleck directed Maj. Gen. William S. Rosecrans to travel to Buell's headquarters, relieve him of command, and personally take command of the newly created Department of the Cumberland and its primary field army. Rosecrans assumed command of the department and the army on October 30. The army was designated the Fourteenth Corps, soon to be renamed the Army of the Cumberland, and it was organized into the Left, Center, and Right Wings.[40]

William S. Rosecrans was forty-three years old at the Battle of Stones River. He graduated from the U.S. Military Academy, where he ranked fifth

Major General William S. Rosecrans, USA, commanding Army of the Cumberland. National Archives.

in his class, in 1842. Commissioned as an engineer officer, Rosecrans served in a variety of assignments, including as a professor at West Point, for eleven years before resigning to pursue a civilian engineering career. In April 1861 he rejoined the army as a colonel. The next month, he was promoted to brigadier general, and in September 1862 he was promoted to major general with a date of rank of March 1862. Prior to assuming command of the Army of the Cumberland, Rosecrans had participated in operations in western Virginia, along the Mississippi, and at the Battles of Iuka and Corinth.[41]

When he informed Rosecrans to take command of Buell's army, Halleck also provided operational guidance. Foremost were the directions that had gone to Buell to promptly occupy East Tennessee. Halleck also urged "the necessity of giving active employment to [Rosecrans's] forces, [as] neither the country or the Government will much longer put up with the inactivity of some of our armies and generals."[42]

Rosecrans could surmise that he would have to begin offensive operations shortly after assuming command. Buell had been relieved not only for not occupying East Tennessee, but also for not being aggressive enough and allowing Bragg's and Smith's armies to escape. Although he didn't mention it, Rosecrans must have known about McClellan's recent removal from command for similar reasons.

Rosecrans did not want to venture into the mountains of East Tennessee any more than Buell did. He was able to sidestep the issue when Confederate cavalry under Forrest and Morgan, Bragg's distant raiding cavalry, attempted to capture the Cumberland River Bridge at Nashville. This action, along with a buildup of Confederate forces in Middle Tennessee, created a situation whereby the Confederates might attempt to capture Nashville. The loss of this strategically and logistically important city would have been a significant reversal of Lincoln's war effort. Thus Rosecrans immediately ordered his army to march to Nashville.[43]

Upon informing Rosecrans of his new command, Halleck strongly suggested that he conduct offensive operations. When Rosecrans had been in command less than a month, Halleck again reminded him that he could not remain at Nashville and had to begin active operations. On November 11 Rosecrans informed Halleck that he soon expected to have the Louisville and Nashville Railroad fully repaired and operational. (It was completed on November 26.) With the army's major supply line open, Halleck could expect that offensive operations were imminent.[44]

Nine days after supply trains began running from Louisville to Nashville, Halleck sent Rosecrans a communication that almost placed both generals in an untenable situation. Halleck began by informing Rosecrans that Lincoln was very impatient with the army's idleness. The troops were still in Nashville, and the campaign season was coming to a close. Halleck further informed Rosecrans that he had been asked twice, presumably by the president or the secretary of war, to designate someone else to command his army. He warned Rosecrans that he would probably be relieved of his command if he did not move very soon.[45]

Rosecrans viewed Halleck's message as an ultimatum; in anger, he replied the same day. After a short review of his supply situation, he informed Halleck that if the administration that had placed him in command had lost confidence in him, it should replace him. He required no other stimulus to do his duty other than knowledge of what that duty was. Rosecrans concluded, "To threats of removal or the like I must be permitted to say that I am insensible." The stage was now set for an either-or situation that could result in Rosecrans's removal or resignation.[46]

The next day (December 5) Halleck replied to Rosecrans in a conciliatory manner, explaining that his first message was not a threat but a statement of facts. He pointed out that on several occasions Lincoln had asked him to account for Rosecrans's remaining in Nashville, and that there were imperative reasons for Rosecrans's army to go on the offense. Halleck stated that he was not told what these reasons were. But he ventured that they were political and concerned Britain and France. The British Parliament was scheduled to meet in the coming January (1863). There was concern that there would be some economic pressure to have Britain join France in recognizing the Confederacy. In Halleck's opinion, Lincoln worried that if Union forces did not hold Middle Tennessee, which they had earlier in the year, it might seem that the Confederacy was gaining on the Union. Halleck concluded by pointing out that, for political reasons, a victory over Bragg's army or the retreat of his men would be more valuable now than later.[47]

The general military situation since the late summer and early fall also caused Lincoln political anxiety. There had been no major successful operations by Union armies since October. In fact, it was just the opposite. Grant's offensive to capture Vicksburg had been halted and then driven back to its starting point. Although Bragg had retreated from Kentucky, Buell had been unable to cut him off or bring him to decisive action, and Bragg's army now occupied Middle Tennessee and threatened Nashville. The Battle of Antietam was a strategic victory but a tactical draw, and Lee's army had escaped back into Virginia. Ambrose Burnside, McClellan's successor, had devised an operation to move on Richmond. But after early success he was now stalled in front of Fredericksburg on the wrong side of the Rappahannock River. Eight days after Halleck wrote Rosecrans, Burnside suffered a crushing defeat, further degrading the administration's strategic situation. Additionally, as a result of Antietam Lincoln had made public the Emancipation Proclamation, which would take effect on January 1, 1863. He was probably thinking that the recent Union reverses had weakened the political impact of the proclamation. It could only be strengthened by a perceived military success.

Options

Rosecrans had two options. He could remain in Nashville, or he could begin a late-season operation and advance south and engage Bragg's army.

Option 1

Rosecrans could continue to bivouac his army at and near Nashville and strengthen his supply line and supply base for a spring 1863 campaign against Bragg. His rationale for doing so would focus on the campaign season's impending close and the risk of exposing his army to unacceptable hardships, including difficulty in obtaining supplies. This decision might be defended with a tactical and logistical argument. Politically, however, it could not be done. Given the situation that had caused Buell's removal from command, there is a high probability that Rosecrans would have been removed as well.

Option 2

Rosecrans could begin a late-season operation south to find and engage Bragg's army. Such an operation would meet Lincoln's expectations for placing Rosecrans in command. Coming at the end of six months of Union reverses, this action would demonstrate that the administration was undefeated, committed to victory, and carrying the fight to the enemy. Commencing a campaign of maneuver at this late date might catch Bragg by surprise— as armies would normally be going into winter quarters.

Decision

On December 26 Rosecrans's army marched south from Nashville to find and engage Bragg's army, which rapidly concentrated at Murfreesboro.

After exchanging messages with Halleck, Rosecrans must have understood that time was running short for him to take action. Concurrently, the logistical and tactical situation began to develop favorably for him over the next few weeks. Immediately after assuming command Rosecrans began reorganizing and revitalizing his force. To logistically prepare his army for an offensive, he had to repair and secure his line of supply, then accumulate sufficient supplies at Nashville to support combat operations.

Rosecrans's main supply route was the 183-mile-long Louisville and Nashville Railroad. In the fall of 1862 this line was the only effective means of moving a large amount of supplies to the army's forward supply base at Nashville. The Cumberland River could be used at other times of the year, but in the fall the water level was too low for the riverboats to reach Nashville. Confederate cavalry operating against the railroad had created a significant break in the tracks between Mitchellville and Nashville. A tunnel thirty-two miles north of Nashville had been obstructed, and there were numerous bridges that needed to be repaired or rebuilt. This break in the line required that supplies be taken off trains and transported thirty-five miles by wagon. This resource-intensive method greatly reduced Rosecrans's ability to build up sufficient supplies at Nashville. However, by November 26 the rail line was completely open, and trains were arriving in sufficient numbers for Rosecrans to reach the level of supplies he needed by the third week of December.[48]

As the logistical situation improved so did Rosecrans's tactical situation in relationship to Bragg's army. Almost as soon as Stevenson's Division departed Murfreesboro for Vicksburg Rosecrans was aware of the reduction in Bragg's infantry strength. Forrest and Morgan were sent off on deep raids into Western Tennessee and Kentucky. As Rosecrans received reports of these cavalry actions, he knew that Bragg's army had again been weakened, and that Bragg's cavalry raiders were too far away to return in time to reinforce Bragg. Rosecrans was confident that he had convinced Bragg that the Union army was settling into winter quarters. After all, Bragg's army had already done so. Therefore, an advance south from Nashville would give him the advantage of attacking a diminished enemy, and he might also gain the element of surprise.[49]

Results/Impact

Rosecrans's decision to commence an offensive operation would bring both armies in contact just outside of Murfreesboro and result in the Battle of Stones River. This engagement would give Lincoln the end of year / beginning of year victory he was looking for. Northern morale would improve, particularly in the Midwest, the home of many of the Army of the Cumberland's soldiers. Internationally, along with the strategic victory at Antietam and the Emancipation Proclamation it would contribute to foreign governments' decisions not to recognize the Confederacy.

Alternate Decision and Scenario

Early January 1863 witnessed severe winter weather that severely hampered or halted operations. Had Rosecrans delayed his offense, there might have been no battle until spring. Without Rosecrans's December 1862 offensive into Middle Tennessee, several alternate scenarios may have developed.

Given the climate of Lincoln's administration in November and December 1862, Rosecrans could have been replaced with another commander. Rosecrans had replaced Buell because, among other things, he refused to follow a direct order to move into East Tennessee. Nor did Buell engage the Confederate forces in East or Middle Tennessee in a decisive battle. As there were several generals, George Thomas among them, who could have replaced Rosecrans, failure to decisively engage Bragg's army before winter could also have resulted in his removal. If Rosecrans or his replacement had followed the December campaign plan in the spring, a battle in the vicinity of Murfreesboro could have developed. But in all probability it would have differed from the one that was actually fought.

Had Bragg remained at Murfreesboro during the winter, he could have used the railroad from Chattanooga to increase his supply and ammunition stocks and his army. This would have given him the capability to conduct offensive operations to recapture Nashville, or to position his army to engage the Union army in a decisive battle for control of the city. In any event, had Bragg moved before the Union commander, there would not have been a Battle of Stones River. Even if not successful, such an operation would have delayed the Army of the Cumberland's advance into Middle Tennessee and made all of the 1863 and 1864 campaigns decidedly different.

Depending on the commander of the Army of the Cumberland in the spring, and the tactical situation that leader faced, there may not have been a battle near Murfreesboro. A Union offensive movement from Nashville could have bypassed Murfreesboro on the west. Thus the Confederate army would have had to redeploy to keep from being cut off. The battle for control of Middle Tennessee might have occurred in the vicinity of Columbia, Shelbyville, or some other suitable defensive position.

However, none of these or any other alternate scenarios came to be history. Rosecrans decided to begin an offensive in late December, giving us the campaign and Battle of Stones River as we know it today. Among all of the critical decisions this one is the most important. Everything in the campaign and battle that developed afterward resulted from this decision.

Bragg Decides to Concentrate at Murfreesboro

Situation

On December 26, when Rosecrans began his movement from Nashville, Bragg's Army of Tennessee occupied a thirty-two-mile front. The center of his position was Lieut. Gen. Leonidas Polk's corps at Murfreesboro. The right was Maj. Gen. John P. McCown's division, located twelve miles east at Readyville. The left was Lieut. Gen. William J. Hardee's corps, situated twenty miles southwest at Eagleville, with one brigade to the north at Triune. Cavalry brigades led by Brig. Gens. John A. Wharton, Joseph Wheeler, and John A. Pegram were positioned to cover the roads north of each location.[50]

Options

In the last days of December 1862, as Rosecrans marched south and southeast from Nashville, Bragg had three available courses of action: retreat, defend, or attack.

Option 1

Bragg could retreat south from his present location and fight Rosecrans at a future date. In this case, the Confederate army would have to retreat approximately thirty miles south to the vicinity of the Duck River. North of the river were the northern ridges of the Highland Rim. These ridges provided good defensive positions and controlled the roads and railroad south to Chattanooga. To maintain contact with Bragg once he retreated, Rosecrans would have to advance into the more difficult terrain of central Tennessee and extend his supply line.[51]

This was a fertile area where Bragg's army could gather food and forage to supplement the supplies that were being sent forward. Unlike the Army of Tennessee's cavalry, the Army of the Cumberland's cavalry did not have the capability for distant raiding operations. Bragg would be assured of a secure supply and communications line back to Chattanooga and locations farther south.[52]

The disadvantages of a retreat were that Bragg would be leaving a location from which he could threaten Nashville and commence offensive operations against that city or southern Kentucky in the spring and summer. From the area of Murfreesboro it was easier for his raiding cavalry, Forrest and Morgan, to continue attacking Rosecrans's overland supply line from Louisville. Although a rise in the Cumberland River would allow supplies to be brought to Nashville by boat, any lowering of the river would again make the overland route the primary supply line. The avenue of approach from Nashville to Chattanooga went into the center of the Heartland. Reaping the full benefits of this crucial area depended on keeping an invading force as far north as possible.

President Jefferson Davis's strategic objective was the preservation of territory. Davis's statement to Johnston and Bragg, not withstanding, when he ordered Stevenson's Division to Vicksburg was that they should, "fight if you can, and fall back [south] beyond the Tennessee [River]", to retreat from Murfreesboro without a fight was contrary to his strategic policy. Davis's policy that no part of the Confederacy would be abandoned without a fight may have been a factor in Bragg's decision.[53]

Option 2

If Bragg didn't retreat he had the options of attack or defense. Before he could consider attack he had to concentrate his army, which by default placed him on the defense.

Bragg lacked sufficient force to block or fight for control of all of the major roads from Nashville. To defend at Murfreesboro or at Eagleville and Triune, the western end of his extended line, meant that one or the other of the positions, because of the road system south from Nashville, was vulnerable to being enveloped or turned. Bragg therefore had to concentrate his army on Rosecrans's primary avenue of approach. Deciding that, although he initially advanced on three routes, Rosecrans would eventually concentrate on Murfreesboro, Bragg ordered the left and right of his army to that location. Although this position had several drawbacks, it gave Bragg four advantages.[54]

First, it provided him a railroad supply line to Chattanooga. In the winter, when traveling on mountain roads to and from that city would be challenging, Bragg would be able to bring forward supplies, ammunition, and reinforcements. Second, it would allow Bragg's army to continue foraging for food in the farming area around Murfreesboro. In a November 24, 1862, letter to President Jefferson Davis, Bragg reported that his troops were securing a rich harvest of supplies. Subsistence was so abundant that a surplus would remain after the soldiers' needs were met. Available items included forage, horses, mules, and material for clothing and tents. Though much had been taken from the area during the late fall and early winter, the growth and harvesting of crops in the spring and summer would replace some of what was consumed. Assuming his army could hold this area, Bragg would be able to gather some of these crops and—just as important—prevent the Army of the Cumberland from acquiring them.[55]

Third, continuing to hold the area around Murfreesboro would keep Union forces out of the center of the Heartland. This stronghold would provide a base of operation from which cavalry, could conduct multiple raids against the Army of the Cumberland's supply lines throughout the winter. And lastly, occupying Murfreesboro would place Bragg in an advantageous position from which to commence offensive operations against Nashville, the Union army, or southern Kentucky in the spring or summer.

Decision

Bragg did not consider retreat a viable option, but if he had, there would have been no Battle of Stones River. In all probability, there would not have been any major combat until the spring of 1863. When Bragg realized that Rosecrans's army was not in winter quarters but was moving south from Nashville, he issued orders that concentrated the Army of Tennessee at Murfreesboro.

Results/Impact

On the morning of Sunday, December 28, both of Bragg's corps were reunited and deployed in positions north and west of Murfreesboro. Bragg's position was divided by Stones River. Hardee's three-division corps was east of the river, while Polk's two-division corps was west of the river. Wharton's cavalry brigade was deployed in front of Polk, Wheeler's cavalry brigade was astride the Nashville Pike, and Pegram's cavalry brigade was positioned across the Lebanon Pike to protect the army's right. The next day Rosecrans advanced until he was in close proximity to Bragg's position. McCown's division was shifted from the right to the left to reinforce Polk's corps. Wharton's brigade took position on the army's left flank, and Wheeler's brigade was withdrawn back through friendly lines. Wheeler's men were then sent to raid Rosecrans's supply line back to Nashville. When Bragg's army concentrated at Murfreesboro, it assumed a defensive posture. Bragg then had the option to remain on the defense or to attack.[56]

Bragg's critical decision whether to remain on the defense or to attack will be discussed in the next chapter.

Harker is Recalled

Situation

Among the critical decisions that shaped the Battle of Stones River, this one concerned the actions and movement of a Union brigade of only 1,747 troops. The tactical situation created by this unit and the courses of action presented to commanders could have changed the battle's sequence of events. The decision had a major influence on how the battle would be fought.[57]

With Bragg's army at reduced strength, with the departure of Stevenson's Division and two cavalry brigades on raids deep behind Union lines, and with sufficient supplies stocked at Nashville, Rosecrans committed his army to an offensive operation. The Army of the Cumberland marched from Nashville in the early morning hours of December 26, 1862. Its three wings were deployed on a wide front as it moved south and southeast along three major routes of

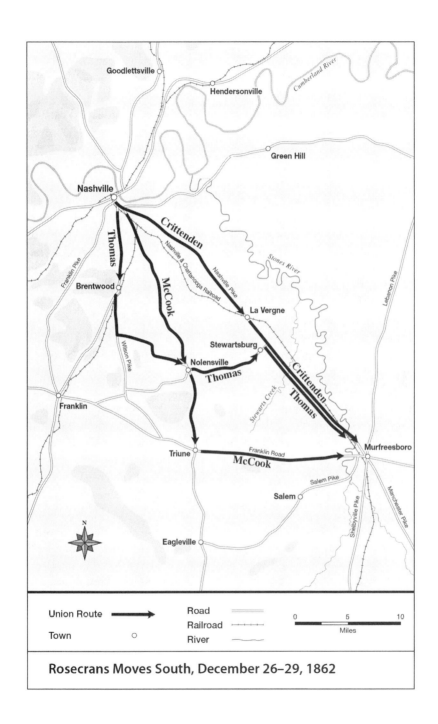

Rosecrans Moves South, December 26–29, 1862

advance. Maj. Gen. Alexander McD. McCook's three-division Right Wing advanced in the center along the Nolensville Pike. Two divisions of Maj. Gen. George H. Thomas's five-division Center Wing advanced on McCook's right (west) on the Wilson Pike. Thomas's remaining divisions were detailed to secure the Louisville and Nashville Railroad and Nashville. On McCook's left (east) Maj. Gen. Thomas L. Crittenden's three-division Left Wing advanced on the Nashville Pike. After Thomas's Center Wing had advanced twelve miles, it turned southeast, passed behind McCook's Right Wing, and moved into a position between the Right and Left Wings. In this tactical configuration Rosecrans continued to advance toward Murfreesboro.[58]

There are four types of offensive operations: movement to contact, attack, exploitation, and pursuit. A movement to contact is conducted by a force when the commander is unsure of the enemy's exact location and strength. An attack, which uses various forms of maneuver, is conducted to destroy enemy troops or render them ineffective. Attacks also capture key terrain. Exploitation often follows a successful attack, and its purposes include preventing the enemy from re-establishing the defense, and capturing objectives deep in the enemy rear area. A pursuit follows a successful attack or a successful exploitation. While the exploitation focuses on the capture of terrain, the pursuit targets the enemy force. Pursuits cut off, capture, or destroy enemy forces that are attempting to escape.[59]

When Rosecrans's army departed Nashville, he had a fairly good understanding of where Bragg's army was deployed. This knowledge made him maneuver on a wide front. However, as Rosecrans did not have the enemy's precise locations and dispositions, he used a *movement to contact*. The use of a movement to contact allowed him to develop the situation as he advanced and protect the Nashville and Chattanooga Railroad with his Left Wing. This railroad went southeast from Nashville, through Murfreesboro, and on to Chattanooga.

As Rosecrans's army advanced farther from Nashville, this railroad assumed greater importance as a major supply line. With the coming of winter, the roads would be difficult, if not impossible, to use for moving supplies to the army. Railroads would provide a better and more economical means of doing so. The lines were not as subject to the ill effects of cold weather as roads, and they also allowed larger quantities of supplies to be transported with less effort.

As Rosecrans moved forward, Bragg consolidated his troops by moving units on the western and eastern part of his line to join the remainder of his army at Murfreesboro. In the late afternoon of December 28, Bragg occupied positions on either side of Stones River, north and northwest of Murfreesboro.[60]

The next day, December 29, Crittenden's Left Wing continued to advance along the Nashville Pike. This unit marched to a position approximately three miles northwest of Murfreesboro. The Left Wing advanced with Brig. Gen. John M. Palmer's three-brigade Second Division on the right of the Nashville Pike. Brig. Gen. Thomas J. Wood's three-brigade First Division was on the pike's left. Brig. Gen. Horatio P. Van Cleve's three-brigade Third Division, the reserve, was following the other two divisions. The advance elements of the Left Wing had been in contact with Brig. Gen. Joseph Wheeler's cavalry brigade and were skirmishing with its soldiers.[61]

Conducting a delaying action, Wheeler's cavalrymen continually fell back toward Murfreesboro. As they came near the town, they broke contact and withdrew. Upon seeing this, Palmer for some reason thought that all Confederate forces were retreating through Murfreesboro. Rosecrans received this erroneous information and ordered Crittenden to immediately occupy the town with one division. Crittenden then planned a two-division attack. Wood's division was to make the main attack on the left (east) of the turnpike, cross Stones River, and occupy Murfreesboro. Palmer's division on the right (west) of the turnpike was to conduct a supporting attack and advance on Wood's flank until his brigades crossed the river. As evening was approaching, both Wood and Palmer requested the order be rescinded as they thought such a move in darkness was hazardous. Crittenden refused, and both divisions moved forward.[62]

Palmer's division moved forward about three-fourths of a mile to one mile, halted, and took up defensive positions. Wood's troops advanced four hundred yards beyond Palmer's.[63]

Wood deployed all three of his brigades on line. Col. George D. Wagner's four-regiment Second Brigade was on the right and next to the turnpike, Col. Charles G. Harker's five-regiment Third Brigade was in the center, and Brig. Gen. Milo S. Hascall's four-regiment First Brigade was on the left. When the order to advance was received, Harker's brigade moved straight forward and crossed Stones River at and on either side of a ford located between the turnpike and McFadden's Ford.[64]

Charles G. Harker was twenty-seven years old when he fought in the Battle of Stones River. In 1858 he graduated sixteenth in his class at the US Military Academy. Commissioned into the infantry, Harker served on the northwest frontier. He returned to the East when the Civil War began, and he was appointed colonel and commander of the Sixty-fifth Ohio Infantry in November 1861. Harker commanded his regiment at Shiloh and Corinth then commanded a brigade at Perryville, Stones River, Chickamauga, Chattanooga, and the Atlanta Campaign. For his conduct at Chickamauga he was

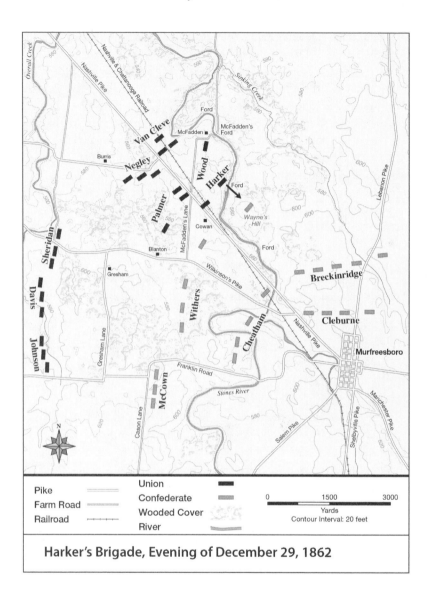

Harker's Brigade, Evening of December 29, 1862

promoted to brigadier general. Harker was killed on June 26, 1864, while leading his brigade in an attack near Kennesaw Mountain, Georgia.[65]

After crossing the river, Harker's lead regiments were at the base of Wayne's Hill, located in the north-center part of the battlefield. The hilltop was relatively flat, measuring approximately 425 yards by 450 yards. Any troops positioned on it had good long-distance observation and fields of fire to the north, west, and south. It was an excellent place for Confederate artil-

Wayne's Hill as it appears today.

lery to fire on Union positions. Especially important was the fact that any artillery, Union or Confederate, on Wayne's Hill could dominate the major avenue of approach along the Nashville Pike and the terrain southwest for a distance of 1,500 to 2,000 yards. As this was part of the area where Bragg's line was located on January 1 and 2, 1863, Union artillery on the hill could deliver enfilading fire and make his position untenable.[66]

Confederate forces east of the river were the three divisions of Hardee's Corps. The front-line division was Maj. Gen. John C. Breckinridge's; all four of his brigades were deployed in a continuous line. Maj. Gen. Patrick R. Cleburne's division was behind Breckinridge's. Hardee's third division, Maj. Gen. John P. McCown's, had been behind Cleburne's. McCown's Division was initially the army reserve, but it had moved west to extend Bragg's left flank.[67]

With its left flank on the river and its center nine hundred yards southwest of Wayne's Hill, Roger W. Hanson's brigade occupied the left of Breckinridge's position. Hanson was a thirty-five-year-old brigadier general, and his unit was known as the "Orphan Brigade" due to its large number of soldiers from Union-controlled Kentucky. Additionally, he had previously served in the Mexican War and the Kentucky legislature. At the war's beginning, Hanson was commissioned colonel of the Second Kentucky. Subsequently, he was captured at Fort Donelson, exchanged, promoted to brigadier general, and given a brigade command. Mortally wounded at Stones River on January 2, 1863, Hanson died two days later.[68]

Brigadier General Roger W. Hanson, CSA,
commanding brigade. Library of Congress.

A minimal number of Confederates were in position on Wayne's Hill on
the evening of December 29. Initially, Hanson had established a skirmish
line between the river and the hill. Later in the day he deployed the four guns
of Capt. Robert Cobb's Kentucky Battery (Cobb's Battery) to firing positions
on the hill. Three infantry regiments, the Sixth Kentucky, Ninth Kentucky,
and Forty-first Alabama, were moved into positions to support the artillery,
and the skirmish line was reinforced.[69]

In preparation to cross the river, Harker deployed three of his infantry
regiments from left to right: the Thirteenth Michigan, Fifty-first Indiana,
and Seventy-third Indiana. Two companies from each regiment were sent
forward as a skirmish line. The three regiments were ordered to ford the river,
form up on the opposite bank, and seize the heights (Wayne's Hill) directly
in front of them. Harker's other two infantry regiments, the Sixty-fourth
Ohio and Sixty-fifth Ohio, and Capt. Cullen Bradley's Sixth Ohio Battery
were held in reserve and ordered to cross the river as soon as possible. The
Sixty-fourth Ohio and Sixty-fifth Ohio followed the other regiment across
the river and assumed a reserve position. Bradley's battery did not have time
to negotiate the waters and remained in a firing position on the west bank.[70]

After the leading regiments crossed the river they were at the northwest
base of Wayne's Hill. Rising forty feet from the river and to a greater height
than any terrain on the battlefield, Wayne's Hill was key terrain.[71]

In the gathering darkness, Harker's skirmish line started across the river
and immediately confronted the Confederate skirmish line. Aggressively

pushing forward, Harker's men drove the enemy back. The Union skirmish-ers were followed by their regiments. Supported by the infantry regiments, Harker's skirmishers pushed the Confederates back up the hill. Seizing the opportunity, Col. Abel Streight, commander of the Fifty-first Indiana, led his regiment in an attack to seize the crest of the hill. Streight's regiment reached the hilltop and almost captured Cobb's guns. Cobb's Battery was saved when the Forty-first Alabama and Ninth Kentucky counterattacked and forced the Fifty-first Indiana to fall back. With the Fifty-first Indiana in its center, the Thirteenth Michigan and Seventy-third Indiana on its left and right, and the support of two other regiments and an artillery battery, a bridgehead began taking shape on the Confederate side of the river. Harker sent back a message that he could hold his position until reinforced. Crittenden and Rosecrans now had the capability to reinforce and expand the bridgehead, seize Wayne's Hill, dominate the left of Bragg's position, and attack the right of the Army of Tennessee.[72]

Options

Harker's successful crossing of the river presented his wing commander, Maj. Gen. Thomas L. Crittenden, with two options. Crittenden could exploit Harker's advantage by reinforcing his troops, or he could order the brigade to cross back to the friendly side of the river.

Ford across Stones River where Harker's brigade crossed on the night of December 28, 1862.

<u>Option 1</u>

To reinforce Harker, Crittenden could send Wood across the river with his other two brigades, either that night or at dawn the next morning, to expand the bridgehead. Then Van Cleve's division could advance, cross the river, and reinforce Wood. Additionally, Palmer's division on the right could move forward along the Nashville Pike and present an additional threat to the Confederate defenders.

<u>Option 2</u>

If Crittenden was not willing to assume the calculated risk of reinforcing Harker, then he could order Harker back across the river. This option would be safest. But it would lose the bridgehead and the element of surprise that Harker had gained from fording the river against minimal resistance.

Decision

After Harker's brigade had crossed the river, Crittenden reconsidered. He decided that Wood and Palmer were correct—continuing the operation in the dark was not a good idea. Crittenden reversed his decision at 10:00 p.m., ordering Harker to withdraw back across the river. The brigade withdrew

Major General Thomas L. Crittenden, USA, commanding Left Wing. U.S. Army Military History Institute.

without complications or interference from any Confederate units. Rosecrans arrived at Crittenden's headquarters and told him he had made the correct decision.[73]

Results/Impact

The decision to withdraw Harker's brigade after it had crossed the river significantly impacted events during the next several days. The immediate threat to Bragg's right flank was removed. This allowed him to move two of the three divisions on his right to his left to be the enveloping force on December 31. Had the order to withdraw not been given, a completely new series of events would have occurred.

Alternate Decision/Scenario

Wood had two other brigades in close proximity to Harker that could have reinforced him. Colonel Wagner's brigade was five hundred yards to Harker's right. From this location Wagner could be positioned to cross the river, either that night or early the next morning. Brigadier General Hascall's brigade was located nine hundred yards to Harker's left, near McFadden's Ford. Likewise, Hascall could have moved to a position to cross the river either that night or early the next morning. Doing so would have provided Rosecrans with an expanded bridgehead on the Confederate side of the river. Palmer's division (three brigades), supported by Negley's division, could hold the position along the Nashville Pike. Van Cleve's division (three brigades), in a reserve position north of the pike and 1,700 yards behind Wood's division, was in an ideal location to move forward, cross the river, and reinforce the units already across. The terrain on the west side of the river provided excellent positions for Crittenden's artillery to cover the daylight crossings (Capt. John Mendenhall used it on January 2) and to cross and support the infantry.

Both the surprise Harker gained when crossing the river and illumination of the moon favored these moves. It was dark a few minutes after 5:00 p.m. on December 29. However, moonrise had been in early afternoon, and moonset would not be until 2:00 a.m. on December 30. There was a three-quarter moon that could provide illumination to facilitate the early movement of reinforcements to exploit Harker's advantage.[74]

But what about the Confederates? On December 29 Bragg had three of his five infantry divisions on the east side of Stones River. One division was in the process of redeploying to the west side. The other two divisions (Polk's Corps) were on the west side of the river and positioned to confront the advance of Rosecrans's Center and Right Wings.

The remainder of Breckinridge's Division was immediately available to confront any Union force building upon Harker's success. Breckinridge could expect to be supported by Cleburne's Division. If necessary, additional combat power could have been added by returning McCown's Division to its previous position. Union forces would have initially been Wood's and Van Cleve's divisions, supported by Palmer's division and perhaps either one or two divisions from Thomas's Center Wing.[75]

Whether Bragg committed one, two, or even three divisions against the Union crossing, he could not afford to ignore this force. A significant fight would have developed for control of Wayne's Hill and the surrounding terrain. This encounter and commitment of troops would have precluded the battle from developing as it did on December 31.

Bragg's plan for December 31 was to conduct an envelopment against Rosecrans's right flank. In order to do this he had to position a preponderance of his combat power west of the river. To accomplish this task, two divisions (Cleburne's and McCown's) of the three located east of the river were withdrawn and moved to the west side. If Bragg had committed one or both of these divisions to a fight for Wayne's Hill, they would not have been available as part of the envelopment. There probably would not have been an envelopment, and Bragg's other divisions would have been hard-pressed to hold off the remainder of Rosecrans's army.

Rosecrans's plan for December 31 was to use part of his army to conduct an envelopment of Bragg's right flank. To do so he would use both the ford Harker used and McFadden's Ford. He was prevented from carrying out his plans because Bragg's envelopment commenced first, had immediate success, and forced Rosecrans to shift troops to his right and center. Had Harker's success in fording the river been exploited, Rosecrans might have turned it into the envelopment he had planned for December 31. However, this scenario did not develop. The order for Harker to recross the river established the tactical deployment and conditions that allowed Bragg, not Rosecrans, to conduct the envelopment on December 31.

CHAPTER 2

THE ARMIES COLLIDE—
WEDNESDAY, DECEMBER 31, 1862

This was a day of tactical maneuvering and intense combat by both sides. General Bragg's envelopment gained early success but ultimately lacked the combat power for victory. Bragg then shifted to frontal attacks against strong reconstituted Union defenses. Initially, Major General Rosecrans faced the potential destruction of his army. However, he rallied units, reestablished his defenses, and successfully held his new position.

Bragg Decides to Attacks Rosecrans's Right Flank

Situation

Maj. Gen. William S. Rosecrans's Army of the Cumberland departed Nashville on December 26, 1862, marching on three separate routes. On the evening of December 30 the soldiers were in position west and northwest of Murfreesboro, facing Bragg's Army of Tennessee. Rosecrans's army was deployed with the three divisions of Maj. Gen. Thomas L. Crittenden's Left Wing in position from McFadden's Ford to just south of the Nashville Pike, a distance of 1,980 yards (1.12 miles). Next were two divisions of Maj. Gen. George H. Thomas's Center Wing. Thomas's wing occupied an 880-yard (0.5 mile) position from Crittenden's right southwest to the Wilkinson Pike. To Thomas's right were the three divisions of Maj. Gen. Alexander McD. McCook's Right

Wing. McCook's position went from the Wilkinson Pike south to the Franklin Road, covering 2,860 yards (1.62 miles).[1]

Offensive tactics call for a main attack and a supporting attack against an enemy position. The main attack is designed to capture the enemy's position or achieve the overall objective. This type of attack usually has the majority of troops assigned to it and claims priority of supporting artillery fire. The reserve is normally positioned to support or exploit the success of the main attack. A supporting attack assists the main attack by making the enemy disperse its force and fight in several locations. Supporting attacks also hold enemy forces in position, cause premature or incorrect commitments of the reserve, and confuse the enemy as to which is the main attack.[2]

Seeing some of the Confederate units shift from his left to his right, Rosecrans correctly surmised that they were weak on their right, or his left. Rosecrans planned his main attack as an envelopment of Bragg's right flank. Two divisions of Crittenden's Left Wing (Wood's and Van Cleve's) were to conduct the envelopment. They were to cross the river at McFadden's Ford and another ford 1,320 yards (0.75 mile) south (where Harker's brigade had crossed on the night of December 29). The next steps involved outflanking and overpowering the defenders, pushing into Murfreesboro, turning west, and moving behind the Confederate center and right. At the same time, Crittenden's other division (Palmer's) and Thomas's Center Wing were to conduct supporting attacks on the remainder of Bragg's right and center, fixing them in position. The main and supporting attacks would force Bragg to either contend with major threats from two different directions or retreat. An additional advantage would be the capture of Wayne's Hill, where Union artillery would be able to place enfilading fire along a significant portion of the Confederate position. As the envelopment proceeded, Crittenden and Thomas could capitalize on the confusion by capturing or destroying the remainder of Bragg's right and center. With Crittenden and Thomas attacking west, Rosecrans could create a major disaster for Bragg by cutting his line of retreat to the Duck River. On the Union right, McCook was ordered to occupy a defensive position. As there was some indication that Bragg might be planning an attack, McCook was also to hold the Confederates in place until they were enveloped or cut off by Crittenden and Thomas. Rosecrans's attack was to commence at 7:00 a.m.[3]

Bragg thought that Rosecrans might attack on December 30. When no attack occurred, Bragg decided to take the initiative and attack Rosecrans the next day. What happened next would completely reverse the armies' roles. Bragg became the attacker, while Rosecrans surrendered the initiative and assumed a defensive role.

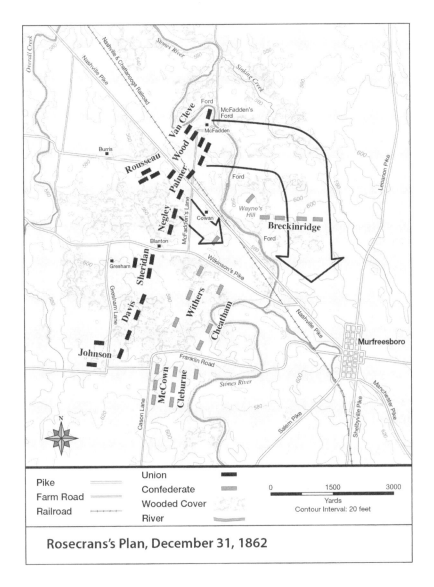

Rosecrans's Plan, December 31, 1862

Options

Bragg had several options to shift from a defensive to an offensive posture. He could attack Rosecrans's center, left, or right.

<u>Option 1</u>

An attack in the center would require Bragg to mass the majority of his army in front of Rosecrans, then conduct a frontal assault to break through the center of the Union position and push into the defenders' rear area. A successful penetration would require Rosecrans to withdraw to favorable terrain behind his present position. At this location he could attempt to reestablish a new viable position. The number of casualties a frontal attack would incur made it a poor choice.

Option 2

Another option for Bragg was attacking Rosecrans's left with his own right. Planned as an envelopment, this maneuver would require significant force to be moved across Stones River, thus dividing Bragg's left and center from his right. Using Wayne's Hill and the adjacent high terrain to the north to cover its movement, Bragg's attack force could be positioned on the east side of the river, north of McFadden's Ford. The 1,400-yard (0.8-mile) area from McFadden's Ford north to Sinking Creek provided sufficient maneuvering space, a ford, and a river crossing for a significant-size attack force. This terrain was not defended by any Union force. Once across the river, the envelopment would be in the left rear area of Rosecrans's army. A strong follow-up might gain the Nashville Pike and drive the Army of the Cumberland away from its lines of supply and communication. Supporting attacks or demonstrations would be necessary to maintain pressure upon the defenders' center and right.

Option 3

Bragg's other option was to attack Rosecrans's right. This attack could be planned as an envelopment as well. Stones River would not hinder this attack, and though the terrain contained wooded areas, it was fairly level and had roads that facilitated movement. Success with this envelopment would place significant Confederate force on the Nashville Pike in Rosecrans's rear area and sever the Union supply and communication lines to Nashville.

Decision

After discarding an attack on Rosecrans's center or left flank, Bragg decided he would attack with his left and envelop Rosecrans's right. Bragg's plan was almost identical to Rosecrans's in that he would envelop the Union right flank. To provide weight to this attack, Bragg repositioned Cleburne's Division from east of the river to an area behind McCown's Division. Hardee was then ordered to take command of these two divisions. Breckinridge's Division remained in position east of the river to protect the army's right.[4]

Had Bragg remained in a defensive position, Rosecrans would have attacked and attempted to envelop the Confederate right. As the army's right

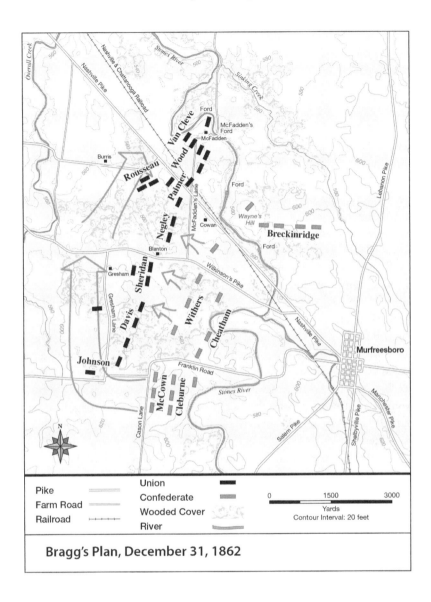

Bragg's Plan, December 31, 1862

had been weakened by the shift of McCown's Division to the left to reinforce Hardee's Corps, Rosecrans would probably have had initial success. If this action could have been converted into a successful envelopment, Bragg would have been forced to retreat, resulting in a Union victory. Perhaps Bragg might have been able to fight a successful defense. In this case both armies would have been checkmated until some future event, such as continued attack or retreat by one or the other of them.

If Bragg had made a different decision at any time during this chain of events, the Battle of Stones River would have been completely different. Bragg's choosing to attack with his left gave us the battle as we know it today. Everything that happened next came from this critical decision.

Results/Impact

As the Army of the Cumberland marched south from Nashville, Bragg had three options: retreat, defend, or attack. He rejected the possibility of retreat. Bragg then ordered his army to concentrate at Murfreesboro, which forced him into a defensive posture, if only temporarily. He subsequently decided to attack, which presented him with three courses of action. He could strike in the center, on his right, or on his left. Bragg made the critical decision to attack Rosecrans's right with his left.

Bragg's main attack was to be commanded by Hardee and carried out by McCown's Division and Cleburne's Division which would follow and support McCown's. This envelopment was designed to collapse the right of Rosecrans's army, pursue it, and capture the Nashville Pike in the rear of the Union army. If Bragg's force could interdict and hold the pike, it would cut Rosecrans's army's lines of supply and communication to Nashville. It would also push the attack's survivors into a pocket formed by the Confederate forces on the north and west and Stones River on the east. Such success would leave Rosecrans with few options. He could attempt to fight his way out, dig in and try to hold out until reinforcements arrived from Nashville, or surrender.[5]

To Hardee's right, Polk's two divisions, Cheatham's and Withers's, were the supporting attack. They were to maintain pressure on Rosecrans's center, hold it in place, and provide direct combat action to help destroy the Army of the Cumberland. Wharton was ordered to conduct a flank guard mission with his cavalry brigade to protect Hardee's left flank. Breckinridge's Division and Pegram's cavalry brigade on the east side of the river would protect the army's right flank.[6]

Bragg Fails to Significantly Weight the Main Attack

Earlier, we discussed the connecting thread that began with Davis's critical decision to send a division from Bragg's army to Vicksburg. The tread runs directly to this decision, where it had primary influence on Bragg. From here, the thread continued on to a critical decision made by Rosecrans.

Situation

Bragg's plan for December 31 was to conduct an envelopment of Rosecrans's right flank, which would carry his attack deep into the Army of the Cumberland's rear area and sever its lines of supply and communication with Nashville. To carry out his plan Bragg had available five infantry divisions, with their artillery, and four cavalry brigades. Two other cavalry brigades (Forrest's and Morgan's) had already been sent on raids deep into the Union rear areas. Bragg's decision about the allocation and use of available combat power (the infantry divisions and cavalry brigades) determined how the battle unfolded and influenced its ultimate results.[7]

Options

Bragg had three options as to allocating combat power for his attack:

1. The main attack with two divisions, the supporting attack with two divisions, and one division to protect the army's right flank.
2. The main attack with three divisions, the supporting attack with one division, and one division to protect the army's right flank.
3. The main attack with three divisions, the supporting attack with two divisions, and a cavalry force to protect the army's right flank.

Option 1

Bragg could position four infantry divisions west of Stones River. Two divisions, McCown's and Cleburne's, would conduct the main attack, the envelopment. McCown's would be the first line of the attack, and Cleburne's would follow in the second line. As McCown's attack would expectedly lose momentum, Cleburne would be available to conduct a forward passage of lines and maintain the tempo of the attack. The objective of the main attack was to cut Rosecrans off from Nashville and drive much of his army up against Stones River.[8]

The supporting attack against the Union center would be conducted by two divisions, with Withers's as the first line and Cheatham's as the supporting second line. The supporting attack did not have to capture the Union positions in front of them to be successful. It was only necessary for them to hold those Union units in position to keep them from reinforcing Rosecrans's right.[9]

The fifth infantry division, Breckinridge's, would continue to occupied positions east of the river, between the river and the Lebanon Pike. Breckinridge would protect the army's right and provide reinforcement west across the river if necessary.[10]

Brig. Gen. John A. Wharton's cavalry brigade would operate on the left flank of the army. There, it would secure the army's left flank and assist the infantry conducting the envelopment. Also operating in this area was Brig. Gen. Abraham Buford's small cavalry brigade. Brig. Gen. John Pegram's cavalry brigade would continue to occupy a position across the Lebanon Pike, east of the river. Pegram would help protect the right flank and provide early warning in the event a Union force maneuvered along that avenue of approach. Also east of the river, Wheeler's cavalry brigade was available to raid Rosecrans's supply trains that were close behind his army, or to assist in securing the army's right flank.[11]

Doctrine states that the main attack should have the priority of combat power, while the reserve should be positioned to support or reinforce the main attack or exploit its success. If Bragg chose this option, the main attack and supporting attack would have equal combat power (two divisions each). In addition, his fifth division east of the river would protect the army's right and be prepared to reinforce west of the river. In other words, one of that division's tasks was to be the army's reserve. However, it was not in a position to effectively sustain or rapidly exploit the success of the main attack. But after allocating his divisions for the main and supporting attacks and protecting the army's right, Bragg would have no other infantry division available for reinforcements.[12]

Option 2

Bragg's second option for force allocation involved the size of the supporting attack. He could allocate only one division for this task—Withers's or Cheatham's. It would probably be Withers's, as it was already positioned along the line of contact. Positioning Cheatham's four brigades behind Cleburne would significantly increase the combat power of the main attack to three divions and provide the capability to respond to unforeseen events.

Although this allocation would significantly weaken the supporting attack, as previously stated, it was not necessary for that attack to overrun or capture the Union positions before it. It was only necessary to hold those Union units in position so they could not reinforce Rosecrans's right or counterattack. Breckinridge's Division and Pegram's Brigade would remain east of the river to protect the army's right flank. Wharton's Brigade would operate on the left flank of the army, and Wheeler's Brigade would be available to raid Rosecrans's supply trains or help secure the army's right flank. For this option to be effective, the decision had to be made and the units repositioned on December 30 or before dawn on December 31.

Option 3

Breckinridge's Division could be moved to the west side of the river and placed behind Cleburne's Division as the reserve. Doing so would have placed Breckinridge in a position to be a true reserve, not one in name only. Breckinridge had five brigades under his command, and all five could have crossed the river. Alternatively, one or two brigades could have been left east of the river while three or four were positioned west to support the main attack. With either all five brigades or only three or four of them west of the river, Breckinridge would have had a significant force that could reinforce the main attack. In addition, this option allocated three divisions to the main attack and would provide a sufficient force to respond to unforeseen events.

The movement of all or part of Breckinridge's Division west of the river raises the question about the security of Bragg's right. There were two cavalry brigades (Pegram's and Wheeler's) east of the river. The reported strength for Breckinridge's four brigades and Brig. Gen. John K. Jackson's brigade (attached) was: Palmer's, 1,575 soldiers; Preston's, 1,951; Adams's, 1,634; Hanson's, 1,893; and Jackson's, 874. Pegram's strength was 480 men, and Wheeler's strength was 1,169 men, providing a combined cavalry total of 1,649. The combined cavalry strength east of the river was slightly larger than two of Breckinridge's brigades (Pillow's or Adams's), only 244 to 302 fewer soldiers than two other brigades (Hanson's or Preston's), and slightly less than double the size of Jackson's Brigade.[13]

Cavalry is assigned an economy of force mission to conduct offensive or defensive operations that will free up infantry for a different mission. In this case, the cavalry would take over the defensive task of protecting the right flank while Breckinridge's Division crossed the river and participated in the main attack.[14]

The decision to move all or part of Breckinridge's Division west of the river needed to be made and carried out on December 30 or before dawn on December 31. After that, it would be too late.

Decision

Bragg decided to allocate two divisions (McCown's and Cleburne's) to the main attack, two divisions (Wither's and Cheatham's) to the supporting attack, and Breckinridge's Division and Pegram's Brigade to protect the army's right. Wharton's Brigade would operate on the army's left flank and support the envelopment. Wheeler's Brigade would raid Rosecrans's supply trains.

If successful, the main attack would envelop Rosecrans's right, penetrate deep in the rear area, cut his supply and communication routes from Nashville, and force much of the Union army up against Stones River.

An effective envelopment had to progress through three successive phases. In the first phase, McCown's Division had to attack in a westerly direction for 1,100 yards (0.6 mile) to destroy or disrupt the right of the Union line. Simultaneously, McCown's three brigades had to turn right (north) 90 degrees on the hinge of the right brigade. In the second phase, the division formation, now facing north, had to continue the attack for 2,650 yards (1.5 miles) to the Wilkinson Pike. During this phase the attack would place sustained pressure on the disrupted and retreating Union regiments, attack and defeat any enemy reserves, and envelop Union forces to the right of the axis of advance. The defenders could either retreat or be cut off and defeated by the envelopment and supporting attack. When it reached the Wilkinson Pike, McCown's Division would probably be low on ammunition and would need to pause and regroup before continuing on.[15]

Phase three would commence with a forward passage of lines by Cleburne's Division, which had been following McCown's in a supporting role. This passage of lines would ensure the attack was continued with a fresh division. Cleburne's Division would then attack in a northeasterly direction for another 2,600 yards to the Nashville Pike and the Nashville-Chattanooga Railroad. Success in phase three would place a significant Confederate force in a blocking position across Rosecrans's lines of supply and retreat. Concurrently, McCown's Division, having resupplied ammunition and reorganized, would also continue northeast, act as a reserve to Cleburne's Division, and be available to reinforce the blocking position in the Army of the Cumberland's rear area. This was the concept, but it didn't exactly happen that way.[16]

Results/Impact

McCown deployed his division with all three brigades in the first line and no reserve. The division's (and the army's) left brigade was Brig. Gen. James E. Rains's four-regiment brigade. To Rains's right was the center brigade, Brig. Gen. Matthew D. Ector's four-regiment brigade. To Ector's right was Brig. Gen. Evander McNair's four-regiment and one-battalion brigade. McNair's right flank was on the east-west Franklin Road. Each brigade had an artillery battery attached, Therefore, three artillery batteries were available to support the infantry.[17]

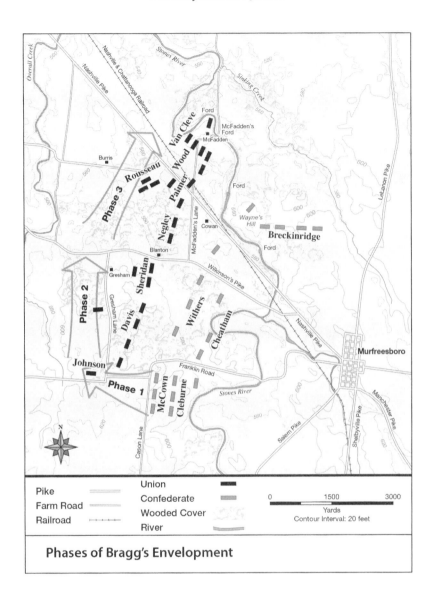

Phases of Bragg's Envelopment

Maj. Gen. John P. McCown graduated from the US Military Academy in 1840 and fought in the Mexican War. He resigned his commission on May 17, 1861, and entered Confederate service as a colonel of artillery. He was promoted to brigadier general in October 1861 and to major general in March 1862. Prior to Stones River he had been at Belmont, New Madrid, Fort Pillow, and in East Tennessee.[18]

Major General John P. McCown, CSA,
commanding division. Library of Congress.

Cleburne deployed his four-brigade division six hundred yards behind McCown's. Cleburne placed three brigades in his first line and one brigade in a supporting (reserve) second line. The division's left brigade was Brig. Gen. St. John R. Liddell's four-regiment brigade. To Liddell's right was Brig. Gen. Bushrod R. Johnson's five-regiment brigade. Next to the right was Brig. Gen. Lucius E. Polk's five-regiment brigade. Polk's right flank was on the Franklin Road. None of the brigades had a reserve because the three brigade commanders deployed all of their regiments in the front line. The division reserve was Brig. Gen. Sterling A. M. Wood's five-regiment brigade, which was positioned behind the right brigade (Polk's) of the first line. Wood did not have a reserve. Three brigades had an attached artillery battery. Brig. Gen. John A. Wharton's cavalry brigade was situated on the left flank of the attack.[19]

Maj. Gen. Patrick R. Cleburne was born in Ireland, and he immigrated to the United States in 1849. Before the war he lived in Arkansas. Cleburne commanded an infantry regiment when the war began and was promoted to brigadier general in March 1862 and major general in December 1862. Additionally, he fought at Shiloh and participated in the Kentucky Campaign. Cleburne was the most effective Confederate division commander in the Western Theater.[20]

The right flank of the Army of the Cumberland was positioned along the Franklin Road 1,100 yards west of McCown's Division. The right unit was Brig. Gen. August Willich's five-regiment First Brigade part of Brig. Gen. Richard W. Johnson's three-brigade Second Division, which was part of McCook's Right Wing. Willich's brigade faced south and west. Brig. Gen. Edward N. Kirk's five-regiment (one regiment guarding the ammunition train) Second Brigade was situated to Willich's left, facing southeast and nearly forming a right angle with Willich. Col. Philemon P. Baldwin's four-regiment Third Brigade was in reserve 1,200 yards behind and north of Willich and Kirk. Two divisions on Johnson's left extended the position north for 2,700 yards (1.5 miles) to the Wilkinson Pike. Brig. Gen. Jefferson C. Davis's three-brigade First Division was to Johnson's left, and Brig. Gen. Philip H. Sheridan's three-brigade Third Division was on Davis's left. Sheridan's left was tied in with the right of Thomas's Center Wing.[21]

Sunrise on December 31, 1862, was at 6:56 a.m. McCown's Division initiated Bragg's plan thirty minutes prior to sunrise, when there was barely sufficient visibility to begin the attack. Moving in the early morning mist, McCown achieved tactical surprise. In a short period of time he broke the right flank of McCook's Right Wing and drove most of Willich's and Kirk's brigades rearward. Phase one of Bragg's envelopment had been successfully completed.[22]

Major General Patrick R. Cleburne, CSA, commanding division. Library of Congress.

Johnson's two brigades (Willich's and Kirk's) did not retreat directly north, the direction McCown now wanted to go, instead angling off to the north-west. Only McCown's right brigade (McNair's) completed the ninety-degree right turn to the north. The center and left brigades (Ector's and Rains's) pursued the fleeing Union troops. This action took a majority of McCown's Division off to the northwest and immediately disrupted Bragg's plan.[23]

As Cleburne's Division, initially following McCown's, made the right turn, Cleburne discovered that his division was no longer in a supporting role but was now in the front line of the attack. After completing the turn Cleburne was oriented north. McCown, who should have been facing north, except for one brigade, was oriented to the northwest and pursuing the retreating Union brigades. McCown's troops had uncovered Cleburne's brigades. Confronted by Johnson's reserve brigade (Baldwin's) and the right of Davis's division, Cleburne had no choice but to take up the attack to the north on either side of Gresham Lane.[24]

Cleburne's attack north successfully drove back the disrupted Union right, even when some units rallied and attempted to fight. As Cleburne progressed north, McCown gained control of his brigades, and they reoriented to the north. Around 9:00 a.m. McCown maneuvered his division on line with Cleburne's. Together they drove Johnson's and Davis's disorganized Union divisions north across the Wilkinson Pike. Phase two of the envelop-

Gresham's Lane today, looking north. Cleburne's Division attacked on either side of the lane.

ment was completed when Cleburne's and McCown's divisions arrived at the Wilkinson Pike between 10:00 and 11:00 a.m.[25]

Johnson's and Davis's regiments continued to retreat northeast to the Nashville Pike, where they were rallied, reorganized, and resupplied with ammunition. Their retreat cleared the way for McCown and Cleburne to exploit the situation and maneuver all the way into the rear area of Rosecrans's army and cut its supply and communication lines to Nashville. In addition, Sheridan's division, the left division of McCook's Wing, had its right flank repeatedly exposed and had been forced, while fighting, to fall back just north of the Wilkinson Pike. The continued maneuvering of Bragg's left would further expose Sheridan's flank. While under frontal attack, Sheridan's division and those to his left (Negley's of Thomas's Center Wing, then Palmer's of Crittenden's Left Wing), would be forced to fall back to the northeast to the vicinity of the Nashville Pike and the Nashville-Chattanooga Railroad.[26]

Upon arriving at the Wilkinson Pike, McCown's Division was forced to halt. The attack in phase one, the misdirected pursuit, and the repositioning on Cleburne's left in phase two had left many of McCown's regiments disorganized and low on ammunition. A division with all brigades committed would normally pause to resupply ammunition and regroup its units after attacking 3,750 yards (2.1 miles).[27]

Phase three of the envelopment would commence with the continuation of maneuvering and pursuit north of the Wilkinson Pike. It was at this point that Cleburne's Division, which was planned to follow McCown's in a supporting role and had not been in contact with the enemy, would conduct a forward passage of lines. Cleburne's Division was then to follow up with a pursuit that would carry it to the Nashville Pike before Rosecrans could move troops to reestablish his right (west) flank.

However, Cleburne's Division had already been in contact with Union brigades since making the ninety-degree right turn that marked the end of phase one and the beginning of phase two. This situation was caused by McCown's pursuit of Willich's and Kirk's brigades as they fled to the northwest. McCown's chase uncovered Cleburne's Division and resulted in its taking up the attack for the 2,650 yards to the Wilkinson Pike. Phase three began not with a forward passage of line by a fresh uncommitted division, but with Cleburne continuing north, after a pause to resupply ammunition, with a division that had already seen considerable fighting.[28]

Shortly after 11:00 a.m., Cleburne had extracted his brigades that had been attacking the right of the new Union position along the Wilkinson Pike. He then maneuvered northeast toward the Nashville Pike. At noon Cleburne's Division, with Col. Alfred J. Vaughan's brigade from Cheatham's

Division, made contact with brigades that Rosecrans had shifted from his left to the right. This fighting occurred halfway between the Wilkinson Pike and the Nashville Pike. Though the combat did not stop Cleburne, it delayed his advance, reduced his combat power, and allowed other Union units to establish a position along the pike. Although some of Cleburne's regiments reached the vicinity of the pike, they were eventually driven back by Union counterattacks.[29]

McCown, in the meantime, maneuvered his division too far to the right (northeast). Instead of following Cleburne, where he might have been in position to reinforce the attack, his division passed to Cleburne's right and struck the Union defenses southeast of where Cleburne did. McCown also was unsuccessful, and he retreated.[30]

As Cleburne's and McCown's Divisions fell back from the Union defenses along the Nashville Pike, any possible success in interdicting Rosecrans's lines of communication and supply and trapping his army faded. Two of McCown's brigades pursued the retreating Union brigades in a northwest direction, and this chase brought Cleburne's Division into the fight sooner than it should have. The pursuit ultimately depleted the combat power necessary for a rapid exploitation to gain the pike in the Army of the Cumberland's rear area.

This prospect is not a certainty, but had McCown's Division completed the right turn at the end of phase one and maneuvered north rather than northwest, Cleburne's uncommitted division would have been in position near the Wilkinson Pike to conduct a forward passage of lines. Cleburne's troops could have rapidly attacked to the Nashville Pike before Rosecrans could reposition sufficient troops to stop them. Followed and reinforced by McCown's resupplied division, and in conjunction with the success of the supporting attack, Bragg's plan had a good chance of success. The probability of success could have been even greater if a third division had been added to the envelopment. The only division available was all or part of Breckinridge's Division from the east side of Stones River. This division's use or misuse will be discussed later.

The mid-December critical decision to detach Maj. Gen. Carter L. Stevenson's division from the Army of Tennessee and transfer it to Vicksburg added complexity to Bragg's choice for allocating of combat power. The consequences of that earlier critical decision can be traced directly to this critical decision.

Bragg's allocation of forces did not allow for adjustments during unexpected events. Consider, for example, McCown's Division not completing the right turn to the north. This circumstance committed Cleburne's Division to the front line of battle earlier than intended. As there was no other division assigned to the main attack and Breckinridge's Division was across the river, there was no way to promptly reinforce the assault and maintain its momentum. The dwindling momentum gave Rosecrans time to shift forces and counter the threat to the right rear of his army.

It is necessary to remember two key points when discussing Bragg's allocation of combat power. One, Bragg had limited forces (five divisions) to execute his plan. Therefore, to properly weight the main attack it was necessary that he be weak somewhere—either east of Stones River or with the supporting attack. The location of that weakness would have to be a calculated risk. Second, to be successful the main attack (the envelopment) needed sufficient combat power to collapse the right of Rosecrans's position and take advantage of that success. It was also necessary for the attack to deal with unforeseen developments, to sustain momentum all the way to the Nashville Pike, and to capture the pike and hold it. Everything depended on the main attack. If it did not succeed, then there was no point in attempting the envelopment.

Bragg's decision on the allocation of combat power for the main attack was critical. That decision created the inability to handle contingencies (McCown's division not completing the right turn), the loss of momentum, and the temporary stopping of the envelopment at the Wilkinson Pike. Rosecrans therefore had the time he needed to shift units to his right. In turn, this circumstance led to his successful defense of the Nashville Pike and the defeat of Bragg's envelopment.

Rosecrans Cancels His Attack

Situation

As Bragg was planning his envelopment for December 31, Rosecrans was doing the same. Rosecrans's plan was almost a reverse image of Bragg's. He planned to envelop Bragg's right in much in the same way Bragg planned to envelop his right. Two divisions were assigned the mission of conducting the envelopment, two divisions composed the supporting attack, three divisions were ordered to defend the army's right, and one division was held in reserve. The day before the attack, the Pioneer Brigade was sent to improve the approaches to McFadden's Ford.[31]

The enveloping force was to cross the river at McFadden's Ford and at another ford 1,300 yards (0.75 mile) farther south. Once across, they would attack Breckinridge's Division and dislodge it from its position. Maneuvering east and turning south, they would then attack Bragg's rear area. This attack would envelop Bragg's right flank, place a significant force in his rear area, and force him to either fight in two directions simultaneously or retreat to avoid being cut off. The envelopment consisted of Brig. Gen. Horatio P. Van Cleve's Third Division and Brig. Gen. Thomas J. Wood's First Division from the Left Wing. Van Cleve's division was to cross Stones River at McFadden's Ford while Wood's division crossed at the ford 1,300 yards to Van Cleve's right.[32]

To the right of the envelopment, Crittenden's third division, Brig. Gen. John M. Palmer's Second Division, and Brig. Gen. James S. Negley's Second Division of Thomas's Center Wing formed the supporting attack. They were to maneuver parallel to the Nashville Pike and hold the center of Bragg's army in position.[33]

To the right of the supporting attack, Maj. Gen. Alexander McD. McCook's three-division Right Wing was to occupy defensive positions to stop maneuvering by Bragg's left and hold those units in position. Maj. Gen. Lovell H. Rousseau's First Division of the Center Wing was held in reserve and positioned behind the supporting attack.[34]

At 7:00 a.m. on December 31 Van Cleve commenced crossing Stones River at McFadden's Ford. By 8:00 a.m. two of his brigades were across the river, and a third was in the process of crossing. Wood was also ordered to cross at the ford south of McFadden's Ford. By 8:00 a.m. Wood's division was in position to cross, and Rosecrans's planned envelopment was commencing. However, events began to develop that would wreck Rosecrans's plan.[35]

Bragg began his attack first. At 6:30 a.m. Bragg's left, McCown's Division followed by Cleburne's, violently struck the right of McCook's position (and Rosecrans's right). The immediate success of this attack collapsed McCook's right and center divisions, driving them back to the northwest and north.[36]

Rosecrans was located behind the army's center and could hear the firing on the right. He thought it was McCook's divisions holding Bragg's left in position. Between 7:30 and 8:00 a.m., a staff officer from McCook's informed Rosecrans that the Right Wing was under heavy attack and needed assistance. Rosecrans thought everything was under control, and he ordered the staff officer to return and tell McCook "to contest every inch of ground." Rosecrans further stated, "If he holds them we will swing into Murfreesboro with our left and cut them off." He then said to his staff, "It is working right." At this point, Rosecrans thought his planned envelopment was still viable.[37]

Soon afterward, a second staff officer from McCook informed Rosecrans of the true situation—the right of his army had collapsed and was being driven rearward. This news confirmed what the army commander was beginning to suspect, as he could hear the sounds of the battle on his right moving north toward the army's rear area.[38]

Options

Rosecrans had three tactical courses of action to choose from:

1. Allow the Left Wing to complete its river crossing and conduct the envelopment into the Army of Tennessee's rear area.
2. Cancel the attacks by the Left and Center Wings. Leave Van Cleve's division across the river to threaten Bragg's right, and send the Pioneer Brigade (fighting as infantry) and two brigades from Wood's division to reinforce the right flank and protect the Nashville Pike.
3. Cancel the attacks by the Left and Center Wings, withdraw Van Cleve back across the river, and send all available forces to reinforce the army's right and defend the Nashville Pike.

<u>Option 1</u>

Rosecrans could opt to complete the river crossing and continue with the envelopment. If the troops moved fast enough, this plan could potentially place a two-division force in the rear of Bragg's supporting attack, and possibly in the rear of the Confederate envelopment. However, this option had a tactical danger. While Rosecrans's left was maneuvering into Bragg's rear area, Bragg's envelopment might successfully reach and cut the Nashville Pike behind Rosecrans's position. Rousseau's division, in reserve, was optimally positioned to deploy and create a blocking position to keep Confederates from reaching the pike. However, these troops were not strong enough to simultaneously block Cleburne's and McCown's attacks. If the division deployed from where it was positioned, it would have faced Cleburne. There would have been a gap between the Union center and Rousseau, the exact area McCown's division later attacked through. If Rousseau moved forward and deployed so that he had contact with the Union center, he would have confronted McCown's division. But Rousseau would also have left an open avenue of approach for Cleburne to maneuver past his right flank and gain the pike.

<u>Option 2</u>

Rosecrans could also cancel the Left Wing's and Center Wing's attacks, leave Van Cleve's division across the river, and send two brigades from Wood's division and the Pioneer Brigade (fighting as infantry) to reinforce the right flank and protect the Nashville Pike. At the same time, Rousseau's division could be ordered forward to extend the army's center farther to the right. An aggressive maneuver by Van Cleve against Breckinridge's Division would hold the unit in position east of the river and keep Bragg from using it to reinforce his left or center. If Van Cleve captured Wayne's Hill, he would be able to deliver enfilading artillery fire on the center of Bragg's army.

A successful limited attack by Van Cleve may have caused Bragg to question if he could continue with his envelopment. Alternatively, it might force Bragg to encounter a developing threat to his right and possibly his rear area from at least one division and, from his perspective, maybe an even larger force. As with the first option, there were several tactical dangers. Van Cleve's division would have been on the other side of Stones River from the rest of the Army of the Cumberland. In the event of a tactical reverse or some other adverse situation, it would have been difficult for Van Cleve to return to the friendly side of the river. With all other available troops committed to reinforcing the army's right, reinforcing Van Cleve would have been next to impossible.

Option 3

If he canceled the attacks by the Left and Center Wings and ordered Van Cleve's division back across the river, Rosecrans would shift his army from the offense to the defense. However, this choice would provide him with uncommitted brigades that he could reposition to the army's right and center, thereby protecting the Nashville Pike.

Decision

Rosecrans decided upon option three, the safest of his choices. He immediately began issuing orders that eventually regained some control of the tactical situation.

Results/Impact

This critical decision stopped the movement of Rosecrans's left and center and placed those units in defensive positions. These positions eventually stabilized and strengthened the army's left. Rosecrans was then able to concentrate on the situation as it developed in his center and right. This critical decision committed Rosecrans's army to fight a defensive battle on December 31. Though it was not a certainty at the time, this decision would establish the tactical situation and follow on critical decisions that gave victory to the Army of the Cumberland.

Rosecrans Shifts Units to the Right

The connecting thread that we wrote about earlier terminates at this decision. The thread directly links Davis's critical decision to detach a division from Bragg's army (Bragg Loses a Division) to Bragg's allocation of combat power for his attack (Bragg Fails to Significantly Weight the Main Attack) and Rosecrans's critical decision to shift units.

Situation

This decision and the preceding one (Rosecrans Cancels His Attack) have a symbiotic relationship. Without the previous decision, there is no option for this decision. When Rosecrans cancelled his attack on the left, it provided him with uncommitted brigades and allowed him to reposition units. Rosecrans's decision also shifted his army from an offensive posture to a defensive one and gave Bragg the tactical initiative. For the remainder of December 31 Rosecrans would respond to Bragg's maneuvering.

The army's defensive position gained Rosecrans two significant advantages. First, the withdrawal of Van Cleve's division to the west side of Stones River created uncommitted units. Rosecrans could redeploy these forces to defend against Bragg's envelopment of his right flank and protect the Nashville Pike. Second, when the Army of the Cumberland was positioned for the December 31 attack, its orientation was an almost straight line. Because of the refusal of its right flank, the Army of Tennessee's position was the inside of an arc. Across the arc's interior, the distance from Bragg's right to his left was shorter than the distance from Rosecrans's left to his right. Prior to his attack, Bragg had the advantage of interior lines. With the early success of Bragg's assault and the collapse of Rosecrans's right then the establishment of a new position along the pike the position of interior lines was reversed. Then there was a considerably shorter distance across the inside of the arc from Rosecrans's left to his right. And the distance from Bragg's right to his left, now along the outside of the arc, was much longer. Rosecrans used this advantage to shift troops from his left to right to confront and eventually stop Bragg's envelopment.[39]

Options

Rosecrans had two options. He could commit his reserve, Rousseau's division, and move it farther west. He could also reposition Rousseau's men to the right of Sheridan's division, thereby extending Sheridan's line, and send other units farther to the right (west) as they became available.

Option 1

Rousseau's troops could be sent to the far right. His division was positioned in the center rear of the army near the intersection of the Nashville Pike and Asbury Road. From that location it could move rapidly to confront Bragg's envelopment. Bragg's envelopment consisted of two divisions, Cleburne's and McCown's. If Rousseau was sent farther to the right, his division would make contact and fight Cleburne's Division. McCown's Division might then maneuver unopposed through a gap between Rousseau's left and Sheridan's right, finding a clear line of approach to the Nashville Pike before other Union units could be repositioned there.

Option 2

Another possibility was sending Rousseau's division to Sheridan's right and the other units farther to the right (west). This option would move Rousseau's division from its reserve position to the right of Sheridan's division. The defensive line would be extended to Sheridan's right, and troops would be positioned to directly confront McCown's Division, which was in the process of flanking Sheridan on his right. Other units from Rosecrans's cancelled envelopment could then be sent to the far right to confront Cleburne's Division.

Decision

Rosecrans decided to send Rousseau's division to Sheridan's right. He directed additional units to the far right as they became available.

Results/Impact

Rosecrans sent Rousseau's division south from its reserve position to a position to the right of Sheridan's division, which had fallen back to the Wilkinson Pike. Rousseau ordered his men forward, and they deployed into a large cedar thicket, engaging in confused fighting with attacking Confederates. Soon after this encounter, Rousseau's division conducted an uncoordinated withdrawal and re-formed along the Nashville Pike. The unit now occupied a defensive position northwest of the Round Forest, facing southwest. With others, Rousseau's troops engaged and repulsed McCown's Division as its brigades came out of the cedars and attacked toward the pike.[40]

When Van Cleve's division returned to the friendly side of the river, Col. Samuel W. Price's Third Brigade was ordered into a defensive position at McFadden's Ford. This brigade was to block an easy route of attack across the river into the army's left. In the event of a large Confederate attack at this

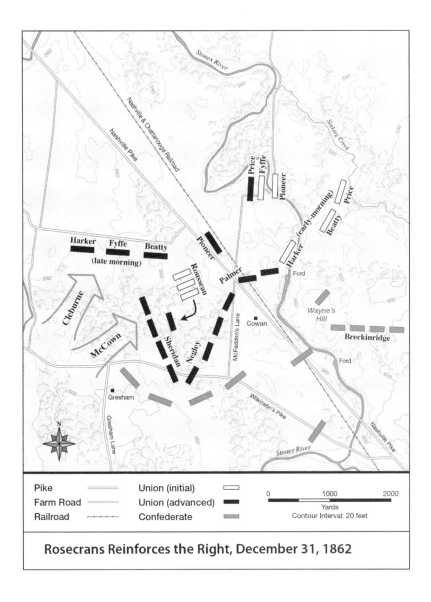

Rosecrans Reinforces the Right, December 31, 1862

location, Price's troops would provide early warning of the threat. Van Cleve's other two brigades were redeployed to the army's right rear area.[41]

Rosecrans used his interior lines and ordered Van Cleve to send Col. Samuel Beatty's First Brigade and Col. James P. Fyffe's Second Brigade to the army's right rear area. Both of these brigades moved to positions west of the pike and south of Asbury Road. The first to arrive was Beatty's brigade, and it deployed and engaged the left regiments of Ector's Brigade, the left

Harker's defensive position after moving to the Union right flank.

of McCown's Division. Fyffe's brigade soon arrived and went into position on Beatty's right. Soon afterward Col. Charles G. Harker's Third Brigade from Wood's division, also sent from the left, went into position south of the Ashbury Road and 250 yards to Fyffe's right. All three brigades were almost immediately attacked by Cleburne's Division of four brigades and Vaughan's Brigade of Cheatham's Division. The Union defenders were driven back. However, they sufficiently disrupted Cleburne's attack so that Confederate regiments that reached the pike were forced to fall back.[42]

Rosecrans also sent one more brigade from his left to the center. Capt. James St. Clair Morton's Pioneer Brigade was ordered to stop work at the ford and follow the three infantry brigades toward the right. The Pioneer Brigade took up a position along the pike that generally corresponds with the present-day location of the National Cemetery. There, it played a significant role in stopping McCown's final attack to gain the Nashville Pike.[43]

Rosecrans's decision to reposition available brigades from the left to his right just barely prevented his line of supply and communication from being cut. Had that happened, his army would have been isolated from Nashville. Rosecrans's advantage with interior lines and McCown's and Cleburne's pause in their attack provided time for Beatty's, Fyffe's, Harker's and Morton's brigades to occupy new defensive positions before the Confederate envelopment reached the Nashville Pike. In conjunction with the one before it (ceasing the attack), this critical decision determined the sequence of the battle on the west and northwest side of the battlefield. It also created a situation in which Bragg had to decide whether to reinforce his left, attack Rosecrans's center at the Round Forest, or cease offensive operations, withdraw his left, and consolidate in a defensive position.

Thomas Decides to Reposition Artillery

Situation

This critical decision demonstrates how a decision concerning a relatively small unit can occasionally have far-reaching consequences. A seemingly minor, almost inconspicuous, decision concerning two artillery batteries was vital to the Army of the Cumberland's successful defense of its position along the Nashville Pike.

When Rosecrans decided to cancel his attack and reinforce his right (both decisions have already been discussed), he ordered Maj. Gen. Lovell H. Rousseau's First Division of Thomas's Center Wing to move forward from its reserve position and extend the right of Brig. Gen. Philip H. Sheridan's position. Sheridan's division began the battle as the left division of McCook's Right Wing. Initially it faced east. As McCook's two other divisions (Johnson's and Davis's) were driven into retreat, Sheridan brought his division back north through a fighting withdrawal that used three defensive positions. At the second position the unit faced south. It was the last organized, combat-effective unit on the Army of the Cumberland's right flank. Sheridan occupied his third defensive position with his three brigades arranged in an inverted *V.* The apex of the position was on the Wilkinson Pike. Sheridan's left was joined with the right of Brig. Gen. James S. Negley's Second Division of the Center Wing. Sheridan's right, stretching back into the cedars north of the Wilkinson Pike, had an open right flank.[44]

Maj. Gen. Lovell H. Rousseau was a Kentucky lawyer and politician who became a successful soldier. He had been at Shiloh and Perryville. Rousseau's division normally consisted of four brigades and three artillery batteries. However, one brigade and a battery had been left behind to assist in guarding the army's supply trains. The other three brigades and two batteries were initially in position just south of Asbury Road and west of the Nashville Pike. (See Map—Rosecrans Reinforces the Right.)[45]

As Sheridan's division was establishing its third position, Rousseau's division was ordered to support it. Rousseau's troops marched south for approximately five hundred yards, turned right, and moved into the cedars to attempt to reinforce Sheridan and extend the Union line north and northwest from his right. Rousseau's unit entered the cedars with two brigades deployed on line and one in reserve. Col. John Beatty's Second Brigade was on the left, and Lieut. Col. Oliver L. Shepherd's Fourth Brigade was on the right. Col. Benjamin F. Scribner's First Brigade was in reserve.[46]

The two artillery batteries tried to accompany the deployed brigades into the cedars. Lieut. Francis L. Guenther attempted to deploy his Battery H, Fifth US Artillery's six guns (four Napoleons and two 10-pound Parrott Rifles) with Shepherd's brigade. Seeing the difficulty the infantry was having in the cedars and knowing it would be an impossible situation for artillery, Guenther went to Rousseau. Finding Rousseau and Thomas together, he informed them that attempting to position his guns in the heavy cedars would probably result in their loss.

Maj. Gen. George H. Thomas graduated from West Point in 1840. He had spent the first fifteen years of his army career as an artillery officer, serving in Florida, the Mexican War, and on the Western Frontier. Thomas had an expert knowledge of how to use and position artillery.[47]

Options

Thomas had three options for his artillery: leave it in the cedars, deploy it along the edge of the cedars, or move it back to terrain with open fields of fire.

Major General George H. Thomas, USA, commanding Center Wing. National Archives.

Nashville Pike final defensive position as seen by the soldiers of McCown's Division.

Option 1

Leaving the artillery in the cedars would provide the Union infantry with close support. However, the field of fire would be very limited; Confederate infantry could come close to the guns before they could be seen. Moreover, it would be difficult for the guns to withdraw rapidly if necessary. This option presented a high risk of some or all of the artillery being overrun and captured.

Option 2

Close-in support could also be provided by redeploying the artillery along the edge of the cedars. Again, the field of fire would be very limited, and Confederate infantry might be able to approach the guns undetected. Yet with an open field behind them, the guns could rapidly withdraw if necessary.

Option 3

Moving the artillery to terrain with open and long-range fields of fire would remove the threat of Confederate infantry approaching unobserved. However, while Rousseau's infantry was in the cedars, they would not receive artillery fire support. Targets could not be identified as friendly or hostile.

Decision

Thomas directed Rousseau to move his artillery out of the trees to good firing positions. Shifting east, Guenther's battery occupied a position in a six-hundred-yard open field between the northeastern edge of the cedars and the Nashville Pike. After firing several rounds at Confederates emerging from the thicket, Guenther moved his battery across the Nashville Pike to a firing position on a small rise of ground (where the National Cemetery is today).[48]

Lieut. George W. Van Pelt was also ordered to move his Battery A, First Michigan Artillery away from the cedars to a better firing position. Van Pelt moved the six 10-pound Parrott Rifles of his battery east, crossed the Nashville Pike, and went into a firing position to Guenther's right on the same rise of ground.[49]

Results/Impact

On this part of the battlefield the small elevation between the railroad and the Nashville Pike was the predominant terrain feature and an ideal position for artillery. The twelve guns of Guenther's and Van Pelt's batteries had excellent observation and a field of fire back across the open ground to the cedars.

Guenther's and Van Pelt's batteries provided the anchor point for the establishment of a final defensive line along the Nashville Pike. They were soon joined on their right by Capt. James H. Stokes's Chicago Board of Trade Battery with six guns (two James Rifles and four 6-pound smoothbore guns) and the three battalions of the Pioneer Brigade. Lieut. Alanson J. Stevens then placed his Battery B, Pennsylvania Artillery with six guns (two James Rifles and four 6-pound smoothbore guns) between Van Pelt's and Stokes's batteries. To Stokes's right, the six guns (four 10-pound Parrott Rifles and two Napoleons) of Capt. George R. Swallow's Seventh Indiana Battery went into a firing position. To Gunther's left, Lieut. George Estep's Eighth Indiana Battery with six guns (two 12-pound howitzers and four 6-pound smoothbore guns) added its firepower to the defenses. These six batteries with a total of thirty-six guns occupied an eight-hundred-yard position parallel to the Nashville Pike. As they formed on the artillery, these cannoneers were initially supported by the Pioneer Brigade, the Second Ohio, and the Thirty-third Ohio. Other regiments eventually rallied and joined in the defense of this position.[50]

No sooner had the artillery and infantry defensive line formed than McCown's Division emerged from the woods 600 yards away on the other side of the open field. Brig. Gen. James E. Rains's brigade was the first to emerge. Without waiting for the other two brigades, it immediately attacked

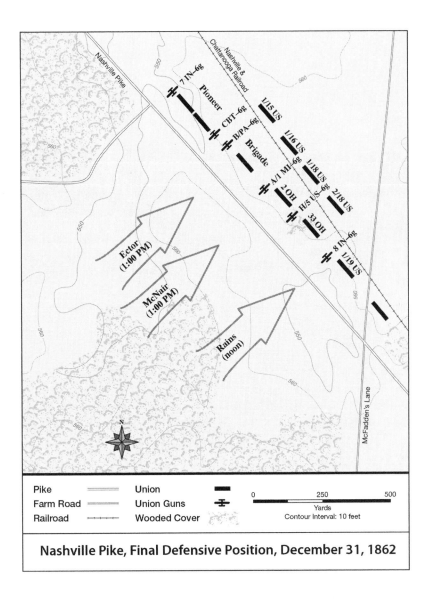

Pike · Union · Union Guns · Farm Road · Railroad · Wooded Cover

0 · 250 · 500 · Yards · Contour Interval: 10 feet

Nashville Pike, Final Defensive Position, December 31, 1862

across the open ground. Swept initially by devastating cannon and then by rifle fire, it was driven back and Rains was killed. Shortly thereafter Brig. Gen. Matthew D. Ector's brigade and Brig. Gen. Evander McNair's brigade (now commanded by Col. Robert W. Harper) emerged from the wood line and attacked across the clearing. The sustained Union cannon and rifle fire from along the pike also drove them back, creating substantial casualties. The

Union view from the Nashville Pike final defensive position. Lieutenant Charles C. Parsons Battery H and M, Fourth U.S. Artillery provided crossfire from a position near the wood at the extreme left of the photo.

intensity of the artillery fire is represented by Estep's Eighth Indiana Battery. The six guns fired 220 rounds of shrapnel, or solid shot, and 70 rounds of canister, often at ranges of fewer than ninety yards.[51]

The repulse of McCown's Division and Cleburne's Division ended Bragg's envelopment of Rosecrans's right and the attempt to sever his army's lines of supply and communication.

Thomas's decision to send Guenther's and Van Pelt's batteries away from the cedars and back to positions along the Nashville Pike was critical. These two batteries became the anchor point upon which four other batteries and many infantry regiments established a final defensive position. From Thomas's decision came the establishment of the strong defensive position along the pike. The successful defense of this position eventually led to Union victory at Stones River.

Alternate Decision/Scenario

If Thomas had chosen any other option, it is doubtful that the Nashville Pike position would have been established in strength when it was. It is possible that Bragg's envelopment would have severed the Nashville Pike. Once the Confederates reached the pike, Rosecrans's army would have been divided into two parts. The northern part would have included the divisions

View from the position of Lieutenant George Estep's Eighth Indiana Battery on the left of the final defensive position along the Nashville Pike.

that had retreated and were attempting to rally and reorganize. The southern part would have included the divisions of the Center and Left Wings that were engaged with Bragg's supporting attack. Those units would have been trapped by Confederate units to their south, west, and north and by Stones River to their east. Their options would have included trying to fight their way out, attempting to escape by crossing the river, or surrendering. The northern segment of Rosecrans's army might have attempted to fight through to the other half. But considering what they had endured, it was more likely that they would have continued to retreat toward Nashville.

This sequence of events would have totally changed the Battle of Stones River and resulted in a victory for Bragg's Army of Tennessee.

Bragg and Polk Repeatedly Attack the Round Forest

Situation

This critical decision, with its accompanying subset of decisions, wasted the combat power of Bragg's only significant uncommitted force. This choice precluded the main attack (the envelopment) from being reinforced, shifted the focus of the battle to the center, and determined the course of the fighting along the Nashville Pike and Nashville-Chattanooga Railroad axis of advance.

The focus of this fighting was the Round Forest, a small wooded area that was slightly higher in elevation than the fields around it. It was located seven hundred yards southeast of where Battery H, Fifth US Artillery and Battery A, First Michigan Artillery, Gunther's and Van Pelt's, established the anchor point (where the National Cemetery is today) for the final defensive line along the Nashville Pike. The Round Forest touched the Nashville Pike on its southwest edge and extended northeast across the Nashville and Chattanooga Railroad to where US Highway 41 is today.[52]

On the morning of December 31, the Army of the Cumberland's left and left center went southwest from McFadden's Ford to and through the Round Forest. The position then crossed the Nashville Pike, continued along McFadden's Lane, and passed through the cedars to the Wilkinson Pike. The area between McFadden's Ford and the Nashville Pike, including the Round Forest, was occupied by Brig. Gen. Horatio P. Van Cleve's Third Division and Brig. Gen. Thomas J. Wood's First Division of the Left Wing. Brig. Gen. John M. Palmer's Second Division of the Left Wing extended the position 500 yards along McFadden's Lane. From Palmer's right the Union position departed from the lane and went along the southeast edge of the cedar thicket to the Wilkinson Pike. Brig. Gen. James S. Negley's Second Division of the Center Wing was positioned in this sector. The army's Right Wing was positioned 2,860 yards southwest from the Wilkinson Pike to the vicinity of the Franklin Road–Gresham Lane intersection.[53]

Rosecrans's plan called for Van Cleve's and Wood's divisions to cross Stones River, capture high ground east of the river, and envelop Bragg's right. Palmer and Negley would move forward simultaneously and hold the center of Bragg's army in position. All of these plans changed when Bragg beat Rosecrans to the punch and began his envelopment of Rosecrans's right. Van Cleve was recalled back across the river, and he then sent two of his brigades to the right. A third brigade secured McFadden's Ford. Wood ordered Brig. Gen. Milo S. Hascall and Col. Charles G. Harker to march their brigades to the army's right flank. At that point, Wood was left with only Col. George Wagner's brigade in the division's original position. The traffic jam on the roads prevented Hascall from moving his brigade to the army's right flank. Instead, his brigade went into position where McFadden's Lane crosses the railroad. Palmer and Negley began their forward movement, but they quickly halted when they heard the heavy volume of fire caused by Bragg's attack to their right. A short time later both divisions moved back to where they had begun the morning.[54]

The departure of the brigades to reinforce the army's right opened a nine-hundred-yard gap between the brigade at McFadden's Ford and Wagner's left.

To cover part of this ground, Wagner shifted his brigade to the left. When this move was completed, his right flank, which had been adjacent to the Nashville Pike, was located next to the northern edge of the Round Forest.[55]

Col. William B. Hazen's Second Brigade of Palmer's division was part of the supporting attack. This brigade initially moved forward but was soon ordered to fall back. When the brigade retreated toward its earlier position, its left was extended into the forest and north of the railroad, where it tied in with Wagner's right. Hazen's new position stretched from the north edge of the Round Forest southwest across the railroad, then through the forest and across the Nashville Pike to McFadden's Lane. There, Hazen's right was in close proximity to Brig. Gen. Charles Cruft's First Brigade of Palmer's division. Negley's division extended the position from Cruft's right to the Wilkinson Pike.[56]

After Rosecrans's right moved back to a final defensive position along the Nashville Pike, the army's position resembled an inverted L. The long part of the L was along the pike, while the short part extended from the pike toward McFadden's Ford. When this position stabilized, Hazen's brigade was at the junction of the two arms of the L and connected them. The loss of the Round Forest would rupture the continuity of Rosecrans's new defensive position.[57]

Bragg's plan of attack was for his left to envelop Rosecrans's right flank, destroy the continuity of the defense on the Union right, and continue the

Nashville Pike today looking south as seen from the vicinity of the Round Forest.

attack to capture and secure the Nashville Pike in the Army of the Cumberland's rear area. This was the main attack. Lieut. Gen. Leonidas Polk commanded the supporting attack by Maj. Gen. Benjamin F. Cheatham's and Maj. Gen. Jones M. Withers's divisions against the center of Rosecrans's position. Two brigades constituted the right of the supporting attack. Along the line of contact was Brig. Gen. James R. Chalmers's brigade of Withers's Division. Behind Chalmers in a supporting position was Brig. Gen. Daniel S. Donelson's brigade of Cheatham's Division. Breckinridge's Division, to the right of Chalmers and Donelson, was across Stones River.[58]

Around 10:00 a.m. Chalmers's Brigade commenced the first attack against Hazen's and Cruft's brigades. Chalmers's five regiments and one battalion had a total strength of 2,000 soldiers. Attacking parallel to the Nashville Pike, they soon encountered an obstacle in the form of the burned Cowan House and its smaller outbuildings. These structures caused Chalmers's battle line to divide into two segments. The Seventh, Forty-first, and Tenth Mississippi Regiments went to the left of the buildings and attacked Cruft's brigade in position along McFadden's Lane. Cruft's position held, causing 353 casualties to the 1,482 soldiers in this part of the attack. The Ninth Mississippi Regiment and Blythe's (Forty-fourth Mississippi) Regiment passed to the right of the Cowan House, attacked astride the pike, and hit Hazen's brigade at the Round Forest. Hazen repulsed the attack. Of the 518 soldiers in this part of the attack, 136 were casualties. Chalmers's total infantry losses in killed, wounded, or missing were 489, including Chalmers and 40 of his officers. These numbers accounted for 24 percent of his brigade's strength. Supporting Chalmers were twelve guns: Garrity's Alabama Battery, Barret's Missouri Battery, and Stanford's Mississippi Battery. Additionally, twelve guns on Wayne's Hill were within range to support the attack. Some of these guns had been firing at targets of opportunity. There apparently was no attempt to coordinate the fire of these guns with Chalmers's attack. More discussion on these guns appears later in the book.[59]

As Chalmers commenced his attack, Donelson moved his brigade forward and occupied the position Chalmers's regiments had just vacated. When Chalmers was repulsed and fell back, Donelson ordered his brigade forward, commencing the second attack against the Cruft-Hazen position. Donelson's five regiments brought 1,400 men to the attack. Going forward from their attack positions, they encountered the same Cowan House obstacle as Chalmers's Brigade. In a repeat of the previous assault, Donelson's Brigade divided into two segments as it passed the dwelling and outbuildings. The Thirty-eighth and Eighth Tennessee Regiments, along with seven companies of the Fifty-first Tennessee Regiment—a force of approximately 1,000

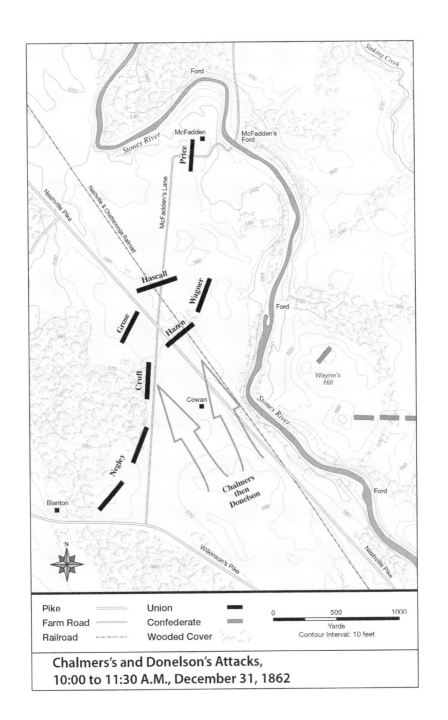

Sinking Creek

Ford

McFadden

McFadden's Ford

Stones River

Price

McFadden's Lane

Nashville Pike

Nashville & Chattanooga Railroad

Hascall

Wagner

Grose

Hazen

Ford

Cruft

Wayne's Hill

Cowan

Stones River

Negley

Chalmers then Donelson

Blanton

Wilkinson's Pike

Nashville Pike

Ford

N

Pike		Union		0	500	1000
Farm Road		Confederate			Yards	
Railroad		Wooded Cover			Contour Interval: 10 feet	

**Chalmers's and Donelson's Attacks,
10:00 to 11:30 A.M., December 31, 1862**

soldiers—passed to the left and attacked Cruft's brigade along McFadden's Lane. Cruft again held his position and repulsed the attack. Three companies of the Fifty-first Tennessee and Sixteenth Tennessee went to the right of the obstacle, attacked parallel to the Nashville Pike, and struck Hazen's brigade at the Round Forest. (One regiment, the Eighty-fourth Tennessee, did not participate in the attack.) This assault was also repulsed. Both segments of Donelson's brigade fell back to their previous positions. Donelson suffered 710 casualties, including 45 officers, among them a regimental commander, 3 field officers, and 5 company commanders. These losses accounted for 51 percent of his command. In addition to the artillery available to support Chalmers's attack, one more unit, Carnes's four-gun Tennessee Battery, was available for Donelson's attack. All total sixteen guns were in position on the west side of the river to support the attack. This was the equivalent of an artillery battalion. Twelve guns were still available east of the river on Wayne's Hill. In total, twenty-eight guns were available and within effective range.[60]

Cruft had again conducted a successful defense, his troops expending an average of fifty rounds per man. But the collapse of Negley's position to the right forced Cruft out of his position. Amidst much confusion, Cruft's and Negley's troops retreated north and northeast to areas on the other side of the railroad, where they reformed.[61]

Cruft's, Negley's, and Sheridan's collapsing defensive positions and Rousseau's failure to reinforce removed all Union forces from the continuation of the defensive line southwest from the Round Forrest. In conjunction with the partial success of Bragg's two-division envelopment, which was approaching the newly established Union defenses along the Nashville Pike, the battle on December 31 was entering a new and final phase.

The attacks against the Round Forest (Hazen's) and McFadden's Lane (Cruft's) positions had been in accordance with Bragg's plan. They were designed to hold Union defenders in position while they were enveloped and cut off. That had been accomplished until Cruft's brigade retreated to a new location. With the formation of Rosecrans's final defensive position, the questions facing the senior Confederate commanders were "What do we do next?" and "What do we do it with?" At this time, a decision was made that would determine the future course of the fighting.

As discussed earlier, had a majority of Breckinridge's Division been committed as a true reserve to the envelopment and positioned behind the two divisions on the army's left, there would not have been any decision to make.

By early afternoon the only uncommitted Confederate force was Maj. Gen. John C. Breckinridge's division. Breckinridge's Division was composed of four brigades and one attached brigade, bringing its effective strength to

7,927. The entire division was on the east side of Stones River, but it had access to a ford that would allow it to cross to positions behind the Confederate line of contact. Breckinridge's mission was to occupy the key terrain of Wayne's Hill, to protect the army's right by occupying the terrain from Wayne's Hill to the Lebanon Pike, and to be prepared to provide units to reinforce combat operations west of the river.[62]

Options

At this point in the battle, Bragg had three options for using Breckinridge's Division: reinforcing the envelopment force, attacking the *L* connection of Rosecrans's new position, or attacking to envelop Rosecrans's left.

<u>Option 1</u>

Bragg could order two to four of Breckinridge's brigades to cross to the west side of Stones River and reinforce the final attacks by the envelopment force (McCown and Cleburne).

To reinforce the two divisions that were conducting the envelopment and located near the Asbury Road, any force from Breckinridge would have to march approximately two and one-half miles after crossing the river to reach an attack position. From this location, troops could support the attack on Rosecrans's rear area to interdict the Nashville Pike. March time to the attack position would be from an hour to an hour and a half for the lead brigade. The following brigades would take slightly longer. Factoring in deployment time, up to three hours could pass between the beginning of the march and the commencement of the attack. With the shorter winter daylight hours, this was a difficult but not insurmountable task.[63]

<u>Option 2</u>

Bragg could allocate any number of Breckinridge's brigades to cross the river and reinforce Polk's supporting attack. The brigades of Breckinridge's Division that reinforced Polk's attack rather than Hardee's would only have to move a short distance after crossing the river to be committed. There was sufficient area for up to four brigades to form behind Chalmers's and Donelson's Brigades. If these reinforcements launched a coordinate attack against the Round Forest position, they might have a good chance of success.

<u>Option 3</u>

Bragg could commit Breckinridge's entire division to an attack west across the river to envelop Rosecrans's left flank.

This plan would require the division's five brigades to cross the river at McFadden's Ford and the area north of the ford. Col. Samuel W. Price's Third Brigade of Van Cleve's division defended this terrain. Across the river there was sufficient space for Breckinridge to attack and attempt to envelop Rosecrans's left. This maneuver would strike the Union position along the Nashville Pike from the rear. With an enemy envelopment of his right in progress and attacks along the center of his position, an attack against Rosecrans's left would have presented him with a whole new set of tactical problems.

Decision

Bragg decided to bring two of Breckinridge's brigades, then two more of Breckinridge's brigades west across the river to reinforce Polk.

Results/Impact

The morning had been a time of confusion and countermanding orders for Breckinridge and his division. Around 10:00 a.m. Bragg had ordered Breckinridge to send at least one, and if possible, two brigades to reinforce the envelopment of Rosecrans's right. Before this could be done, Bragg received information that a Union force east of the river was preparing to attack. He sent a staff officer to Breckinridge with orders cancelling the movement to reinforce and outlining a strike on Union troops east of the river. Bragg subsequently learned that no Union attack was forming in that area. A staff officer was again dispatched from army headquarters, this time with orders for Breckinridge not to attack, but to send two brigades west of the river to reinforce Polk. Soon afterward, another order arrived to dispatch two more brigades to Polk.[64]

The first of Breckinridge's brigades to cross the river was Brig. Gen. Daniel W. Adams's three-regiment, one-battalion brigade, which numbered 1,634 soldiers. Completing the crossing around 1:00 p.m., Adams formed his unit in the area where the Nashville Pike and Nashville-Chattanooga Railroad cross each other. With the arrival of Adams, Polk fixated on capturing the Round Forest position and issued orders accordingly from that time until late afternoon.[65]

Polk commanded Adams to attack the Round Forest Position. Moving astride the pike and railroad, Adams commenced his assault at 2:00 p.m. With his right flank next to the river, he confronted the Round Forest defenders straight on. Caught in a frontal enfilading fire from his right, Adams's attack was halted. The brigade suffered 544 casualties—33 percent of its strength—including Adams and 25 other officers.[66]

Crossing the river right behind Adams were the 874 officers and men of Brig. Gen. John K. Jackson's three-regiment, one battalion brigade. Forming his battle line to the left (west) of the pike, Polk ordered Jackson to attack on Adams's left. Passing through Chalmers's and Donelson's heavily damaged brigades, Jackson's attack progressed between the converging McFadden's Lane and Nashville Pike. He struck the defensive position almost at the point where the lane and pike intersected—the junction of the two arms of Rosecrans's position. Like Adams's on his right, Jackson's Brigade was unable to breach the defenses. After a short period of time, the troops broke contact and fell back. The casualties for this small brigade totaled 307—35 percent of its strength—and included 3 regimental commanders and 27 other officers.[67]

The artillery available to support Adams's and Jackson's attacks was substantial. Added to the sixteen guns of the four batteries west of the river that had supported the previous attack were Humphrey's Arkansas Battery, Fifth Company of the Washington Artillery (-), a section of Semple's Alabama Battery, and a section of Lumsden's Alabama Battery, for a total of fourteen more guns. A total of thirty guns were west of the river to provide fire support. Apparently no effort was made by Bragg, Polk, or anyone else to coordinate the fire of these guns on a specific target or targets and increase the probability of success. An additional twelve guns were located across the river on Wayne's Hill. These cannon from Semple's Alabama Battery (-), Lumsden's Alabama Battery (-), a section of Fifth Company, Washington Artillery, and Cobb's Kentucky Battery supported Breckinridge's Division and were in excellent firing positions. Breckinridge, or whomever he designated, should have coordinated the fire of these guns with those on the west side of the river. The artillery east and west of the river were positioned so that they had the capability to place cross fire on the Round Forest position. Again, lack of proper coordination and command and control let this advantage slip away. Used properly these forty-two guns, the equivalent of two and one-half artillery battalions, might have made the difference.[68]

Adams and Jackson attacked a much more formidable position than Chambers and Donelson did. During the two hours between the end of Donelson's attack and the beginning of Adams's and Jackson's, the Round Forest position had become stronger. In fact, the longer the fighting went on, the stronger the position became. During the lull in action, Wager, who was on Hazen's left and facing the river, pivoted on his right regiment, swinging the center and left regiments forward and to the right so that the left of his line was anchored on the river. This maneuver closed off an area of ground that allowed any attacking force next to the river to maneuver around the left of Hazen's and Wagner's defenses. It also allowed Wagner's left regiments to

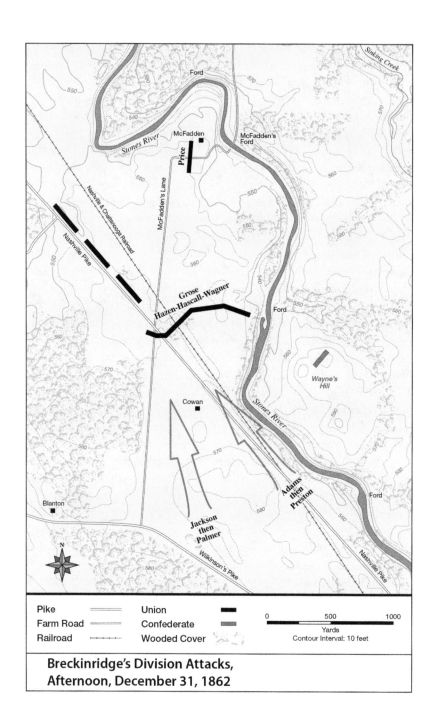

Breckinridge's Division Attacks,
Afternoon, December 31, 1862

place an enfilading cross fire into the right of any force attacking Hazen. In addition, the four regiments of Brig. Gen. Milo S. Hascall's brigade, which had been unable to reinforce the right due to clogged roads, became available to reinforce Hazen and Wager. Hascall, the senior officer, also assumed responsibility for coordinating the defense of the Round Forest and the adjacent area. Later, regiments from Grose's brigade and Sheridan's division that had retreated to the vicinity of the pike and railroad were resupplied with ammunition and rejoined the fight for the Round Forest.[69]

With Bragg's approval, Polk continued uncoordinated frontal attacks against the Round Forest. While Adams and Jackson were attacking and being repulsed, two more of Breckinridge's brigades crossed to the west side of the river. Maj. Gen. Breckinridge accompanied these units. As they completed the crossing, the brigades formed an attack formation where the pike and railroad crossed. Col. Joseph B. Palmer's five-regiment brigade, comprising 1,575 men, formed to the left (west) of the pike. Brig. Gen. William Preston's four-regiment brigade, with a strength of 1,951 soldiers, formed on Palmer's right between the pike and the river. At 3:30 p.m. both brigades commenced their attacks.[70]

As they viewed the numerous dead and wounded covering the ground their brigades were crossing, both commanders realized the strength of the Union position and the small probability they had of success. As a result, neither commander pressed the attacks as hard as the previous ones; after a brief exchange of fire, they broke contact and fell back. Palmer's Brigade had 23 casualties (1 percent of its strength), and Preston's Brigade lost 163 men (8 percent of its strength).[71]

The available supporting artillery peaked with Preston's and Palmer's assaults. To support these attacks, thirty-four guns were available west of the river, and twelve guns were positioned on Wayne's Hill.[72]

When the sun went down on the last day of 1862, Polk had ordered four successive major frontal attacks against the Round Forest position. The assaults deployed six brigades with a total strength of 9,434 officers and men. Total casualties numbered 2,236, or 24 percent of the units' strength.

The first two attacks, by Chalmers and Donelson, were designed to hold Union defenders in place and keep pressure on the Round Forest position. Chalmers and Donelson achieved their goal of preventing Union troops from reinforcing Rosecrans's collapsing right or strengthening the final defensive line along the Nashville Pike. They even drew more Union regiments to the Round Forest, stopping their deployment elsewhere.

To accomplish his mission it was necessary for Polk to keep the Union regiments at the Round Forest. To do that, he had several options for the employment of available infantry and artillery. Polk could have used Chalmers's and Donelson's Brigades in a coordinated effort to threaten another major attack or to conduct limited attacks against the defenders to hold them in place. Coordinated use of his artillery, and perhaps of Breckinridge's guns across the river, would have given warning that a major attack might be about to commence. To take advantage of Chalmers's and Donelson's threats, Breckinridge's Division would have to move to Bragg's left or left center to reinforce the attacks against the Nashville Pike defensive position.

Another choice for Polk would have been waiting until all four of Breckinridge's brigades were across the river, then committing them all to an attack to break the Union defenses. While using the concept of mass for an attack, this course of action had its own problems. The cedar forest to the west of the pike and the river to the east provided an avenue of approach that restricted maneuver. While not as good an option as the first course of action, it was certainly better than the decision that was chosen.

With Bragg's concurrence, Polk ignored both options and continued frontal attacks against the Round Forest position. The assaults were carried out by the first two brigades of Breckinridge's Division to cross the river. Polk then followed up this attack with another one by the next two brigades to cross the river.

Polk's decision that afternoon demonstrated a fixation on attacking the Round Forest. He had forgotten that this defensive position was not the army's objective; interdicting and holding the Nashville Pike north of the Round Forest was. Polk's decision ignored the principle of massing maximum combat power at a decisive point. It also ignored the axiom "Reinforce success, not failure."

Polk's decisions set the course of the fighting on the Confederate right center for the afternoon of December 31. These choices resulted in a series of frontal attacks, as brigades became available, against a strong defensive position. The piecemeal commitments of six brigades in fruitless and costly attacks along the Nashville Pike axis of advance only resulted in a waste of rather significant combat power. The same mistake was made eight months and twenty days later at Chickamauga. There, on September 20th, Polk massed eight brigades to envelop Thomas's left (north) flank in Kelly Field and cut one of Rosecrans's lines of supply, communication, and retreat to Chattanooga. The striking power of Polk's force dissipated when it was committed piecemeal. Ironically, several of these brigades were the same ones that had attacked the Round Forest.[73]

Rosecrans Decides to Remain

Situation

Sunset at 4:42 p.m., followed by darkness thirty minutes later, brought the fighting on December 31 to a close. Combat between the armies had begun ten hours before with Bragg's attempt to envelop Rosecrans's right flank and sever the Nashville Pike. This almost successful attack was halted by redeploying Union brigades from the army's left to its right. In the center the attack had been successful in driving back the defenders. But the prize of the Nashville Pike had again been unattainable. The right center of Bragg's army had taken many casualties in repeated futile frontal assaults against the Round Forest defenders. As darkness closed in, Bragg's divisions broke contact, withdrew a short distance, and established a consolidated position. The right of the Army of Tennessee was anchored on Wayne's Hill. From there the position crossed the river and extended west for 2,600 yards (1.5 miles). Cavalry covered the left and right flanks.[74]

The day's fighting had cost Bragg 8,534 casualties; 25 percent of the 33,475 officers and men committed to the battle. Of the 104 guns in the twenty-four artillery batteries, only three were reported as disabled, and none were captured. Bragg's supply situation remained adequate. There had been no cavalry operations against his ammunition and supply trains, and he still had a resupply capability. Overall, the Army of Tennessee, although bruised and somewhat battered, had the capability to conduct a defensive operation or carry out limited attacks. Bragg decided to wait and see if Rosecrans would retreat or remain in position.[75]

With the coming of night, Rosecrans's position continued to resemble an inverted *L*. The left was at McFadden's Ford. From the ford the defenses reached generally south for 1,300 yards (0.75 mile) to the vicinity of the Round Forest and Nashville Pike. From this location, it extended northwest for 2,300 yards (1.3 miles) parallel to the pike.[76]

The Army of the Cumberland had 8,580 soldiers killed or wounded on December 31. This number accounted for 21 percent of the officers and men committed to the fight. When the captured were tabulated later, the figure was even higher. Some of the losses were offset by the arrival of three units from Nashville. Col. Moses B. Walker and four of the five regiments of his brigade joined the Union troops in the early afternoon. Col. John C. Starkweather's four-regiment brigade arrived in the late afternoon. Brig. Gen. James G. Spears's five regiment brigade escorting a 303-wagon supply train arrived on the morning of January 3, 1863.[77]

On December 31 Rosecrans had positioned twenty-six batteries with 149 guns at Stones River. Twenty-eight guns were captured and one was disabled, accounting for a 19-percent loss of artillery firepower. Twenty-two of the captured guns and the sole disabled one came from seven of the nine batteries of the Right Wing. McCook's wing saw an artillery firepower reduction of 44 percent. The other guns captured were in three of the six batteries of Thomas's Center Wing; six guns were captured for a 19 percent loss of artillery firepower. Crittenden's Left Wing reported no guns lost or disabled. In addition to the army's twenty-nine-gun artillery reduction, 557 artillery horses had been killed, wounded, or reported missing.[78]

Rosecrans's supply situation was tenuous at best. His infantry had fired enormous amounts of ammunition; some estimates go as high as two million rounds. On December 31 the artillery had fired approximately 18,000 rounds. Before the battle was over a total of 20,307 were fired.[79]

Confederate cavalry raiders behind Union lines had discovered and destroyed several supply trains with needed ammunition and rations. Reports state that between 106 and 114 wagons were destroyed. This loss represented a significant reduction in Rosecrans's logistical capability. The ability to resupply ammunition was not critical, but it was not what was normally desired for continuing combat operation.[80]

During the fighting on the right, Capt. Gates P. Thruston, who was in charge of McCook's ammunition train, moved seventy-six ammunition wagons out of harm's way and parked them near Rosecrans's headquarters. He did so with difficulty and the help of Federal cavalry. Although there are reports of batteries not receiving a full resupply of ammunition, this train and other ammunition wagons provided sufficient infantry and artillery ammunition for another day's fight. Yet even with this ammunition, some batteries, such as Capt. William E. Standart's Battery B, First Ohio, only had sufficient rounds to fill their limbers but not their caissons.[81]

On New Year's Eve night 1862 and New Year's Day 1863 Bragg was faced with a decision. While not as successful as he had planned, Bragg realized he had done considerable damage to the Army of the Cumberland. His soldiers had inflicted a substantial amount of casualties and captured twenty-eight pieces of artillery. His supply situation was satisfactory and units were resupplied with ammunition. Thus situated, Bragg had three tactical options: attack, defend, or retreat.[82]

Bragg had suffered casualties to the extent that resuming the attack was not his best option. Because of his success, limited as it was, he did not believe there was a need to retreat. Throughout the night he received reports of the sounds of wagons behind the Union lines proceeding north on the Nashville

Pike. Bragg reasoned that if Rosecrans was preparing to retreat, he would be sending his supply trains north on the pike prior to the departure of his combat elements. Bragg didn't know that the wagons moving on the pike were empty and returning to Nashville for more ammunition and supplies or were transporting wounded. In Bragg's estimation the Army of the Cumberland would commence a retreat within the next twenty-four to thirty-six hours. As such a retreat would give Bragg an undisputed victory, he decided to remain on the defense. If the combat along Stones River was to continue, it was going to be Rosecrans's decision.[83]

Options

Rosecrans faced the same choices that Bragg did: attack, defend, or retreat.

Option 1

To attack, Rosecrans could either cross Stones River to strike Bragg's right or launch an offensive on Bragg's left flank. The losses in men and materiel would have caused Rosecrans to think hard before choosing this option. However, on January 1 he did send a division across McFadden's Ford to occupy a portion of the higher terrain west of the river.

Option 2

Several factors suggested that the army should hold a defensive position where it was. During the afternoon Rosecrans had been minimally reinforced with the arrival of two infantry brigades; Walker's and Starkweather's. In addition, the Right Wing's ammunition train escaped capture, and other ammunition supply trains were safe. Rosecrans had ordered this ammunition to be issued, and he estimated that it would allow him to fight one more day. Orders had been issued to send more ammunition forward from Nashville. And if necessary, some of the units protecting Nashville could be used to reinforce the position at Stones River. The longer Bragg waited to resume the offense, if he ever did, the stronger Rosecrans's position would become due to the extra supplies, ammunition, and troops from Nashville. By remaining where it was, the army would continue to hold the terrain and that part of the railroad that had been gained since they departed Nashville on December 26.

Option 3

Rosecrans's third option was to retreat to a new position. The new location would need to be at least several miles behind the previous one, either where Overall Creek intersected the Nashville Pike, or eight miles back to Stewarts

Creek, or perhaps even closer to Nashville. Choosing this option would place Rosecrans's army in a better position and lessen the distance that reinforcement, supplies, and ammunition had to travel. But it would be an admission of defeat, and it would surrender the battlefield to Bragg's army. Such an admission, in conjunction with the failure of Grant's first attempt to capture Vicksburg, the calamitous Union defeat at Fredericksburg, and Buell's failure to aggressively pursue, trap, and destroy Bragg and Kirby Smith's armies as they retreated from Kentucky, would bring severe political repercussions to Lincoln's administration, both at home and abroad. Not the least of these consequences would be the weakening of the Emancipation Proclamation that was to go into effect the next day. Lincoln had issued the proclamation after the strategic victory at Antietam in mid-September 1862. But there had been no major Union victories since then.

Decision

Late on the night of December 31, Rosecrans brought his wing commanders and others to his headquarters at the Daniel cabin for a meeting. (The Daniel cabin does not exist today. It was located 0.75 mile north of the National Cemetery gate on the west side of the Nashville Pike.) Accounts of what transpired during this meeting are varied.

Like many recollections dating from years after an event, these differ to some degree. Rosecrans had decided against attacking Bragg the next day. The casualties reported by his subordinates and the large expenditure of ammunition did not make this option particularly viable. Discussion centered on whether the army should remain in a defensive posture or retreat. Rosecrans asked his subordinate commanders what plan they recommended. Maj. Gen. Thomas L. Crittenden (Left Wing) either deferred to Rosecrans and offered no suggestion or stated that the army should remain in position. Maj. Gen. George H. Thomas (Center Wing) stated, "This army does not retreat." Maj. Gen. Alexander McD. McCook (Right Wing) contended that the army should retreat to Nashville and wait for reinforcements. His opinion was seconded by Brig. Gen. David S. Stanley (Cavalry).[84]

Rosecrans asked his subordinate commanders to wait at his headquarters while he made a reconnaissance along the pike. He rode the short distance to Overall Creek and saw torches and small fires. Though he assumed that the flames were guiding Confederate forces into his rear area, they were in fact Union cavalry disobeying Rosecrans's orders and lighting fires for warmth.[85]

Assuming the pike was or would soon be blocked, Rosecrans returned to his headquarters, announced that the army would remain on the battlefield, and ordered all the reserve ammunition issued.[86]

Monument indicating the location of Rosecrans's headquarters beside Nashville Pike.

Results/Impact

Rosecrans's decision to keep the Army of the Cumberland on the battlefield gave us the Battle of Stones River that we know of today. Because of that decision, the combat between the two armies continued for two more days and eventually resulted in a Union victory. Had Rosecrans decided to retreat, the battle would have ended the next day as a Confederate victory. Bragg would have been in position to move on Nashville in the spring, or Union operations would have had to repeat the events of the last week of 1862. The political repercussions in the North would have been disastrous to Lincoln.

CHAPTER 3

THE BATTLE CONTINUES—
FRIDAY AND SATURDAY,
JANUARY 2 AND 3, 1863

Three critical decisions were made on these two days. One of them renewed the fighting with an attack, one defeated the attack, and one brought the Battle and Campaign of Stones River to a conclusion.

Bragg Decides to Attack Rosecrans's Left Flank

Situation

On the first day of 1863 both armies remained in close proximity to each other. The commanders used the previous night and that day to make adjustments to their positions.

Maj. Gen. William S. Rosecrans abandoned the Round Forest position and brought the center of his line back 250 yards. The troops on the left of his line were withdrawn 500 yards. When the adjustment was completed, the Union position stretched southwest from McFadden's Ford for 1,100 yards (0.62 mile). At that point it intersected with the Nashville Pike between the Round Forest and the present-day National Cemetery. From this point it generally paralleled the pike for 1,000 yards (0.6 mile) to the northwest, then intersected with Asbury Lane. Three hundred yards west of this juncture,

Rosecrans's defensive position again extended northwest for 900 yards (0.5 mile). Cavalry covered the right flank. The left flank at McFadden's Ford, a potential avenue of approach to the Union rear area, was covered by an infantry brigade and artillery. This alteration gave the Army of the Cumberland a more compact and cohesive defensive position.[1]

Gen. Braxton Bragg consolidated his position facing Rosecrans by withdrawing the left wing of his army that had almost reached the Nashville Pike. Those units fell back to positions eight hundred yards north of the Wilkinson Pike. Palmer's Brigade of Breckinridge's Division was sent back across the river to reinforce Hansen's Brigade in the vicinity of Wayne's Hill. On January 1 Bragg's right flank was anchored on Wayne's Hill. From this point it reached west to Stones River. From the river, crossing the Nashville Pike and the railroad, it continued west for three thousand yards (1.7 miles), nearly reaching present-day Interstate 24. Cavalry was positioned on each flank.[2]

During the night of December 31, Bragg had received reports of wagons traveling north and away from Rosecrans's position. Bragg believed that Union supply wagons were moving in preparation for a retreat by Rosecrans's combat elements. The next morning Confederate skirmishers were sent forward, and they discovered that the Army of the Cumberland was still in position.[3]

On New Year's Day, Capt. Osborn F. West's Ninth Mississippi Battalion from Chalmers's Brigade was sent forward on a reconnaissance along the Nashville Pike. West's battalion reached and occupied the Round Forest but was later driven back by the Fifty-first Indiana. At midmorning on January 2 in this same area, twenty-two guns from Stanford's, Carnes's, Turner's, Scott's, and Robertson's Batteries astride the Nashville Pike engaged the eighteen guns of the Sixth Ohio, Eighth Indiana, and Tenth Indiana Batteries located north of the Round Forest. The Ninth Mississippi Battalion's forward movement to the Round Forest and the artillery attack in the same area would confirm for Bragg that Rosecrans's army had not retreated.[4]

On January 1 a troop movement on Rosecrans's left set the stage for a renewal of the fighting the next day. On Thursday, Rosecrans ordered Van Cleve's division, commanded by Col. Samuel Beatty since Brig. Gen. Van Cleve was wounded, to cross Stones River at McFadden's Ford and occupy the high ground east of the river. These movements were accomplished without any enemy opposition. Occupation of this key terrain gave Rosecrans several tactical advantages. It provided him a lodgment area east of the river. There, he could renew his original plan for December 31—enveloping Bragg's right flank. Occupying this key terrain also afforded Rosecrans the capability to dominate Bragg's right and enfilade it with artillery. Making this part of Bragg's position untenable would force a withdrawal of the right, and subsequently the remainder of the Confederate army, to new positions. There is no evidence that this was Rosecrans's intention when he sent troops across the river, but he possessed the capability and might have realized and acted upon it.[5]

Early on, neither Bragg nor Rosecrans fully realized the advantages of occupying Wayne's Hill and the high ground north of it. Instead, both commanders concentrated on the fight on the west flank and in the center. Rosecrans probably did not understand the importance of Wayne's Hill and the higher terrain north of it until sometime on January 1. When he did, he ordered a division across the river at McFadden's Ford to occupy this key terrain north of Wayne's Hill. Bragg did not reach the same understanding until the morning of January 2. The high ground east of the river provided a position for the Army of Tennessee to launch an attack across the river and into the Union left flank and rear areas. Conversely, it provided the Army of the Cumberland a position from which to attack the Confederate right flank or conduct an envelopment leading to Bragg's rear area. This is what Rosecrans had intended to do on December 31 until he was preempted by Bragg's attack on his right flank.

Wayne's Hill, just south of this important high ground, was within the Confederate lines and had been occupied by Hanson's Brigade and supporting artillery. From the hill the advantages of the high ground to the north were obvious. That this information was not previously communicated up the chain of command to the army commander is indicative of a breakdown in the command and communications functions.

On the morning of Friday, January 2, it was discovered and reported to Bragg that the high ground east of McFadden's Ford was occupied by a Union division. This information forced Bragg to make a decision that would affect renewal of combat and the remainder of his operations at Murfreesboro.[6]

Options

With a Union division, and perhaps others to follow, on the dominant terrain on his right, Bragg was forced to make another critical decision. Doing nothing was not an option, but Bragg could either withdraw or attack.

Option 1

Bragg could order his army to withdraw from its current position to a new one. This withdrawal would have to be to defensible terrain, if it could be found, somewhere south of Murfreesboro. Realistically, Bragg might have to march his army at least as far as the Duck River, thirty miles south of Murfreesboro, to find the terrain he needed. If he decided on this plan of action, he would be abandoning the battlefield and admitting defeat. As a result, President Lincoln would have the victory he so desperately need after a series of Union defeats. Lincoln would also gain political support for the Emancipation Proclamation, which had gone into effect on January 1. Bragg probably did not consider these potential ramifications, but they would still have been a consequence of this choice.

Bragg would also have another problem. On the night of December 31 he sent a telegram to the Confederate War Department claiming victory over the Union army. This premature telegram was released, and news of his triumph at Murfreesboro was announced in many newspapers. The negative repercussions of a retreat after this announcement would be momentous.[7]

<u>Option 2</u>

Bragg's other course of action was to remain in position and recommence offensive operations. Reconnaissance toward the center of Rosecrans's position had shown a strong defense in place. He had already tried to envelop the Union right with his left. Although he had almost been successful, his maneuver had been stopped and his troops thrown back. His attacking units were then withdrawn to just north of the Wilkinson Pike. Bragg probably thought his men lacked the strength to again attack a likely reinforced Union right. His only other option then would be attacking Rosecrans's left.

If successful, this offensive would recapture the key terrain east of Stones River. Occupying this high ground would provide an attack position for a later strike across the river at McFadden's Ford, if desired. It would remove the lodgment area east of the river that Rosecrans could use to envelop the Army of Tennessee's right. Of immediate benefit, success would give the Confederates control of this terrain and remove the Union capability to enfilade the right of Bragg's defenses with artillery. It would also provide a good position for Bragg's artillery to enfilade part of Rosecrans's position.

Decision

Bragg was not ready to concede victory to Rosecrans and abandon his position; therefore, the high ground east of the river had to be captured and occupied. Around noon, Bragg decided he would attack the Union left positioned on the high ground just east of Stones River. His next step was allocating units for the assault.[8]

During the fighting on December 31, three of Maj. Gen. John C. Breckinridge's brigades and an attached brigade had been sent west across the river. There, they unsuccessfully participated in the attacks against the Round Forest. That night, Col. Joseph B. Palmer's brigade, was sent back across the river to reinforce Brig. Gen. Roger W. Hanson's brigade. The following day, two other brigades, Brig. Gen. Daniel W. Adams's and Brig. Gen. William Preston's, recrossed the river. By early afternoon Breckinridge's Division had been reassembled with four of the five brigades under his command in attack positions near Wayne's Hill. Breckinridge's mission was to attack the Union force head on and recapture the higher terrain east of the river that overlooked McFadden's Ford. To support the infantry, Breckinridge had artillery from five batteries and a section from another battery, for a total of twenty-four guns. In addition, Bragg ordered Capt. Felix H. Robertson to take his battery and two sections of Capt. Henry C. Semple's Alabama Battery, cross the river, and join Breckinridge's assault. Thirty-four guns were available to support the attack.[9]

Results/Impact

Bragg's decision to attack renewed the fighting for another day. He must have considered that he had to eliminate the Union threat of enveloping his right flank. He also had to control the higher ground on his right to prevent Rosecrans from placing artillery there and enfilading the Confederate position. Union artillery on the higher terrain would have forced Bragg's army to fall back to a different position somewhere south of Murfreesboro. Conversely, Confederate artillery on the higher terrain would provide Bragg a significant advantage. His guns would be able to enfilade part of Rosecrans's defenses. He might also force Rosecrans to move to a different location, probably five miles north along Stewarts Creek. Either side's departure from the battlefield, if only for a few miles, would have been perceived as a victory for the other side. At 4:00 p.m. Breckinridge's Division commenced its attack. What happened next was the most spectacular use of artillery in the Western Theater during the war.

Mendenhall Reinforces with Artillery

Situation

Van Cleve's division, commanded by Col. Samuel Beatty after Van Cleve was wounded, occupied the high terrain east of McFadden's Ford, which was Breckinridge's objective. Van Cleve's division had originally been designated to lead Rosecrans's December 31 attack across the river at McFadden's Ford. This offensive was to envelop Bragg's right flank. Yet with Bragg's earlier envelopment of Rosecrans's right, Van Cleve had been recalled. Two of his brigades, Col. James P. Fyffe's and Col. Samuel Beatty's, had been involved in heavy fighting when they were sent to their army's right to halt Bragg's envelopment. A third brigade, Col. Samuel W. Price's, remained to guard

McFadden's Ford and the army's left flank. On January 1 the division had been reunited, and it again crossed the river at McFadden's Ford and occupied the higher terrain on the east side. At the time of Breckinridge's attack two brigades, Price's on the right and Fyffe's on the left, were deployed in a defensive position. Beatty's brigade (now commanded by Col. Benjamin C. Grinder), was held in reserve. One six-gun battery of artillery, Lieut. Cortland Livingston's Third Wisconsin, supported the infantry.[10]

Also on January 1 two brigades of Brig. Gen. John M. Palmer's division were moved to McFadden's Ford to support Beatty. Col. Samuel Grose's brigade crossed the river and occupied a position north of the ford and to Beatty's left rear. Brig. Gen. Charles Cruft's brigade occupied a position west of the river, where it covered the ford.[11]

At midday on January 2, Rosecrans placed additional forces in the vicinity of McFadden's Ford; Brig. Gen. James S. Negley's division was positioned west of the crossing. Negley deployed Col. John F. Miller's brigade on the left and Col. Timothy R. Stanley's brigade on the right to support the artillery.[12]

Major General Breckinridge deployed his division with two brigades in the front line and two in the supporting line. In the first line, Brig. Gen. Roger W. Hanson's five-regiment brigade was deployed on the left, and Palmer's five-

Major General John C. Breckinridge, CSA, commanding division. Library of Congress.

regiment brigade, now commanded by Brig. Gen. Gideon J. Pillow, was deployed on the right. In the supporting line, Brig. Gen. Daniel W. Adams's three-regiment, one-battalion brigade, commanded by Col. Randall L. Gibson, was on the left behind Hanson's Brigade. Brig. Gen. William Preston's four-regiment brigade was on the right behind Pillow's Brigade. The infantry was supported by thirty-four guns from eight batteries.[13]

Breckinridge had timed his attack so that it was launched in the last hour of daylight. As his leading brigades came out of the woods, where they had formed, they came under artillery fire. Hanson's Brigade on the left marched directly toward Price's position. Ordered not to fire until they were within one hundred yards of the defenders, and then to deliver one volley and charge with the bayonet, Hanson's troops moved steadily across the open ground.[14]

Price's regiments held their fire until the attack was ninety to sixty yards away, then delivered a devastating volley that temporarily stalled the Confederates. Rallied, they again continued to advance. The Union position began to crumble as the front-line regiments retreated through those behind them, and Price ordered his regiments back. At this point, Brigadier General Hanson was mortally wounded. He died two days later.[15]

On Breckinridge's right, Pillow's Brigade hit Fyffe's position. As Fyffe's left extended past the Confederate right, his left regiments placed flanking fire into the attack. A regiment from Preston's supporting brigade with Captain Wright's Tennessee Battery maneuvered to attack Fyffe's flank regiments, driving them back. The remainder of Preston's Brigade moved forward with Pillow's, and both units continued the attack. On the left, Col. Gibson moved Adam's Brigade into line with Hanson's, and they moved forward.[16]

Colonel Beatty committed his reserve brigade to stop the overwhelming Confederate attack. The troops were initially successful, but they were soon flanked, and they also joined in the retreat. After thirty minutes of intense combat, Breckinridge had captured the key terrain east of the river. Darkness was not too many minutes away. Though success was within the Confederates' grasp, what happened next changed everything.[17]

When Van Cleve's division crossed Stones River on January 1, one of its three divisional artillery batteries, Lieut. Cortland Livingston's Third Wisconsin Battery (four 10-pound Parrott Rifles and two 12-pound howitzers), went with the infantry. The second battery, Lieut. Alanson J. Steven's Twenty sixth Pennsylvania Battery (two James Rifles, and four 6-pound smoothbores), moved from its December 31 fighting position, near the present-day National Cemetery, south to a position near the turnpike. The third unit, Capt. George R. Swallow's Seventh Indiana Battery (four 10-pound Parrott Rifles and two 12-pound Napoleons), moved to the plateau above McFadden's Ford.

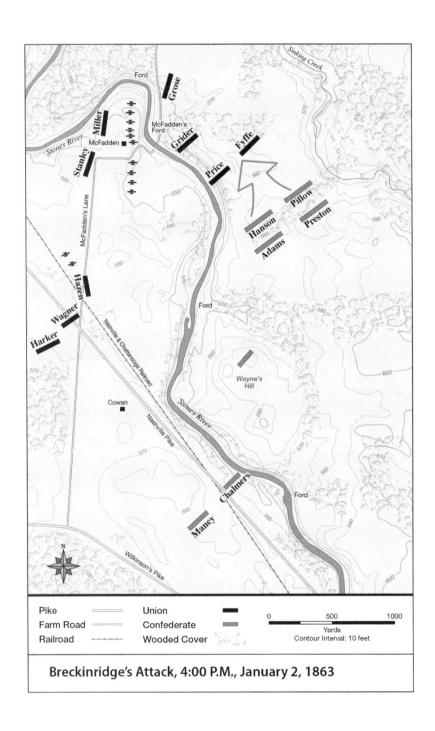

Breckinridge's Attack, 4:00 P.M., January 2, 1863

Confederate regiments were seen crossing Stones River in the vicinity of the Nashville Pike. About the same time, Confederate artillery was spotted moving about on Wayne's Hill. Some of the batteries commenced reconnaissance by fire, and this activity gave Union commanders warning of a possible Confederate attack.[18]

Options

With the Confederate movement across the river, Capt. John Mendenhall, the Left Wing's chief of artillery, had to consider the best use of his available artillery. Mendenhall had two options. He could leave the artillery positioned as it was, or he could concentrate artillery at McFadden's Ford.

Option 1

Maintaining the artillery's position would provide continuous coverage of the Left Wing's location. It would ensure that the entire position would have artillery fire support in the event of multiple Confederate attacks.

Option 2

Concentrating artillery at McFadden's Ford would greatly increase the guns defending the crossing. The risk would be leaving much of the Left Wing's defensive position without artillery support in the event of several simultaneous Confederate attacks.

Decision

With enemy activity increasing east of Stones River, Captain Mendenhall decided to concentrate artillery at McFadden's Ford. An 1851 graduate of the US Military Academy, Mendenhall was thirty-three years old when the Battle of Stones River took place. Prior to the war he had served on the western frontier and in Florida. Mendenhall had been a battery commander at Shiloh and in the Kentucky Campaign, and he became the Left Wing's chief of artillery just before the fighting at Stones River.[19]

Results/Impact

By midafternoon eighteen guns had joined the six guns that were already at the ford. The first of these were the batteries in Negley's division with whatever guns had survived the fighting on December 31. They included: Lieut. Alexander Marshall's Battery G, First Ohio (a 12-pound howitzer and a 6-pound Wiard Rifle); Capt. Frederick Schultz's Battery M, First Ohio (three

Captain John Mendenhall, USA, Chief of
Artillery, Left Wing. National Archives.

guns, see footnote); and Lt. Alban A. Ellsworth's Battery B, First Kentucky
(one 10-pound Parrott). These batteries' six guns went into firing positions to
the left of the Seventh Indiana Battery. They were positioned from right to left
as follows: G, First Ohio; M, First Ohio; then B, First Kentucky.[20]

Next were the twelve guns in two of the three batteries from Palmer's
division. Lieut. Charles C. Parsons's Batteries H and M, Fourth US (four
3-inch Ordnance Rifles and four 12-pound howitzers) went into position to
the right of the Seventh Indiana Battery. To Parsons's right Lieut. Norval
Osburn deployed his Battery F, First Ohio (four guns, see footnote). The
spacing between these batteries was sufficient to allow additional guns to be
deployed. At the commencement of Breckinridge's attack, Mendenhall had
twenty-four guns in position at McFadden's Ford. More were to come.[21]

The Confederate attack commenced at 4:00 p.m., and it broke the Union
defenses east of the river in about thirty minutes. Van Cleve's division retreated and began to cross to the west side of Stones River. Breckinridge's brigades moved into the defender's position; their mission was complete. Confederate forces now occupied the key high ground, and a Union counterattack
could probably not be organized before it was dark (sunset was at 4:44 p.m.,
darkness at 5:12 p.m.). The nighttime hours could be used to mass artillery so
that Rosecrans's position could be dominated and partially enfiladed the next
morning. It was even possible for Bragg to attack again on January 3. But in
the next twenty to thirty minutes, all these advantages disappeared.[22]

Center of Mendenhall's artillery position looking north. The guns represent Captain George R. Swallow's Seventh Indiana Battery. Trees to right not there.

The key terrain Breckinridge's infantry had just captured was nine hundred to one thousand yards from Mendenhall's artillery above McFadden's Ford. The terrain had several rolling depressions that could have provided protection from the Union guns. Elated over their victory, the Confederate brigades rushed forward in pursuit instead of consolidating their gains.[23]

Additional batteries arrived just prior to the Confederates' unorganized pursuit. The third battery from Palmer's division, Capt. William E. Standart's Battery B, First Ohio (three guns, see footnote), became the left of Mendenhall's artillery line when it went into a firing position to the left of Battery B, First Kentucky. Capt. James H. Stokes's Chicago Board of Trade Battery (two James Rifles, and four 6-pound smoothbore guns) unlimbered between Parsons's and Osburn's batteries. A battery from Wood's division, Lieut. George Estep's Eighth Indiana Battery (two 12-pound howitzers and four 6-pound smoothbore guns) became the right of the position above McFadden's Ford when it occupied a position to the right of Osburn's F, First Ohio. One last battery was added to the position when Lieutenant Livingston's Third Wisconsin Battery recrossed the river ahead of the retreating infantry. The Third Wisconsin's six guns went between Swallow's and Parsons's batteries. These units' twenty-one guns increased the total number of guns at McFadden's Ford to forty-five.[24]

Farther to the right were the six guns (two James Rifles and four 6-pound smoothbores) of Lieut. Alanson J. Stevens's Twenty-sixth Pennsylvania Battery.

Center of Mendenhall's artillery position looking south. The guns represent Capt. James H. Stokes's Chicago Board of Trade Battery.

Lieutenant Stevens was joined by Capt. Cullen Bradley's Sixth Ohio Battery (four 10-pound Parrott Rifles and two 12-pound Napoleons). These two batteries were able to place enfilade fire into the left of the Confederate infantry. With these batteries' twelve guns, Mendenhall had massed fifty-seven guns to defend the ford and the terrain to either side of it.[25]

As Breckinridge's infantry pursued Van Cleve's troops off the higher terrain, they descended into an open area between the high ground and the river. It was nine hundred to one thousand yards from the recently captured higher ground to the Union position at McFadden's Ford. The attacking infantry would be partially protected by the steep slope of the terrain once they reached the river. However, they would still be subjected to rifle fire from the infantry supporting the artillery. Before this protection could be reached, the troops had to cross the open area between the higher ground and the river. This area was a killing zone for Mendenhall's guns, which opened fire. The next fifteen to twenty minutes provided a tremendous display of the power of artillery when massed and positioned under the central command and control of a tactically proficient artillery officer.

Each gun firing at a rate of 2 rounds per minute meant that 57 guns fired 114 rounds for every minute of the infantry attack. This pace lasted from fifteen to twenty minutes. Therefore, between 1,710 and 2,280 rounds were fired into the compact and rapidly disorganized mass of Confederate infantry!

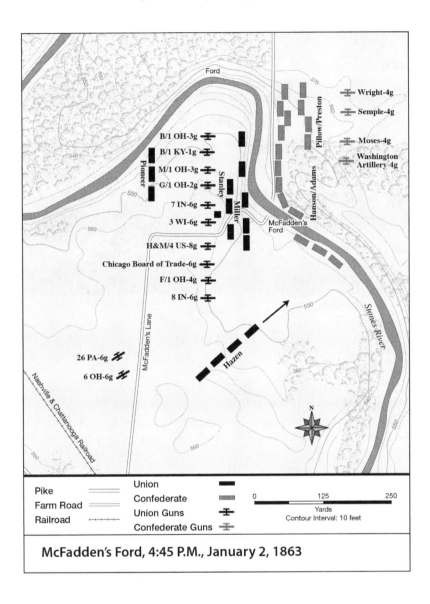

McFadden's Ford, 4:45 P.M., January 2, 1863

Lieut. Edwin Porter Thompson of Company E, Sixth Kentucky Infantry (Confederate) recalled the events of that day: "The very earth trembled as with an exploding mine, and a mass of iron hail was hurled upon [us]. The artillery bellowed forth such a thunder that men were stunned and could not distinguish sounds. There were falling timbers, crashing arms, the whirring of missiles in every direction, the bursting of the dreadful shell, the groans of

McFadden's Ford today.

the wounded, the shouts of the officers mingled in one horrid din that beggars description."[26]

The sustained deadly fire from Mendenhall's guns stopped, broke up, and then repulsed Breckinridge's infantry. Negley's two brigades (Stanley's and Miller's), which had been supporting the artillery, counterattacked, driving the Confederates back to the higher ground and beyond. As it became dark, the key terrain east of the river was again occupied by Union troops.[27]

Capt. Mendenhall's critical decision to reinforce the position above McFadden's Ford set the course of the fighting late on the afternoon of January 2. It was a decision that had to be made and mostly carried out prior to Breckinridge's attack. If Mendenhall had waited until the attack began, the concentration of artillery probably would not have had as many guns as it did. In order to position ten batteries on the small plateau above McFadden's Ford before or just as Breckinridge began his attack, Mendenhall had to conceptualize the information he was receiving about Confederate infantry movement and artillery firing early in the afternoon. Once he understood what was probably about to happen, he needed to aggressively issue orders, and supervise the placement of the batteries to defend the ford and the areas to the left and right. His successfully accomplishing this created a strong artillery position, supported by infantry, that was able turn Breckinridge's quick success into defeat.

If the Confederate infantry had not been stopped and turned back before crossing the river, an entirely different scenario may have developed late on

View from McFadden's Ford of the center Union artillery position.

January 2 and the next morning. Possession of the high ground east of the river would have provided Bragg a position from which his artillery could enfilade part of Rosecrans's defensive position. Confederate infantry west of the river near the ford would have provided a lodgment that could have been reinforced during the night. The advantageous artillery and infantry positions would have given Bragg the ability to attack again on January 3. This additional assault would have extended the fighting for at least another day. It might also have resulted in the battle being a Confederate victory as Rosecrans fell back to better positions along Stewarts Creek.

Because of Mendenhall's decision this scenario, or some variation of it, did not occur. When the artillery and infantry weapons ceased firing in the early evening hours of January 2, even though the commanders may not have realized it, the Battle of Stones River was over.

Bragg Decides to Retreat

Situation

As night fell on Friday, January 2, 1863, Bragg was faced with the reality that his second offensive operation within three days had failed. His first attempt to defeat Rosecrans's Army of the Cumberland on Wednesday had come very close to success. The envelopment of the Union right (west) flank had resulted in the complete disruption of that section of Rosecrans's position, the rout of most of McCook's Right Wing, and the cancellation of a Union envelopment against Bragg's right. Although in partial disarray, Confederate divisions had penetrated into the Army of the Cumberland's rear areas and threatened its lines of supply and communication to Nashville. For a time it appeared that Bragg's Army of Tennessee would have a major victory. However, the arrival of reinforcements from the Union left brought Bragg's envelopment to a halt. During the night his left divisions drew back and consolidated their position with the divisions on the right.

Bragg was certain that he had achieved a major victory. Throughout the night, the sounds of Union troop and wagon movements suggested that Rosecrans was retreating. The Confederate army commander expected that daylight on Thursday (January 1, 1863) would confirm his belief. Much to Bragg's surprise, dawn found Rosecrans still in position.

On Wednesday night Bragg had sent an optimistic telegram to Gen. Samuel Cooper, the adjutant general, in Richmond.

> Murfreesboro, Tenn.,
> December 31, 1862.
>
> We assailed the enemy at 7 o'clock this morning, and after ten hours' hard fighting have driven him from every position except his extreme left, [where] he has successfully resisted us. With the exception of this point, we occupy the whole field. We captured 4,000 prisoners, including 2 brigadier-generals, [28] pieces of artillery, and some 200 wagons and teams. Our loss is heavy; that of the enemy much greater.
>
> BRAXTON BRAGG,
> General, Commanding
> General S. COOPER[28]

This telegram, viewed in Richmond as the announcement of a major battlefield victory, was released to newspapers throughout the South. The premature declaration returned to haunt Bragg.

Both armies used Thursday to adjust their positions and conduct limited resupplying. Significantly, one of Rosecrans's position changes involved sending a division across Stones River at McFadden's Ford to occupy the key high ground to the east. Occupying this terrain would allow Rosecrans to dominate the right of Bragg's position with artillery fire and move more troops across the river to envelop Bragg's defenses.

When Bragg was informed of the Union force east of the river, he ordered Maj. Gen. John C. Breckinridge to attack, capture, or drive off the Union troops and then occupy the key terrain. If successful, Breckinridge would enable Bragg to protect his position and dominate much of Rosecrans's position with artillery fire. He would also occupy an excellent area to commence an infantry attack, heavily supported by artillery, against the Union left. Although initially successful, Breckinridge's attack was stopped and driven back with heavy losses. As the Confederates retreated, Union forces once again crossed Stones River and reoccupied the key high ground.

Bragg had attacked Rosecrans's army twice. Both attacks had nearly succeeded, but they had ultimately been halted and repulsed by the Union defenders. The cost to the Army of Tennessee had been high; 10,266 officers and men were killed, wounded, or captured. These casualties accounted for 27 percent of the army's total strength. The leadership loss at the brigade level included two commanders who were killed or who died of wounds, and three who were wounded. Ten regimental commanders were killed or died of wounds, sixteen were wounded, and two were captured. These casualties were the equivalent of the brigade and regimental leadership structure for two divisions. In addition, several thousand rounds of artillery ammunition and somewhere in the vicinity of several million small-arms rounds had been fired. Two failed attacks and significant casualties, and ammunition consumption were pushing Bragg to decide what to do next.[29]

Reports indicated that the Army of the Cumberland was being reinforced. In addition, rain was increasing the water level and flow rate of Stones River. If it continued rising, the river would create a water barrier dividing the Army of Tennessee into two mutually unsupportable parts.

The Union army could be resupplied much faster from its forward supply base at Nashville than the Army of Tennessee could bring supplies from Chattanooga. The city was one hundred miles away from Stones River, and some of the provisions had to travel over mountain roads.

During the early evening of January 2, Bragg had decided to maintain his position where it was. Later that night, he received a message from two of his division commanders, Maj. Gens. Jones M. Withers and Benjamin F. Cheatham, and endorsed by their corps commander, Lieut. Gen. Leonidas Polk. The message urged Bragg to retreat because many of the units were unreliable and others were demoralized. Bragg's initial response to Polk was, "We shall maintain our position at every hazard." Regardless of his first answer, the dispatch caused Bragg to reevaluate his position and his next course of action.[30]

Options

Bragg had three options: attack, defend, or retreat.

<u>Option 1</u>

There were two possible courses of action if Bragg decided to attack. He could reinforce Breckinridge's Division on his right and confront the Union force that had reoccupied the key high terrain east of McFadden's Ford. If the river continued to rise, a quick retreat or reinforcement of this force would be difficult and might lead to its destruction or capture. To achieve the combat power necessary, Bragg would need to move one or more divisions from the left to his right. A reduction in strength on the left might cause Rosecrans to take the initiative and attack the Confederate left; and then there was all that Union artillery just west of the river.[31]

Another course of action would have been to attack Rosecrans's right or right center to rupture his defensive position and force a retreat. Both of these attack scenarios were fraught with danger for the Confederate army. If he reacted quickly enough, Rosecrans had the capability to overwhelm Bragg's weakened left as he struck with his reinforced right. In the other scenario Rosecrans had a good chance to defeat Bragg's attack against his right or right center.

All things being equal, the attack option did not favor Bragg. What about defense?

<u>Option 2</u>

The defense creates conditions for a successful counteroffensive to regain the initiative. The defense also retains key terrain or denies a vital area to the enemy. The question was: What could Bragg have accomplished by continuing to occupy a defensive position outside of Murfreesboro?[32]

Bragg could resupply and reinforce to regain the capability for offensive operations. The Army of Tennessee would be close to Rosecrans's Nashville supply base when spring, and a renewal of the campaign season, came. The Confederate army would be in a threatening position that provided a start point for further northward offensives. In addition, Bragg would still occupy and control territory in northern Middle Tennessee and block avenues of approach into the north central Heartland.

However, several factors suggested that maintaining a defensive position was not Bragg's best course of action. As mentioned earlier, heavy rains were raising the Stones River's level and currents. High, fast-moving water had the potential, at least for the short term, to divide Bragg's army. Of additional consideration was the troops' level of ammunition and supplies. The Army of

Tennessee's major supply depot was some one hundred miles south in Chattanooga. Since arriving in northern Tennessee, requisitions upon civilians for food and forage had just about eliminated that population as a supply source. Moreover, the number of casualties had greatly reduced the army's combat effectiveness, and Bragg could not expect reinforcement anytime soon. Conversely, Bragg was receiving reports of Rosecrans's heavy reinforcements. Rosecrans was receiving reinforcements, but not to the extent that Bragg had been advised.[33]

Remaining in position meant that Bragg would in all probability be passing the initiative over to Rosecrans. The Army of the Cumberland had withstood severe casualties (30 percent of its effective strength) and consumed large amounts of ammunition. But the army was beginning to recover. In the afternoon of December 31, Col. Moses B. Walker's five-regiment brigade with the Fourth Michigan Battery (six guns) arrived in the army's rear area. This was followed by the arrival that evening of Col. John C. Starkweather's four-regiment brigade. On the morning of January 3, Col. James G. Spears's six-regiment brigade, along with two sections (four guns) of the Tenth Wisconsin Battery and a 303-wagon supply train, also arrived. Rosecrans had received three reinforcing infantry brigades (about 4,500 troops), two artillery batteries (ten guns), and a significant amount of supplies within a relatively short period of time. The 4,500 soldiers made up for about 33 percent of the 13,249 casualties incurred between December 31 and January 2. The ten guns replaced 35 percent of the twenty-nine guns lost or disabled. This offset wasn't great, but it was enough to constitute a strong defense and planning for offensive action could begin.[34]

There were additional units that Rosecrans could use as reinforcements. A two-brigade division (eight regiments, an additional artillery battery, and a three-battery artillery reserve) was garrisoning and protecting Nashville. Twenty-five miles north of Nashville, a two-division force of four brigades (totaling seventeen regiments) and four batteries of artillery were positioned in the vicinity of Gallatin, Tennessee, to secure the railroad and the tunnel. Within forty-eight to seventy-two hours, the division at Nashville could move to join Rosecrans. At the same time, one of the divisions near Gallatin could march to Nashville and protect that valuable city and supply base. Even if the railroad supply line from Louisville to Nashville was disrupted, Rosecrans had accumulated five weeks of supplies at Nashville. Those supplies would support his army until February. In addition, with the winter and spring rains the Cumberland River would be navigable. Supplies could be brought from Louisville to Nashville by boat on the Ohio and Cumberland Rivers.[35]

Within a short period of time the arrival of the division from Nashville, in conjunction with the earlier three brigades, would give Rosecrans the capability for an offensive. Taking the initiative, Rosecrans could again maneuver against Bragg's defensive position. The most likely course of action would be leaving enough troops in front of Bragg to fix his army in position and maneuver against him with a significant force. The most likely maneuver and attack would be either an envelopment of Bragg's left (west) flank or a turning movement. A road network to the west and the south existed to support such operations. Either action had the potential to cut off the Army of Tennessee's line of retreat, inflict severe casualties, and render it combat ineffective. Bragg may have considered all of these factors or just some of them. But, if he decided that remaining on the defense in his present location was not a viable option, only one choice remained.

Option 3

If he could not attack or defend where he was, Bragg's sole option was retreat. The factors in favor of this decision were the condition of his army (casualties and men now becoming sick because of the continued cold rain), the rising water level of Stones River, the lack of food with his deployed units, and the reports that Rosecrans was receiving substantial reinforcements. Rosecrans's reinforcements were far less extensive than Bragg believed.[36]

Decision

Bragg decided that he would retreat. At noon on January 3 orders were issued for the army's trains to begin moving south, and at 11:00 p.m. the infantry began to retreat. Wheeler's cavalry occupied the former infantry positions for one day to cover the retreat and then departed.[37]

Results/Impact

Polk's Corps retreated on the Shelbyville Pike, while Hardee's Corps used the Manchester Pike. The army's initial destination was the Elk River, some fifty miles south of Murfreesboro. When Bragg realized that Rosecrans was not pursuing, he decided to halt and position his army along the Duck River, thirty miles south of Murfreesboro. This fertile agricultural area was a source of food and forage. Within a month the Army of Tennessee was established in positions along the river. A cavalry covering force was situated to the north, and a forward supply depot was located eighteen miles south at Tullahoma. Bragg's army would remain in this position until early summer.[38]

This critical decision by Bragg brought the Stones River battle and campaign to an end. It gave the battlefield to Rosecrans, who claimed victory.

CHAPTER 4

CONCLUSIONS

Although many important decisions were made prior to, during, and just after the Battle of Stones River, sixteen of them were critical decisions that shaped history and gave us the battle as we know it today. Of these sixteen, two were organizational decisions, four were operational decisions, and ten were tactical decisions. Viewing the decisions from the levels of command, there were two national-level decisions, ten army-level decisions, and four at the wing or corps level. Seven were made by a Union commander, and nine were made by a Confederate commander.

Confederate Army Reorganized: National-Level Organizational Decision

President Jefferson Davis realized that two separate armies in Tennessee would only lead to defeat in detail. He therefore combined the two armies of Gen. Braxton Bragg and Maj. Gen. Edmund Kirby Smith into one unit, renamed it the Army of Tennessee, and placed Bragg in command. This critical decision shaped the course of the Battle of Stones River, and it influenced the other major battles in Tennessee and Georgia in 1863 and 1864.

Bragg Loses a Division:
National-Level Organizational Decision.

President Davis detached Maj. Gen. Carter L. Stevenson's division from the Army of Tennessee and sent it by railroad to Lieut. Gen. John C. Pemberton for the defense of Vicksburg. Except for one brigade, Stevenson's Division arrived too late to help in the fight for Vicksburg in 1862. The reduction of Bragg's army by 7,500 to 10,000 troops (depending on the source) was a significant loss in strength that caused him to reorganize his troops in two corps instead of three. The loss of Stevenson's Division limited Bragg's tactical options on December 31, 1862. Had Stevenson's Division been present, it might have provided the additional combat power Bragg's envelopment needed. In a completely different scenario, Stevenson's Division might have joined with Breckinridge's Division, crossed Stones River and enveloped Rosecrans's left at the same time that his right was being enveloped. A double envelopment would have been extremely difficult to stop. Troops sent from the Union's left to its right would have been engaged and held in position by the second attack.

Bragg Orders the Cavalry to Raid:
Army-Level Operational Decision.

Bragg ordered part of his cavalry on raids into Western Tennessee and central Kentucky. Brig. Gen. Nathan B. Forrest's raid into Western Tennessee helped defeat Maj. Gen. Ulysses S. Grant's central Mississippi campaign against Vicksburg by destroying the railroad supply line necessary to sustain Grant's operations. Brig. Gen. John H. Morgan's raid into Kentucky destroyed segments of the Louisville and Nashville Railroad, but Rosecrans had already positioned sufficient supplies at Nashville to support his army for five weeks. These raids reduced Bragg's strength when he most needed it. The intelligence that a large contingent of cavalry and an infantry division were not with Bragg was one of Rosecrans's considerations in commencing offensive operations.

Rosecrans Moves South:
Army-Level Operational Decision.

Rosecrans was under pressure from the Federal government to move south against Bragg before winter made it impractical. When he had stockpiled sufficient supplies and ammunition and realized that Bragg's army had been reduced in strength, Rosecrans marched his army south from Nashville and engaged Bragg's Army of Tennessee. Had he not made this critical decision, both armies would have stayed where they were through the winter and into the spring. There may or may not have been a Battle of Stones River. But there was a battle, and all of the critical decisions that followed came from this one decision.

Bragg Decides to Concentrate at Murfreesboro: Army-Level Operational Decision.

When Rosecrans started maneuvering south from Nashville, Bragg's army was located in a thirty-two-mile-long position extending from Eagleville through Murfreesboro to Readyville. Once he determined the axis of Rosecrans's advance, rather than retreat farther south, Bragg ordered his corps to concentrate at Murfreesboro, assume a defensive posture, and await developments. This concentration was completed on December 28. Bragg's decision ensured that a battle would be fought at Murfreesboro.

Harker is Recalled: Wing/Corps-Level Tactical Decision.

On December 29, 1862, Rosecrans's army was approaching Murfreesboro. Late in the afternoon, under the impression that Confederates were retreating from the town, Col. Charles G. Harker's brigade of Wood's division was ordered across Stones River to occupy Wayne's Hill. Harker accomplished the crossing in the dark, engaged the enemy force on Wayne's Hill, and established a bridgehead that might have been exploited to some advantage. Concerned about Harker's brigade, Left Wing commander Maj. Gen. Thomas L. Crittenden made the critical decision to order Harker to recross the river. Harker brought his brigade back, and the bridgehead was lost. Had Harker's brigade continued to defend the bridgehead, other brigades could have been sent across the river. Bragg could not have ignored a substantial Union force near or on Wayne's Hill. Rather than attack on the western end of the battlefield, Bragg would have had to contain or defeat that portion of Rosecrans's army on the east side of the battlefield. The Battle of Stones River would have been entirely different from that point on.

Bragg Decides to Attack Rosecrans's Right Flank: Army-Level Tactical Decision.

Bragg thought Rosecrans was going to attack him on December 30. When that did not happen, he decided to attack instead. Bragg planned to conduct an envelopment that would dislodge Rosecrans's right. To exploit this success, he would attack all the way to the Nashville Pike to cut off and trap a majority of the Army of the Cumberland. The Confederate envelopment preempted Rosecrans's plans and set the course for a major portion of the combat on December 31.

Bragg Fails to Significantly Weight the Main Attack: Army-Level Tactical Decision.

This decision concerned the allocation of combat power for the envelopment. With the loss of Stevenson's Division, Bragg's army only had five infantry divisions on December 31. Two divisions were assigned to the main attack (the envelopment), and two divisions were allocated to the supporting attack. The fifth division was to remain east of Stones River, protect the army's right flank, and be prepared to provide reinforcements when necessary. The problem was that the main assault did not have enough combat power to deal with unexpected events. Either Breckinridge's Division east of the river should have provided three or four brigades, or one of the divisions in the supporting attack should have been designated as a reserve behind the envelopment. As Bragg failed to make these assignments, the main attack was not significantly weighted. When McCown's Division went off course and Cleburne's Division had to take up the attack early, there were no additional units to maintain momentum when McCown and Cleburne had to temporarily stop along the Wilkinson Pike.

Rosecrans Cancels His Attack: Army-Level Tactical Decision.

Major General Rosecrans had also planned to attack on December 31. His plan was a mirror image of Bragg's; he planned an envelopment of the Confederate right with his left. Bragg's attack commenced prior to Rosecrans's. As it became evident that the Union right was collapsing and retreating, Rosecrans had to decide whether to continue his offensive and hope to force Bragg to stop and redeploy units, or to stop his own troops and shift them to defensive operations. Rosecrans's decision to cancel his attack allowed him to redeploy brigades from his left to reestablish the defense on his right.

Rosecrans Shifts Units to the Right: Army-Level Tactical Decision.

This critical decision immediately followed the previous one. As Rosecrans's units on the left were halted and not in contact with a major Confederate force, some of them were available to reinforce the Union's center and the right. Three brigades from Rosecrans's left were deployed in front of Cleburne's Division, slowing its attack until a defensive position was established along the Nashville Pike.

Thomas Decides to Reposition Artillery:
Wing/Corps-Level Tactical Decision.

This decision initially seemed inconsequential, but it ultimately had a significant impact on the battle. When Maj. Gen. Lovell H. Rousseau's division reinforced the center of the Union defenses, it entered a cedar forest. One of the artillery battery commanders observed that his battery could not deploy in this heavily wooded area. Maj. Gen. George H. Thomas made the critical decision to recall the artillery and send it to the open ground behind the division. Lieuts. Francis L. Guenther and George W. Van Pelt moved their batteries (H, Fifth US and A, First Michigan) to the small rise of ground between the Nashville Pike and the railroad tracks, where the National Cemetery is located today. At that site they went into firing positions covering the ground across the open fields to the cedar woods. This position became the anchor point for Rosecrans's final defensive line. Gunther and Van Pelt were soon joined by four other batteries, which brought the total number of guns to thirty-six. The Pioneer Brigade's three battalions then went into position with the artillery, and infantry units retreating from the cedars rallied at this position. When the three brigades of McCown's Division attacked across the open field, the Union position was strong enough to repel them and protect the Nashville Pike, which was Rosecrans's line of supply, communication, and if necessary, retreat.

Bragg and Polk Repeatedly Attack the Round Forest:
Corps-Level Tactical Decision.

Lieut. Gen. Leonidas Polk oversaw the supporting attack against the Union center while the main attack, the envelopment, proceeded against Rosecrans's right. Polk had two divisions for the supporting attack. The right of Polk's assault was along the Nashville Pike. When the right and right center of the Union army was driven back, Rosecrans's troops established a final defensive position along the Nashville Pike. The Union army's defensive position then resembled an inverted *L*. The long part of the *L* was along the Nashville Pike, and the short part went from the pike to McFadden's Ford. The junction of the two defensive lines was at the Round Forest, adjacent to the pike.

As part of the supporting attack, Polk made four successive assaults against this position. The first attack was by Brig. Gen. James R. Chalmers's brigade, and the second was by Brig. Gen. Daniel S. Donelson's brigade. Both attacks were repulsed with heavy losses. Shortly afterward, brigades from Breckinridge's Division began crossing Stones River. Rather than send these brigades to support the main attack, Bragg turned them over to Polk. Four of Breckinridge's brigades conducted unsuccessful repeated attacks against the Round Forest defensive position. Polk's critical decision to continue assaulting the Round Forest fixed the pattern of combat in the center for the afternoon of December 31. Due to this decision, no reinforcements were committed to the main attack, which required additional combat power to successfully complete the envelopment.

Rosecrans Decides to Remain: Army-Level Tactical Decision.

Darkness brought an end to the combat on December 31. Rosecrans's army, especially its Right Wing, was heavily battered and bloodied. But the defenders had managed to hold on, and in the vicinity of the Round Forest they gave better than they got. The choice facing Rosecrans was retreating back up the Nashville Pike to defensible terrain or remaining where he was. Casualties and ammunition expenditure might suggest a retreat. However, a modest reinforcement of two infantry brigades arrived. These reinforcements gave Rosecrans the margin he thought necessary to remain in position. Had he decided to retreat, the battle would have been over and declared a Confederate victory. Coming after the Union defeats in December, this triumph would have been politically disastrous for the Lincoln administration. Rosecrans's critical decision to remain pushed the combat into another two days and eventually resulted in a badly needed Union victory.

Bragg Decides to Attack Rosecrans's Left Flank: Army-Level Tactical Decision.

On January 1, 1863, Rosecrans sent a division across Stones River at McFadden's Ford to occupy key high ground. This terrain provided two advantages. First, Union artillery positioned there could deliver enfilading fire along the right half of the Confederate position. Second, this terrain could provide a staging area for an attack against the Confederate right flank. The next day Bragg, when he realized what Rosecrans had done, made the critical decision to attack the Union division east of the river. Bragg's decision renewed combat operations on the afternoon of January 2. Had he not made it, the only decision left would be who would retreat—the Army of the Cumberland or the Army of Tennessee.

Mendenhall Reinforces with Artillery: Wing/Corps-Level Tactical Decision.

Bragg responded to Rosecrans's placing a division east of the river by launching an attack to regain that high ground. Indications of this attack were witnessed earlier in the day—Confederate brigades had crossed the river and assembled close to Wayne's Hill. In response to this intelligence, Capt. John Mendenhall, chief of artillery for the Left Wing, began sending batteries to level ground overlooking the river and McFadden's Ford. Other batteries were positioned so they could move to this area if necessary. Mendenhall initially assigned 5 batteries with 18 guns to reinforce the 1 battery with 6 guns that was already there. Just before the attack and during its early stages, an additional 4 batteries with 21 guns were brought into firing position. Thus, 45 guns were placed near the ford. Two more batteries with 12 guns were positioned south of the ford to deliver flanking fire into the Confederate attack. Mendenhall employed, in total, 57 guns against Breckinridge's attack.

The attack was successful in capturing its initial objective, the important high terrain east of the river. When the offensive progressed toward the river, it came within range of Mendenhall's artillery. Within twenty minutes the attack was halted, broken up, and driven back. Union infantry then crossed the river, counter attacked the Confederates, and reoccupied the high ground. Captain Mendenhall's early response to indications of a Confederate attack was crucial; it led him to position a large amount of artillery where it reversed the initial success of Breckinridge's attack. The artillery's success allowed an infantry counterattack to recapture key terrain. It also kept Bragg's artillery from occupying the higher ground and dominating a large portion of Rosecrans's position.

Bragg Decides to Retreat: Army-Level Operational Decision.

Bragg's Army of Tennessee had been in contact with Rosecrans's Army of the Cumberland for four days. On two of those days Bragg launched attacks that had been defeated with heavy casualties. The weather was cold, and the rain and sleet continued. Many soldiers were sick, rations with the soldiers were in short supply, and a considerable amount of ammunition had been fired. In addition, the rain was increasing the Stones River's level and rate of flow. This circumstance threatened to create an unfordable barrier that would divide the Confederate army. Bragg therefore made the critical decision to retreat south. This decision brought an end to the Battle of Stones River and gave Rosecrans the victory.

Afterward

On the evening of January 2, 1863, Gen. Braxton Bragg initially decided to remain on the defense near Murfreesboro. However, he reevaluated the situation the next day. A number of factors changed Bragg's mind: high casualty numbers, increasing sickness among his soldiers, food shortages within the combat units, a perception that the Union army was being heavily reinforced, and the rising level of Stones River. A retreat was ordered for January 3.[1]

The army's trains were positioned south of Murfreesboro, and they commenced moving at midday. At 11:00 p.m. the infantry and artillery began leaving their positions and marching south in a cold, drenching rain. Polk's Corps retreated on the Shelbyville Pike, while Hardee's Corps marched on the Manchester Pike. Wheeler's and Wharton's cavalry brigades occupied the abandoned infantry positions and covered the retreat. The next morning the cavalry departed and proceeded south as the rear guard for the Army of Tennessee.[2]

As the retreat began, Bragg did not have a firm destination for his army. He first stopped his soldiers at the Duck River, thirty miles south of Murfreesboro. Polk's Corps was at Shelbyville, and Hardee's Corps was stationed twenty miles to the east at Manchester. Bragg then decided to continue the retreat to the Elk River, fourteen miles farther south. Two days later he changed his mind and ordered Polk's Corps back to Shelbyville. Hardee's Corps was to continue on to Tullahoma. Although Bragg had protected his army by retreating, he had also given up an additional thirty miles of the avenue of approach into the north-central Heartland.[3]

Over the next few months the Army of the Tennessee refined its positions. The two infantry corps covered an area twenty miles wide. The cavalry occupied a seventy-mile covering force position north of the infantry. Additionally, a supply depot was established at Tullahoma on the Nashville–Chattanooga Railroad. Bragg's army remained in these locations for the remainder of the winter and through the spring.[4]

January 4 revealed that the Confederate army was no longer at Murfreesboro. Later in the day, Col. Timothy R. Stanley's brigade of Negley's division was sent forward along the railroad and the Nashville Pike. Stanley's reconnaissance proceeded to the site where the railroad and pike crossed Stones

River. Here, it halted while the First Battalion from the Pioneer Brigade was brought forward to repair the railroad trestle.[5]

The next day, Negley, reinforced with Brig. Gen. James G. Spears's brigade, was ordered to cross Stones River with his division and occupy Murfreesboro. He accomplished this task by 9:00 a.m. Shortly thereafter, Brig. Gen. David S. Stanley's cavalry crossed the river and conducted reconnaissance for several miles on the roads leading south from the town. Before night, Maj. Gen. Lovell H. Rousseau's division crossed the river and joined Negley's in Murfreesboro.[6]

After Murfreesboro was secured, Rosecrans conducted a limited pursuit, then ceased major operations and placed his army in winter quarters. A look at the army's tactical and supply situation provides us with some clues as to Rosecrans's thought process leading to this decision. When Bragg retreated, Rosecrans could tactically claim victory. The victory at Stones River came after a previous month with disastrous Union defeats. Rosecrans's end-of-the-year triumph was turned into a strategic political advantage. In conjunction with the Battle of Antietam and the issuing of the Emancipation Proclamation, victory at Stones River played a major role in preventing Great Britain from recognizing the Confederacy. It also boosted Northern civilians' morale, especially in the midwestern states that many of the Army of the Cumberland's soldiers called home.[7]

Rosecrans's casualties had been significant. The 13,249 killed, wounded, and missing accounted for 31 percent of the troops engaged. Casualties among the brigade and regimental leadership had also been high. Even though Rosecrans had been reinforced by three brigades, effective strength was still a factor to be considered. In addition to the aforementioned casualties, 557 artillery horses and 1,334 mules had been lost, twenty-eight artillery pieces had been captured, one artillery piece had been rendered unserviceable, and 229 wagons had been lost. Two million rounds of small arms and 20,307 rounds of artillery ammunition had been fired and needed replacing.[8]

The weather before and during the battle had been some of the worst that any Civil War army had endured. On most days a cold rain fell, and at night it turned to sleet and frozen mud. Under these conditions, traveling the roads to pursue Bragg's army would have difficult if not impossible.

The condition of the supply line from Nashville to the army would have been of great concern. Prior to leaving Nashville, Rosecrans had accumulated enough supplies to last for five weeks. The day after the battle, he estimated there were sufficient provisions at Nashville to last until January 25. The problem was forwarding these supplies to his army in a sustainable manner and replenishing the depot at Nashville. The weather had not made the roads from Nashville unusable, but the movement of wagons was difficult. The best way to transport supplies to the army was by the Nashville-Chattanooga Railroad. However, the tracks from Nashville to Murfreesboro were in disrepair or had been destroyed. Rosecrans estimated that that section of the railroad would be operational by February 6. But it wasn't until February 12 that he reported it usable.[9]

Restocking the depot at Nashville depended upon the railroad from Louisville. The 183-mile-long Louisville and Nashville Railroad had been a favorite target of Confederate raiders. Repairing this supply line had been a top priority for Rosecrans when he assumed command in late October 1862. He had achieved this goal on November 26, and a surplus of supplies and provisions for the army had begun to arrive. Once a sufficient supply reserve had been accumulated at Nashville, Rosecrans commenced offensive operations. Now a large quantity of those supplies had been used, and it was necessary to ensure a steady flow into Nashville and then on to the army at Murfreesboro. This necessity again gave Rosecrans concern about the Louisville and Nashville Railroad. Confederate raiders had attempted to cut this vital route, and combat units were needed for its protection. With the rise of the Cumberland River, additional supplies were being transported by steamer from Louisville. However, this was dependent upon rains to keep the river high enough, and attempts were also being made to interdict river traffic.[10]

As Rosecrans reviewed his situation he knew that he would have to move forward another twenty-five to thirty miles to effectively pursue the Army of Tennessee. Because of casualties, many of his units were approaching marginal combat effectiveness. The winter weather and the condition of the roads would make continuous resupply of the army difficult at best. Before he could even consider moving forward, sufficient supplies and reinforcements would have to be brought from Nashville. This could not be done effectively until the railroad from Nashville was repaired and operational. Rosecrans believed this could be accomplished by February 6 (actually, the task was not completed until February 12). This would give Bragg over a month to establish and improve his defensive positions. Additional supplies would be required to restock the Nashville depot to assure the army's sustainment. Given the troops' casualty and reinforcement situation, the condition of the roads and railroad, the winter weather, and the supply situation, Rosecrans decided that his army had accomplished enough.

The area of the Duck River and its adjacent valley was one of the most agriculturally productive in Middle Tennessee. Remaining in this location allowed the Army of Tennessee to gather subsistence for men and animals. In addition, the land on either side of the Nashville and Chattanooga Railroad from Shelbyville to Stevenson, Alabama, was agriculturally productive. In this area and in other areas in Middle Tennessee and northern Alabama, sufficient food, forage, and livestock could be obtained by purchasing agents. The Nashville and Chattanooga and the Western Atlantic Railroads were used to bring additional subsistence, supplies, and ordnance forward from Atlanta and Chattanooga.[11]

Bragg's troop strength just prior to the battle at Stones River was 37,317. His losses numbered 10,266. By mid-June, the returning wounded and new recruitment had brought his effective strength to 43,089. Some of his brigades were stronger then than they were before the fighting at Stones River.[12]

In mid-March an inspection by Col. William Preston Johnston, an aide to President Jefferson Davis, showed the Army of Tennessee to be well clothed, healthy, and disciplined. Sufficient rations were kept with the troops, and a reserve was stored at various locations. Johnston's report noted that there were sufficient small arms, with 140 rounds per man; 40 rounds in the cartridge boxes; and 100 rounds in the regimental wagons. There were 125 pieces of artillery, and the ammunition boxes for the limbers and caissons were full. An additional reserve of 50 rounds per gun was held in the depot at Chattanooga.[13]

The remainder of winter and early spring was used to prepare the Army of the Cumberland to resume combat operations when the weather became warmer and the roads were passable. Rosecrans focused on reorganization, reinforcement, and the establishment of sufficient reserves of supplies and ammunition.

War Department General Order Number 9, dated January 9, 1863, officially renamed Rosecrans's command the Army of the Cumberland, a name that had been used unofficially since Rosecrans assumed command. This order was followed on February 2 by Rosecrans's order organizing the army from wings into corps. The wings were redesigned as the Fourteenth Corps (Center Wing), the Twentieth Corps (Right Wing), and the Twenty-first Corps (Left Wing). The corps commanders were Maj. Gens. George H. Thomas, Alexander McD. McCook, and Thomas L. Crittenden.[14]

The commander of the Department of the Ohio was made responsible for securing the Louisville and Nashville Railroad. Troops that Rosecrans had used for providing security were thus freed and brought south. In addition, a three-division corps was formed from troops in Kentucky, placed under the command of Maj. Gen. Gordon Granger, and sent to Nashville. Granger's corps would eventually be the Reserve Corps. At the beginning of his next campaign, Rosecrans's infantry strength had been increased to 66,013.[15]

Rosecrans also used this time to strengthen his cavalry. A constant problem for Rosecrans before and during the Battle of Stones River was the lack of cavalry. Just prior to the battle, the Army of the Cumberland's cavalry included 3,200 effective troopers. These numbers did not provide the capability Rosecrans needed for reconnaissance and security operations. Conversely, the Army of Tennessee's cavalry numbered 9,837. Of this number, 4,327 were retained close to the army for normal reconnaissance and security missions, and 5,600 were used for deep raiding missions against Union supply lines and depots.[16]

Rosecrans set about increasing his cavalry organization, and by early spring he had an effective cavalry strength of 4,961. In mid-February he mounted Col. John T. Wilder's infantry brigade. In May this brigade was equipped with repeating rifles. It became one of the most, if not the most, effective brigade-size unit in the war.[17]

At the commencement of the battle along Stones River, the Army of the Cumberland committed twenty-six batteries with 143 guns. Toward the end of the fighting, two additional batteries with ten guns arrived on the battlefield. Before beginning his next campaign, Rosecrans had increased his artillery to thirty-four batteries with 195 guns.[18]

While strengthening and refurbishing his army, Rosecrans also improved his capability to provide sufficient supplies, rations, and ammunition to his army during sustained operations. To this end, he concentrated on the lines of supply and forward supply depots. The section of the Nashville and Chattanooga Railroad extending to Murfreesboro was repaired and operating by mid-February. These tracks provided the capability to move large amounts of supplies and ammunition from Nashville to the army's forward area. As long as the Louisville and Nashville Railroad's tracks and bridges could be protected and the Cumberland River was navigable, large amounts of supplies and ammunition could be brought to the depot at Nashville and then forwarded to the army.[19]

To further increase his resupply capability Rosecrans constructed the largest enclosed earthen fortification of the Civil War. Named Fortress Rosecrans and sited on the northern edge of Murfreesboro, this structure was a depot for the forward distribution of food, weapons, supplies, and ammunition. The fortress was enclosed with three miles of earthen works. The two hundred acres inside these walls could shelter fifteen thousand troops and store sufficient supplies to sustain the Army of the Cumberland for three months. The bridges crossing Stones River were protected, and the railroad from Nashville went directly through the fortification. Fortress Rosecrans would play a predominant role in Rosecrans's 1863 campaigns and in Maj. Gen. William T. Sherman's Atlanta Campaign.[20]

Rosecrans's victory was politically and strategically significant. The resulting battle gave Lincoln a victory as the new year of 1863 arrived. It strengthened his position politically when the British Parliament met in January, it provided increased legitimacy for the Emancipation Proclamation that went into effect on January 1, 1863, and it helped bolster Northern morale, especially in the midwestern states, from which many of the Army of the Cumberland's soldiers hailed. Eight months later Lincoln was still expressing his appreciation to Rosecrans for his victory at Stones River. In a letter dated August 31, 1863, he wrote, "I can never forget, whilst I remember anything, that at the end of last year and the beginning of this, you gave us a hard earned victory, which, had there been a defeat instead, the nation could have scarcely lived over."[21]

Strategically Stones River provided an irreversible Union penetration into Middle Tennessee. Nashville was secured. Using the Cumberland River and the Louisville and Nashville Railroad, the city was developed into a significant supply depot. This depot was the base of supply for the Union advance into southern Tennessee and Georgia. A significant forward supply base was developed at Murfreesboro, and Rosecrans used it to support his Tullahoma and Chickamauga Campaigns.[22]

The Confederate victory at Chickamauga notwithstanding, the Army of the Cumberland commenced a series of campaigns in the early summer of 1863 that took it deep into the Heartland and captured the critical rail junction at Chattanooga. As part of Sherman's campaign the next year, the Army of the Cumberland pierced even deeper into the Heartland. During this operation, Atlanta was captured; the Confederacy's last north-south and east-west rail junction, manufacturing center, and strategically and politically significant city. All of these events flowed from Rosecrans's victory at the Battle of Stones River.

APPENDIX I

BATTLEFIELD GUIDE TO THE CRITICAL DECISIONS AT STONES RIVER

Begin your battlefield tour of the critical decisions at the National Park Visitor Center. Before you depart for your tour, you may wish to visit the museum and bookstore and view the short film.

There is value in being close to the place where a critical decision was made or carried out. Insomuch as modern construction allows, seeing the terrain as the decision maker and those that executed the decision provides a perspective that can't be gained by reading or studying a map. This appendix provides a battlefield tour that will place you on the ground where critical decisions were made, or carried out as near to these locations as possible.

The tour is designed to trace the decisions in chronological order. Driving and walking instructions will move you around not only the Stones River National Battlefield, but also the adjacent areas that were part of the 1862 battlefield. Orientating information is provided for each stop, including which direction to face, what units were in your vicinity, the critical decision that was reached, and the resulting action and consequences of that decision. Wherever possible, primary source material has been used to allow the battle's participants to tell you what happened. If you need more information, read the decision discussion in the appropriate chapter. Some words in the primary material are spelled differently than they are today, but they have been left as they were written by the battle's participants. For example, the present-day spelling of *re-enforce* is *reinforce*. Driving, walking, and positioning directions appear in bold type.

Stones River was a fluid battle. Therefore, when looking at the maps in this appendix you must remember they present a brief snapshot in time of many unit movements. The maps are designed to be a frame of reference that will allow you to visualize the events that transpired as you read accounts of the fighting.

Maps in books are normally oriented so that the tops of the pages correspond to the direction of north. Some maps in this appendix depart from that practice. One of the basic rules of map reading is that you orient the map with the terrain. As you stand at a particular location, you will read instructions informing you where to walk, where to position yourself, and which direction to face. When you then look at the map for that stop, it will be correctly oriented with the terrain. It will not be necessary for you to rotate the book, even when you page back and forth between the text and the maps. Additionally, the maps contain compasses indicating north.

A majority of the Stones River critical decisions were made within the confines of the 1862 battlefield. However, five of the decisions that shaped the battle were not made on or in close proximity to the battlefield. It is not practical for the tour to include these critical decisions as stops. However, it would be beneficial for you to review these decisions prior to beginning the tour.

The first critical decision was President Jefferson Davis's; he combined Gen. Braxton Bragg's Army of the Mississippi with Maj. Gen. Edmund Kirby Smith's Army of Kentucky. Operations in Kentucky by both armies, with the commanders supposedly cooperating, revealed the problems caused by an absence of unity of command and a clear hierarchy of authority. Davis's critical decision removed this ambiguous command structure and consolidated both forces into the Army of Tennessee under Bragg's command. The result was one Confederate army of sufficient strength, under a single commander, to confront the Union army as it marched south from Nashville. The organization of these troops determined how they would be deployed in the battle.

The next critical decision was also made by Jefferson Davis. In early November 1862 Maj. Gen. Ulysses S. Grant commenced operations to capture Vicksburg, Mississippi. In response, the Confederate commander, Lieut. Gen. John C. Pemberton, called for reinforcements.

In December 1862 Davis was on an inspection trip through the Western Theater. At Murfreesboro, he informed Bragg of his intent to send one of his divisions to Pemberton. Bragg strongly objected. He also pointed out that

Brig. Gen. Nathan Bedford Forrest's cavalry, then on a raid into Western Tennessee, would destroy Grant's supply line or so severely damage it that he would have to cancel his advance and retreat back north. Davis appeared to have deferred his decision. But a few days later, when he met Gen. Joseph E. Johnston, the department commander, at Chattanooga, he ordered Maj. Gen. Carter L. Stevenson's division to be sent to reinforce Pemberton. The loss of this division significantly reduced Bragg's infantry strength, caused a further reorganization of his army from three to two corps, and had a decided effect on the deployment of Bragg's troops for the December 31 battle. Bragg's losing this unit also influenced the commander of the Army of the Cumberland, Maj. Gen. William S. Rosecrans, to commence combat operations south from Nashville.

Bragg made the third critical decision before the battle, and it concerned his cavalry. When the Army of Tennessee was restructured Bragg divided his cavalry into two major organizations. One group, under the command of Brig. Gen. Joseph Wheeler, was to remain in close proximity to the army and perform the traditional roles of reconnaissance, guard, and economy of force missions. The other group was for distant raiding operations in the enemy's rear areas. This force consisted of two cavalry brigades commanded by Brig. Gen. Nathan Bedford Forrest and Col. (soon to be Brig. Gen.) John Hunt Morgan. Both of these brigades were on raids into Western Tennessee and central Kentucky at the time of the battle. Their departure removed an additional 5,600 troops from Bragg's immediate control, severely limiting his options for allocating combat power for his December 31 attack. The brigades' departure also factored into Rosecrans's decision to begin combat operations against Bragg's army.

The fourth critical decision, made away from the battlefield and before the battle, was reached by Maj. Gen. William S. Rosecrans. Rosecrans assumed command of the Army of the Cumberland on October 30, 1862. Soon afterward he began to receive numerous communications from Maj. Gen. Henry W. Halleck, the general-in-chief, urging him to move out of Nashville and begin an offensive against Bragg's army.

It wasn't that Rosecrans didn't want to commence offensive combat operations, but he was confronted with a logistical problem that had to be corrected first. Nashville was his forward supply depot. Supplies, food, and ammunition came from Louisville, Kentucky, either by river or by railroad. Supply by river followed the Ohio River to the Cumberland River and then to Nashville. However, a lack of rain meant that the Cumberland was too low for steamboats to use. This left the 183-mile-long Louisville and Nashville Railroad as the only route. Sections of the tracks were in disrepair or had been damaged by Confederate raiders. As a result, it was not until November 26 that the rail line opened and supplies began arriving in sufficient quantity at Nashville. Rosecrans calculated he needed five weeks of supplies, food, and ammunition before he could begin offensive operations. This amount would provide him with a sufficient reserve in case the railroad was interrupted again. By the third week of December Rosecrans had the logistical reserves that he required. He also knew that Stevenson's Division had departed and that Forest and Morgan were raiding in Western Tennessee and central Kentucky. These forces were too far away to return in time to reinforce Bragg. Taking all of these events and other planning factors into account, Rosecrans ordered his army to depart Nashville on December 26, find the Confederate army, and engage it.

The final critical decision made away from the battlefield was Bragg's, and he chose to concentrate his army in the vicinity of Murfreesboro. Bragg was in the process of placing his army in winter quarters. His soldiers occupied a thirty-two-mile front beginning at Eagleville in the west, running through Murfreesboro, and reaching Readyville in the east. When he learned of Rosecrans's movements south from Nashville, Bragg ordered his army to concentrate in the Murfreesboro area. This measure initially placed him in a defensive position, but it also gave him the option to attack Rosecrans. These last two critical decisions brought the two armies into battle just outside of Murfreesboro.

The road that passes by the Visitor Center is the Old Nashville Highway. In 1862 it was the Nashville Pike. In the midafternoon of December 29, 1862, the advanced guard of the Army of the Cumberland's Left Wing was advancing along this road and skirmishing with Brig. Gen. Joseph Wheeler's cavalry brigade as it conducted a delaying action. You will now join the Union advance guard and drive to Stop 1.

* * *

Drive 120 yards to the park entrance gate and the intersection with the Nashville Pike, today's Old Nashville Road. Turn right onto the Nashville Pike and drive southeast for 0.7 mile to the access road for Thompson Lane. The access road is on your right just after you go under the overpass. Turn right onto the access road and drive for 0.1 mile to the intersection with Thompson Lane. Turn right onto Thompson Lane, stay in the right lane, and drive north for 0.3 mile to the intersection of US Highway 41 (NW Broad Street). Turn right onto US 41, stay in the right lane, drive southeast for 0.1 mile, and turn right into a trailhead parking area for the Stones River Greenway. After turning right make an immediate left turn and park. If you drive across the river you have gone too far. Leave your car and walk 40 yards down the path

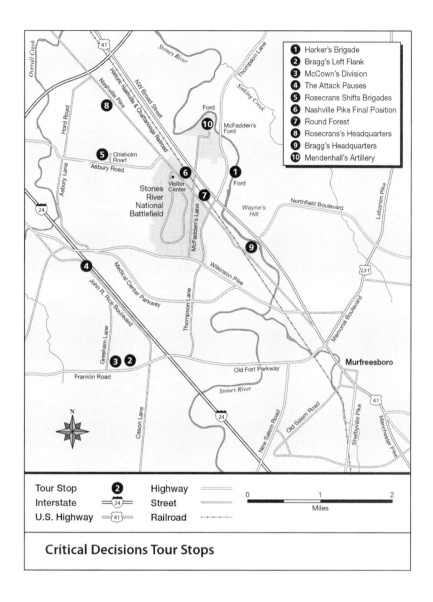

Tour Stop ❷   Highway
Interstate ⟦24⟧   Street
U.S. Highway ⟨41⟩   Railroad

0   1   2
Miles

Critical Decisions Tour Stops

to the walking trail along Stones River. At the walking path turn left and walk north for 560 yards (0.3 mile) to the wayside and marker on your right for Harker's crossing. Face to your right (southeast) and find a position where you can see the ford and terrain across the river. Depending on the time of the year, the vegetation can make navigating the terrain slightly challenging. Be careful of the steep river bank and wet, slippery ground.

Stop 1—Harker is Recalled, December 29, 1862

As you face the ford, Wayne's Hill is across the river and to your right front, where the Stones River Country Club is today. The clubhouse is 650 yards from your location, and in 1862 it was the top of Wayne's Hill. This hilltop was a forward position for Maj. Gen. John C. Breckinridge's division and was occupied by elements of Brig. Gen. Roger W. Hanson's brigade. The open area on the other side of the river was a cornfield in 1862.

At the center of the position were the four guns (two 12-pound howitzers and two 6-pound smoothbore guns) of Capt. Robert Cobb's Kentucky Battery. The artillery was supporting three infantry regiments: the Sixth Kentucky, Ninth Kentucky, and Forty-first Alabama. A strong skirmish line was deployed across the river from where you are located. The remainder of Hanson's Brigade and the other four of Breckinridge's brigades were positioned behind Wayne's Hill and to the southeast and east. Maj. Gen. Patrick R. Cleburne's division was positioned behind Breckinridge's.

Since departing Nashville on December 26, Maj. Gen. Thomas L. Crittenden's Left Wing of the Union Army of the Cumberland had been advancing on the Nashville Pike. Crittenden's advance units had been in contact with Brig. Gen. Joseph Wheeler's cavalry brigade, which had conducted a series of delaying actions. In the late afternoon of December 29 the Left Wing reached a position 900 yards (0.5 mile) behind you. Brig. Gen. John M. Palmer's three-brigade Second Division was positioned to the right (southwest) of the Nashville Pike, close to where the Round Forest is. Brig. Gen. Thomas J. Wood's three-brigade First Division was directly behind you and to the left (north) of the Nashville Pike. Brig. Gen. Horatio P. Van Cleve's Third Division was positioned 1,300 yards (0.75 mile) behind the forward divisions.

Palmer's and Wood's divisions had been skirmishing with the Confederate cavalry until Wheeler broke contact and withdrew along the Nashville Pike to Murfreesboro. This withdrawal was reported to Maj. Gen. William S. Rosecrans as the Confederates were retreating. Rosecrans immediately ordered Crittenden to occupy Murfreesboro with one division. Crittenden decided to advance with two divisions, Palmer's on the right and Wood's on the left.

Wood had deployed all three of his brigades on line. Col. George D. Wagner's Second Brigade was on the right and near the pike. Brig. Gen. Milo S. Haskell's First Brigade was on the left and in position to cross in the vicinity of McFadden's Ford, which was 1,100 yards (0.6 mile) to your left. Col. Charles G. Harker's Third Brigade, in the center, was positioned to cross the river where you are. Harker had deployed three of his regiments in the first line. From left to right they were the Thirteenth Michigan, Fifty-first

Indiana, and Seventy-third Indiana. Each of these regiments sent forward two companies as a skirmish line. Behind them were the Sixty-fourth Ohio, Sixty-fifth Ohio, and the Sixth Ohio Battery, with four 10-pound Parrotts and two Napoleons. By the time the units were formed, it was dark.

Earlier, Brig. Gens. Palmer and Wood, not wanting to undertake a major maneuver at night, had appealed to Crittenden to rescind Rosecrans's order. Crittenden had refused to do so. Shortly thereafter, Palmer and Wood again appealed to Crittenden to cancel the order, and this time he agreed. But it was too late, for Harker's brigade had commenced crossing Stones River.

Report of Col. Charles G. Harker, USA, Commanding Third Brigade, First Division, Left Wing, Army of the Cumberland

We took up a position near Stones River, about [650] yards to the left of the Nashville and Murfreesboro pike, the Second Brigade, Colonel Wagner commanding, being on the right, and the First Brigade, General Hascall commanding, being on the left, and somewhat to the rear, owing to the conformation of the ground.

We remained in this position until about dark, when we received orders to proceed to Murfreesboro. Stones River being fordable in our front, we at once commenced crossing the stream. Throwing a strong line of skirmishers over the stream, orders were given to the Fifty-first Indiana, Thirteenth Michigan, and Seventy-third Indiana Volunteers to cross simultaneously, form on the opposite bank, press forward, and seize the commanding heights beyond, while the Sixty-fourth and Sixty-fifth Ohio, with Bradley's battery, were directed to follow as rapidly as possible.

The skirmishers had barely left the bank of the river before they were vigorously attacked by those of the enemy, concealed in a thicket and behind a fence in our front. Our skirmishers, in no way daunted by this fierce assault of the enemy, pressed gallantly forward, driving the foe until they came upon the enemy in force.[1]

The first Union troops across the river were the skirmish line. Company commander and Medal of Honor recipient Capt. Milton T. Russell described his company's actions as part of the skirmish line. His account provides unique insight into combat at the company level.

Colonel Charles G. Harker, USA, commanding brigade. National Archives.

Narrative of Capt. Milton T. Russell, USA, Commanding Company A, Fifty-first Indiana Infantry, Third Brigade, First Division, Left Wing, Army of the Cumberland

About nine o'clock on December 29, 1862 an orderly came quietly along the line of sleeping soldiers and in a low tone called my name and said that Colonel [Abel D.] Streight [the regimental commander] wanted to see me. I went a short distance with the orderly and found the colonel and Colonel Harker standing by their horses in consultation. They had just returned from a reconnaissance. The colonel said, "Russell, take your Company A, move quietly to the front until you come to the river (which was about 200 yards in our immediate front), wade across, form your company on the [east] bank and wait for further orders." . . . This move was necessary in order to fully develop the enemy's position. It required but a moment to return to my company and form it in line, as the men had rolled up in their blankets without removing any of their clothing. Without further ceremony the company moved off. As we left the regiment, the officers were busy forming the men into line to support us. We moved down and crossed the river, wading it with the water in some places up to our hips. Talk about cold water or a cold bath, it was so cold that our teeth chattered!

As the company was nearing the opposite shore a terrific volley was fired from behind a rail fence not over forty steps in our front. The enemy being on higher ground than we, fired too high, their bullets taking effect in the regiment that was standing in line where

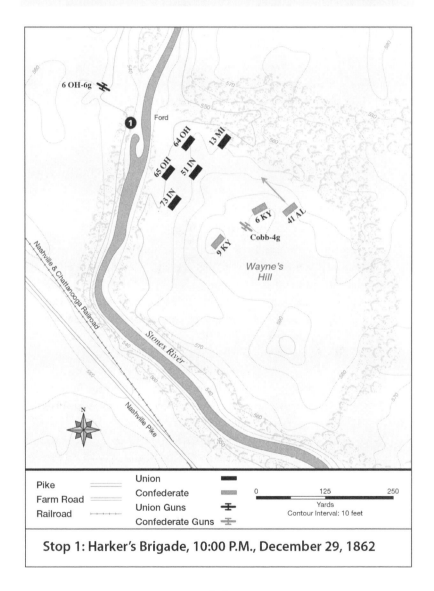

Stop 1: Harker's Brigade, 10:00 P.M., December 29, 1862

we left them on the opposite side of the river. There were but two ways out of the trap; one was to recross the river, the other was to advance. There was only a second in which to decide which horn of the dilemma to take. It flashed through my mind that their guns were empty, ours loaded. I gave the command: "On right into line, double-quick, charge"; and in less time that it takes to tell it, we were over that fence. My boys emptied their guns, fixed bayonets, and went at them. . . . Before I could bring the men to a halt the rebel [skirmish] line was driven back 400 yards.[2]

The skirmish line was followed across the river by the remainder of the Fifty-first Indiana and the Thirteenth Michigan and Seventy-third Indiana on its left and right. An attempt was then made to capture and secure the top of Wayne's Hill.

Report of Col. Able D. Streight, USA, Commanding Fifty-first Indiana Infantry, Third Brigade, First Division, Left Wing, Army of the Cumberland

I received orders to cross the river, preparatory to moving upon Murfreesboro. Being fully aware that the enemy occupied the opposite bank, and as none of our troops had at that time crossed the river, it became necessary to proceed somewhat cautiously, in order to avoid the danger of running into an ambuscade; consequently I deployed Companies A and F to act as skirmishers, and ordered them to cross in advance and engage the enemy briskly, and, if possible, to seize the heights on the east side of the river.

No sooner had my skirmishers crossed than the enemy opened a brisk fire from under cover of a strong fence but a few yards distant. My skirmishers were ordered forward at a double-quick, and charged upon the enemy, who instantaneously fled from their hiding places. At this moment it became evident, from the brisk firing of the enemy, that large numbers of them were concealed in the standing corn on the hill side; and fearing that my skirmishers would be overwhelmed, I ordered the whole regiment forward at a double-quick, but before the regiment had entirely crossed the river,

Captain Russell informed me that the enemy was advancing in line of battle just beyond the crest of a ridge, about 400 yards to our front.

I at once determined to seize the crest before the enemy could get there, if possible; consequently the whole line was ordered forward on the run, and although the whole ridge seemed to issue forth a continuous flame of fire, not a man faltered, but each seemed to strive to reach the desired point in advance of his comrades. The boldness of the movement, and the alacrity with which it was executed, together with the brisk and well-directed fire of my men, struck terror to the enemy, who fell back in great confusion at our approach. I was at this moment ordered to advance no farther, but hold my position. I then ordered my men to lie down, so as to conceal them as much as possible, and in a few moments the enemy was plainly seen advancing upon our position. They were allowed to advance to within 30 paces, when fire was opened upon them with such effect that they hardly waited to reply, but broke and fled again. Re-enforcements soon arrived on my right and left.[3]

Streight's attack secured part of Wayne's Hill. Captain Cobb's battery was saved from being overrun and captured by the arrival and counterattack of the Ninth Kentucky, and Forty-first Alabama.

Harker's first three regiments were soon joined by the remaining two, and a strong position was established on the open ground in front of you.

Report of Col. Charles G. Harker, USA—continued

The skirmishers were soon supported by the front line of the brigade. The enemy seemed to have been entirely disconcerted by this bold movement of our troops, and fell back in confusion. In this movement our loss was 2 men killed and 3 wounded. This slight loss must be attributed to the able manner in which the officers of the brigade conducted their commands. A prisoner taken reported an entire division of the enemy on my front; movements along my entire front and flanks indicated that a strong force was near me. I reported this to the general commanding the division, at the same time stating that I could hold the position until re-enforced.[4]

Crittenden's Left Wing now had a bridgehead on the Confederate side of the river. This advantage could have been exploited that night and early the following day by crossing additional troops into the bridgehead and expanding it. Additional crossings could also have been made in the vicinity of McFadden's Ford, to your left. By dawn the majority of Wood's division could have been in position on the far side of the river. The bridgehead could have then been further expanded by crossing Van Cleve's division.

General Bragg could not have ignored this Union movement; and would have had to respond with a strong force. The Battle of Stones River could have commenced on the terrain in front of you on December 30. However, this advantage was not exploited, and the critical decision was made to withdraw Harker's brigade that night. There would not be any major combat on the other side of the river until January 2, 1863.

Return to your car for the drive to Stop 2.

Drive from the parking area back to US 41 / NW Broad Street and turn right. Drive southeast for 2.2 miles to the intersection with Old Fort Parkway / Memorial Boulevard. Turn right onto Old Fort Parkway and drive west for 2.7 miles. In 2.1 miles you will cross over Interstate 24. Old Fort Parkway will become the Franklin Road. Continue on for 0.6 mile and turn right into the parking lot. Park, leave your car, and face east, the direction you just came from.

Stop 2—Bragg Attacks Rosecrans's Right Flank

You are standing between the Confederate and Union positions as they were in the predawn hours of December 31, 1862. The ground all around you was farmland, cornfields, and wooded areas. Six hundred yards in front of you, where Cason Lane is today, was the left of the Army of Tennessee. Bragg had positioned two divisions there. They were the main attack forces, and they were to conduct an envelopment of the Union right.

Maj. Gen. John P. McCown's three-brigade division was positioned from the Franklin Road south (to your right) for 1,200 yards along Cason Lane. All three brigades were deployed in the first line of the attack. Their order from your left to your right was as follows: Brig. Gen. Evander McNair's four-regiment, one-battalion brigade; Brig. Gen. Matthew Ector's four-regiment brigade; and Brig. Gen. James E. Rains's two-regiment, two-battalion brigade. An artillery battery supported each brigade.

Maj. Gen. Patrick R. Cleburne's four-brigade division was positioned immediately behind McCown's. Three units were deployed from the Franklin Road south: Brig. Gen. Lucius E. Polk's five-regiment brigade, Brig. Gen. Bushrod R. Johnson's five-regiment brigade, and Brig. Gen. St. John R. Liddell's

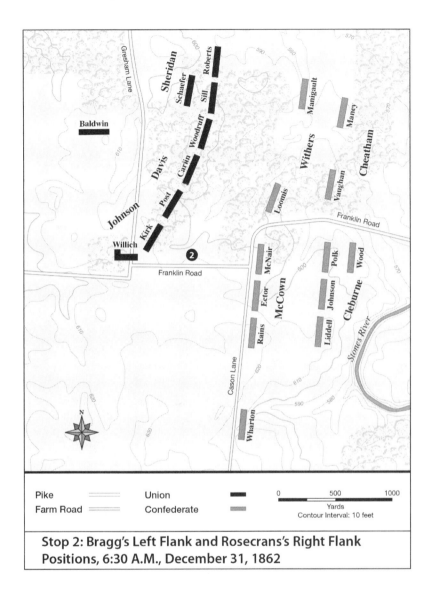

Stop 2: Bragg's Left Flank and Rosecrans's Right Flank Positions, 6:30 A.M., December 31, 1862

four-regiment brigade. Brig. Gen. Sterling A. M. Wood's four-regiment, one-battalion brigade maintained a second reserve line behind Polk's Brigade. An artillery battery supported each brigade in Cleburne's first line. Wood's artillery, Semple's Alabama Battery was on Wayne's Hill supporting Hanson's Brigade. Brig. Gen. John A. Wharton's cavalry brigade was positioned to the left of McCown's division to protect the left flank and exploit any advantage that developed.

North of the Franklin Road was the center of Bragg's army and the supporting attack. Maj. Gen. Jones M. Withers's four-brigade division was positioned from a location 600 yards in front of you to the north and northeast for 3,100 yards (1.75 miles). Maj. Gen. Benjamin F. Cheatham's four-brigade division was deployed behind Withers's. The extreme right of the Confederate line was Breckinridge's Division on the other side of Stones River.

Turn around so that you are now facing west.

Look west along the Franklin Road and at a distance of 500 yards (0.3 mile) you can see a church steeple on the same side of the road where you stand. This is the Franklin Road Baptist Church. The church's site today was the location of the right (west) flank of the Army of the Cumberland in 1862. Maj. Gen. Alexander McD. McCook's three-division Right Wing was the right of the Union army. The right division was Brig. Gen. Richard W. Johnson's Second Division. Johnson had deployed two brigades in a defensive position and maintained one brigade as a reserve.

Brig. Gen. August Willich's five-regiment First Brigade was in the vicinity of present-day Franklin Road Baptist Church and was facing south. This brigade was the right flank unit of the Union army. To Willich's left (your right as you view it) was Brig. Gen. Edward N. Kirk's five-regiment Second Brigade. Kirk's position went from the Franklin Road toward the northeast and was to your front and right front. The reserve brigade, Col. Philemon P. Baldwin's four-regiment Third Brigade, was positioned 1,200 yards north behind Willich and Kirk.

Brig. Gen. Jefferson C. Davis's three-brigade First Division was positioned to the left of Johnson's division. The right of Davis's division was 400 yards to your right, and the division's position extended northeast. To Davis's left, Brig. Gen. Philip H. Sheridan's three-brigade Third Division occupied an area stretching northeast to the Wilkinson Pike. McCook's three divisions covered a frontage of 2,860 yards (1.6 miles). From McCook's left at the Wilkinson Pike, the Union position continued northeast with the Center and Left Wings for 3,000 yards (1.7 miles), reaching the vicinity of McFadden's Ford.

At 6:30 a.m. on December 31, 1862, McCown's and Cleburne's Divisions commenced their attack under the overall command of Lieut. Gen. William J. Hardee. Moving forward from their attack positions, they passed through and on either side of your current location, violently hitting the right of the Union position. Shortly thereafter, Withers's and Cheatham's Divisions, to your right, moved forward and attacked the position of the Union Center and Left Wings.

Report of Lieut. Gen. William J. Hardee, CSA, Commanding Hardee's Corps, Army of Tennessee

McCown advanced with his division against the enemy, about 600 yards distant, with McNair on the right of Ector [in the center] and with Rains' brigade on the left. The division of Major-General Cleburne was about 500 yards in rear of McCown, as a second line. The two divisions were posted on the left of Lieutenant-General Polk's command. The troops advanced with animation and soon became hotly engaged. The enemy were broken and driven through a cedar brake after a rapid and successful charge by McCown's command, in which Brigadier-General [August] Willich and many prisoners were taken.

I had ordered McCown and Cleburne, as they crushed the line of the enemy, to swing round by a continued change of direction to the right, with [McNair's Brigade] as a pivot, while Wharton was to make a diversion on their flank and rear. This was done by Cleburne, but was not so promptly executed by McCown, on account of the position of the enemy in his front. McCown continued westward, fighting toward Overall's Creek, far to our left, while Cleburne, executing the maneuver, changed his direction northeastwardly toward the Wilkinson turnpike, which placed him on the right of McCown and filled the interval between McCown and Polk. The line, now single and without support, engaged and drove the enemy with great carnage through the fields and cedar brakes which lie between the [Franklin] and Wilkinson roads.[5]

Return to your car for the drive to Stop 3.

Drive to the Franklin Road, turn right, and drive west for 0.2 mile to the intersection with Grisham Lane. Turn right onto Grisham Lane and immediately turn right into the parking area. Park so that you do not block traffic, then leave your car and find a safe place to stand so that you can look north along Gresham Lane. Be careful—there is traffic in both directions on Grisham Lane and in the parking area.

Stop 3—McCown's Division Goes Astray

At this stop you can begin to see the consequences of Bragg's critical decision concerning the allocation of combat power. His choice meant that the Confederates had insufficient forces in the main attack.

The road leading north from your location is Gresham Lane; it was here in 1862. Two hundred and fifty yards to your left (west) you can see the spire of Franklin Road Baptist Church. Although the church was not there in 1862, it marks the vicinity of the Right Wing's right flank, and of the Army of the Cumberland's right. This unit was Brig. Gen. August Willich's First Brigade, whose position faced south and was generally along the Franklin Road. Two hundred yards to your right, the left flank of Willich's brigade joined with the right flank of Brig. Gen. Edward N. Kirk's Second Brigade. Both of these brigades were a part of Brig. Gen. Richard W. Johnson's Second Division. Kirk's position was at a forty-five-degree angle to Willich's and extended to your right front (northeast) for 600 yards. Johnson's other brigade; Col. Philemon P. Baldwin's Third Brigade, was in a reserve position 1,200 yards north of your location.

Maj. Gen. John P. McCown's three-brigade division was the first line of the Confederate attack. His center and left brigades, Rains's and Ector's, passed behind your location, then struck and enveloped Willich's brigade. McCown's right brigade, McNair's, struck Kirk's brigade. This area is where McCown's division was to execute a right wheel and attack north. As the right of the Union line retreated to the northwest, it was pursued by Rains's and Ector's Brigades. They did not complete the turn. McNair's Brigade did complete the turn, and it engaged other Union units as the defensive line fell back and tried to form a new position.

Report of Maj. Gen. John P. McCown, CSA, Commanding McCown's Division, Hardee's Corps, Army of Tennessee

My men advanced steadily, reserving their fire until they were but a short distance from the enemy's position. A volley was delivered, and their position and batteries taken with the bayonet, leaving the ground covered with his dead and wounded, leaving also many prisoners in our hands; among them Brigadier General [August] Willich. . . . The enemy made several attempts to rally, but failed, being closely pressed by my men, their defeat becoming almost a rout. The enemy was pressed near a mile. The force of the enemy in my front prevented me throwing forward my left wing as soon as instructed by Lieutenant-General Hardee.[6]

Maj. Gen. Patrick R. Cleburne's four-brigade division followed McCown's. It was also to make a right turn and continue to follow McCown's Division

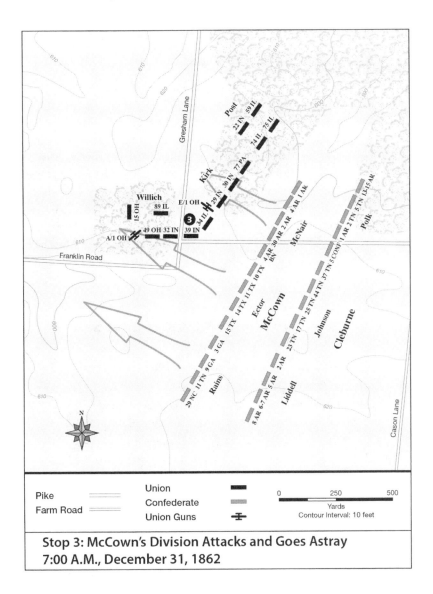

Stop 3: McCown's Division Attacks and Goes Astray
7:00 A.M., December 31, 1862

north. As McCown reached the vicinity of the Wilkinson Pike, 2,650 yards
(1.5 miles) north of your location, it would need to stop, regroup, and resupply ammunition. At that location Cleburne's Division would conduct a forward passage of lines and continue the attack. However, because Rains's and
Ector's Brigades pursued retreating Union units to the northwest, they did
not complete the right turn. This incident left only McNair's Brigade in position to continue the attack north. It also exposed Cleburne's Division to the

fire of the Union defenders who were now north of you and facing south. Cleburne was forced into the front line of the attack.

After Cleburne's Division completed its right turn, it was deployed facing north. Brig. Gen. Bushrod R. Johnson's brigade was attacking on either side of Gresham Lane. To Johnson's left was Brig. Gen. St. John R. Liddell's brigade. McNair had positioned his brigade on Liddell's left and was also attacking north. These brigades attacked Col. Sidney Post's First Brigade of Brig. Gen. Jefferson C. Davis's division and Baldwin's brigade, which had moved forward from its reserve position. Post's brigade had been enveloped on its right by the attack and had repositioned to a south-facing position astride Gresham Lane 500 yards in front of you. Baldwin's brigade was in a position west of Gresham Lane, to Post right rear, and was 1,100 yards to your left front. Cleburne's other two brigades, Brig. Gen. Lucius E. Polk's and Brig. Gen. Sterling A. M. Wood's, were attacking to the right of Johnson's Brigade.

Report of Maj. Gen. Patrick R. Cleburne, CSA, Commanding Cleburne's Division, Hardee's Corps, Army of Tennessee

It was not yet clear day when I received orders from General Hardee to advance. Swinging to the right as I moved forward, I rapidly communicated these instructions to brigade commanders, caused my division to load, and moved forward, stepping short upon the right and full upon the left, so as to swing round my left as directed. . . . My whole division was now advancing in line of battle, gradually wheeling to the right as it advanced. My left had not moved half a mile when heavy firing commenced near its front, supposed to be McCown's division engaging the enemy. A few moments more, and the enemy's skirmishers opened fire along the right and left center of my division, indicating that instead of being a second line supporting McCown's division, I was, in reality, the foremost line on this part of the field, and that McCown's line had unaccountably disappeared from my front. Skirmishers were immediately thrown forward, and I pressed on, continuing the difficult wheel under fire, through a country cut up with numerous fences and thickets. . . . I encountered his first solid line of battle at an average distance of three-fourths of a mile from the scene of my bivouac of last night. The left of this line (opposite Wood's and Polk's brigades) stretched through a large cedar brake; the right (opposite Liddell's and Johnson's) through open ground. In many parts of the brake the enemy found natural breastworks of limestone rock. In the open ground he covered most of his line behind a string of fence. Opposite my left, where the ground was open, a second line of the enemy, supported by artillery, could be seen a short distance in rear of his first. Here was my first important fight of the day. It extended along my whole line, and was participated in by McNair's brigade, of McCown's division, which had been placed on my left, and which a few moments before had surprised and driven the enemy from the ground over which my left had passed. The fight was short and bloody, lasting about twenty-five minutes, when the enemy gave way, both in the cedars and open ground, and fled back on his second line, which was immediately encountered in the woods, pastures, and open ground in rear of his former position. His second line soon gave way, and both went off together.[7]

Cleburne's attack drove the Union defenders in front of you to the north, and it enveloped the Union position to your right front.

Return to your car for the drive to Stop 4.

Depart the parking area and drive north on Gresham Lane for 1 mile to its intersection with John R. Rice Boulevard. In almost 0.3 mile you will pass Clairmont Drive on your left. At this point you are at the center of the position of Post's brigade. Nearly 0.4 mile farther on, you will pass Braxton Bragg Drive on your left. After Baldwin's brigade moved forward from its reserve position, it was deployed where Braxton Bragg Drive is today. In another 0.3 mile you will be at the intersection. In 1862 Gresham Lane continued across present-day Interstate 24. It then went on through the modern shopping center to the Wilkinson Pike. Turn left onto John R. Rice Boulevard and drive northwest for 0.6 mile to an old road on your right. Turn right onto this road and stop. If you wish, get out of your car and face north.

Stop 4—The Attack Pauses

The road 250 yards in front of you that goes from your left to your right was the Wilkinson Pike in 1862. As Cleburne's Division continued attacking north, it reached this location. The entire right of the Union position had collapsed, and the defenders were in retreat north of the Wilkinson Pike.

You are at the left of Cleburne's Division. Liddell's Brigade was where you are. To your right were Johnson's, Polk's, and Wood's Brigades. The right of Cleburne's Division had turned farther to its right and was maneuvering east and parallel to the Wilkinson Pike. This maneuver was targeted against Sheridan's division, which had been the left of the Right Wing but was now the right unit of Rosecrans's defenses. Sheridan's division was 1,800 yards to your right. Cleburne pulled these units back and redirected them north. To your left was McNair's Brigade of McCown's Division. McCown's other two brigades, Rains's and Ector's, which had pursed retreating Union units to the northwest, were redirected back north. They joined McNair along the Wilkinson Pike.

The Confederate situation along this section of the Wilkinson Pike demonstrates the consequences of Bragg's critical decision as to the allocation of combat power to the main attack. When Bragg formulated his plan for enveloping Rosecrans's right, five infantry divisions and four brigades of cavalry were at his disposal. This does not count Forrest's and Morgan's cavalry brigades on deep penetration raids into Western Tennessee and central Kentucky. Two of the remaining four cavalry brigades were on a raid against Rosecrans's supply line from Nashville and were not available for the December 31 attack. Bragg allocated two infantry divisions, McCown's in the first line and Cleburne's in the second and supporting line, to the main attack (the envelopment). Two infantry divisions, Wither's and Cheatham's, constituted the supporting attack. The fifth infantry division, Breckinridge's, was positioned across Stones River to secure the right flank One brigade each from the two remaining cavalry brigades was positioned on each of the army's flanks. As the combat progressed, most of Breckinridge's Division was brought to this side of the river and committed to action in the center. Perhaps a better use of this division would have been to position it, minus a brigade or two to protect the right flank, as a reserve for the main attack. Doing so would have provided sufficient troop strength to respond to unforeseen problems, such as the premature commitment of Cleburne's Division.

McCown's Division was in the front line of Bragg's main attack. Cleburne's Division initially was in the second line of the main attack. Had all of McCown's Division made the right turn north and generally followed the axis of advance paralleling Grisham Lane, it would have arrived at this location. As with any attack of this distance and intensity, McCown's units would have been disorganized and low on ammunition. This was a good location for them to pause, reorganize, and resupply ammunition. While McCown was doing this, Cleburne's Division, which would have been following, could have executed a forward passage of lines and taken up the attack. This action would have maintained a constant pressure on the retreating Union Right Wing units.

As you have seen at Stop 3, because two of McCown's brigades, Rains's and Ector's, had pursued the retreating Union defenders to the northwest, Cleburne had been forced to bring his division into the first line shortly after the attack commenced. As a result, the main attack arrived along the Wilkinson Pike with both divisions committed and no reserve to maintain the momentum that had been achieved. Both Confederate divisions were disorganized to some degree. Furthermore, some brigades needed to be reoriented to the original direction of attack, and many units were low on ammunition. McCown's two brigades that pursued the retreating Union forces to the northwest caused the situation that forced a pause in the attack and gave Rosecrans time to shift units and readjust his defenses.

Another possible use for Breckinridge's Division was to have it conduct a demonstration or even a limited attack against Rosecrans's units near McFadden's Ford to hold them in position. There will be more discussion of this option at the next stop.

Return to John R. Rice Boulevard and drive north for 0.3 mile to the intersection with Fortress Boulevard / Medical Center Parkway. Turn right and drive 0.4 mile to the intersection with Asbury Lane. Turn left onto Asbury Lane. Be careful—do not turn on to the I-24 access road. Drive north on Asbury Lane for 1.3 miles to the intersection with Asbury Road. Turn right onto Asbury Road and drive east 0.6 mile to Chisholm Road (on your left). Turn left onto Chisholm Road, drive to the T-intersection with Cimarron Trail, make a U-turn, and drive back south toward Asbury Road. Be careful of traffic and children. Stop prior to reaching Asbury Road. Do not pull off to the side of the road, as there is a steep drop. If it is convenient, get out of your car and stand where you can safely see south across the field on the other side of Asbury Road.

Stop 5—Rosecrans Shifts Brigades

In 1862 the ground all around you was open countryside and fields of cotton and corn. Eight hundred yards south of your location was the northern edge of a large wood east of Asbury Lane. Northeast of you was a cedar woods that ran along the sides of the Nashville Pike.

The Nashville Pike is 1,050 yards (0.6 mile) northeast from this location. Any sizeable Confederate force reaching and holding the pike would be in the Army of the Cumberland's rear area and would have cut its lines of supply and communication to Nashville.

Rosecrans had also planned an offensive operation for the morning of December 31. In a mirror image of Bragg, he planned to conduct an envelopment of the Confederate right. Two divisions of the Left Wing, Brig. Gen. Thomas J. Wood's First Division and Brig. Gen. Horatio P. Van Cleve's Third Division, were given this mission. Before they could fully commence the envelopment, Bragg struck the Union right.

When Rosecrans began to understand the magnitude of the disaster on his right flank, he began shifting units from his left to his right to establish a new defensive position in this area. He could effect this transfer because there had been no aggressive movement by Breckinridge's Division, which was across Stones River from Rosecrans's Left Wing.

Report of Maj. Gen. William S. Rosecrans, USA, Commanding Army of the Cumberland

The movement began on the left by Van Cleve, who crossed at the lower fords. Wood prepared to sustain and follow him. The enemy, meanwhile, had prepared to attack General McCook, and by 6.30 o'clock advanced in heavy columns.

Within an hour from the time of the opening of the battle, a staff officer from General McCook arrived, announcing to me that the right wing was heavily pressed and needed assistance. . . . Soon after, a second officer from General McCook arrived, and stated that the right wing was being driven – a fact that was but too manifest by the rapid movement of the noise of battle toward the north.

General Crittenden was ordered to suspend Van Cleve's movement across the river, on the left, and to cover the crossing with one brigade, and move the other two brigades westward across the fields toward the railroad for a reserve. Wood was also directed to suspend his preparations for crossing, and to hold Hascall in reserve. At this moment fugitives and stragglers from McCook's corps began to make their appearance through the cedar-brakes in such numbers that I became satisfied that McCook's [Right Wing] was routed. I, therefore, directed General Crittenden to send Van Cleve in to the right of Rousseau; Wood to send Colonel Harker's brigade farther down the Murfreesboro [Nashville] pike, to go in and attack the enemy on the right of Van Cleve's [two brigades].[8]

Rosecrans ordered Van Cleve to leave one brigade to guard McFadden's Ford and send the other two to the right. Col. Samuel Beatty and Col. James P. Fyffe immediately began moving toward where you are now. Wood was also

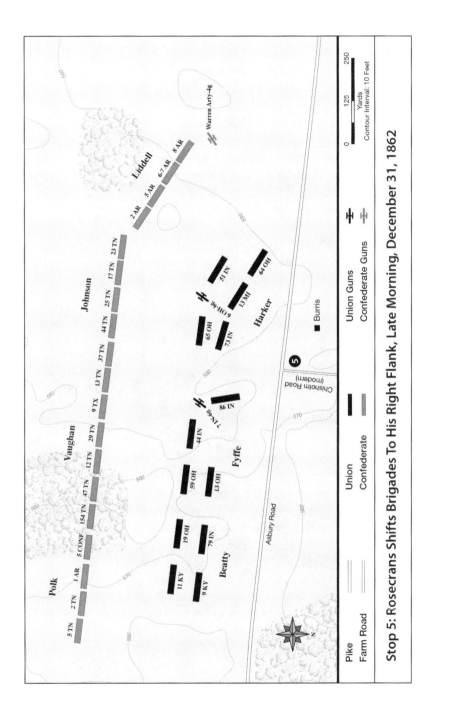

Polk

Vaughan

Johnson

Liddell

5 TN
2 TN
1 AR
5 CONF
154 TN
47 TN
12 TN
29 TN
9 TX
13 TN
37 TN
44 TN
25 TN
17 TN
23 TN

2 AR
5 AR
6-7 AR
8 AR

Warren Arty-4g

51 IN
64 OH
9 OH-68
13 MI
65 OH
73 IN

Harker

86 IN
7 IN-58
44 IN
59 OH
13 OH

Fyffe

19 OH
79 IN

11 KY
9 KY

Beatty

Chisholm Road (modern)

Asbury Road

Burris

N

Pike
Farm Road

Union
Confederate

Union Guns
Confederate Guns

0   125   250
Yards
Contour Interval: 10 Feet

Stop 5: Rosecrans Shifts Brigades To His Right Flank, Late Morning, December 31, 1862

ordered to send two brigades to the right, and he dispatched Brig. Gen. Milo S. Haskell's and Col. Charles G. Harker's units. The roads were clogged with advancing and retreating troops, preventing Haskell from completing the move. He returned to a position between the Round Forest and today's National Cemetery. However, Harker's brigade accomplished the move to this location.

Harker's five regiments and supporting artillery battery took up a defensive position in the field in front of you. Two hundred and fifty yards to Harker's left were Fyffe's brigade and Beatty's brigade to Fyffe's left. Soon after assuming their new positions, they were struck by three of Cleburne's brigades and Col. Alfred J. Vaughan's brigade from Cheatham's Division.

Report of Col. Charles G. Harker, USA, Commanding Third Brigade, First Division, Left Wing, Army of the Cumberland

About 8 a.m., December 31, I received orders from General Wood, commanding division, to cross the river with my command. The movement was commenced, in obedience to General Wood's order, but was suspended for a few moments by an order emanating from Major-General Crittenden, commanding the left wing. While awaiting further orders, Major-General Rosecrans passed my command, and gave me direct instructions to proceed immediately to the support of the right wing of our army, which was yielding to the overwhelming force of the enemy at that point.

On approaching the right, much confusion was visible; troops marching in every direction; stragglers to be seen in great numbers, and teamsters in great consternation endeavoring to drive their teams they knew not whither. My progress was impeded by the confusion. . . . The brigade was, however, pressed on to a position on the extreme right of our line, Colonel Fyffe's brigade, of General Van Cleve's division, being immediately upon our left.

About this time a battery from the enemy, situated in a cornfield, and nearly opposite my right flank, opened upon my command with canister. In order to get a commanding position for artillery, and at the same time guard well my right flank, which I was fearful the enemy would attempt to turn, I moved the command a little to the right.

While this movement was being executed, a staff officer from the command upon my left reported a strong force of the enemy in his front. I replied that my right was in danger, and that a strong force and battery was in front. No sooner had I taken a position on the crest of the hill than a most vigorous engagement commenced. The position selected for my brigade proved a most fortunate one. The enemy was completely baffled in his design to turn my right; not only [was the battery] in my front silenced and the enemy there repulsed, but a most destructive fire from Bradley's [Sixth Ohio] battery played upon the heavy columns of the enemy then pressing the troops upon my left. This engagement had continued about twenty minutes, when it was reported to me that the troops on my left had given way, and that the enemy was already in rear of my left flank, and about 200 yards from it, pouring a destructive cross-fire upon my troops.[9]

Maneuvering against Harker's front and his right were Brig. Gen. Bushrod R. Johnson's brigade and Brig. Gen. St. John R. Liddell's brigade.

Report of Brig. Gen. Bushrod R. Johnson, CSA, Commanding Johnson's Brigade, Cleburne's Division, Hardee's Corps, Army of Tennessee

An order now came to me from General Cleburne to move my brigade to support General Liddell. After marching some 400 yards by the left flank, we moved to our front and passed north through a long wood lot projecting into open fields. Having received a message from General Liddell, through Colonel Kelly, who was wounded, to the effect that the aid of my brigade would rout the enemy, we came up with General Liddell's brigade on an ascent beyond the edge of the woods. General Liddell's command now yielded the ground to my men, and reformed under the brow of a small hill, to the top of which my command ascended.

Before us was now an open field, declining in front. At the foot of the declivity, at the distance of about 400 yards, was a battery, strongly supported by infantry. My command steadily advanced, fighting under fire from the battery and infantry. The battery was soon silenced, and our men advanced in double-quick time to a position behind a fence and a ledge of rocks. In front, about 80 yards,

Brigadier General Bushrod R. Johnson, CSA, commanding brigade. Library of Congress.

was a cedar glade, in the edge of which the enemy were now seen lying close together along a ledge of rocks. Under cover of the fence and rocks our men took deliberate aim and poured upon the enemy a destructive fire, which was returned with spirit. The conflict lasted some twenty minutes, when the enemy arose to retire. At this moment a volley was discharged upon them with remarkable effect, and our men rapidly advanced to the cedars, capturing the fine battery of Parrott guns [actually two guns] against which they had been fighting, and which was now in position on the adjacent flanks of the Twenty-third and Seventeenth Tennessee Regiments. The men of my brigade then took shelter behind the ledge of rocks at the edge of the glade, and were well covered from the enemy's fire. All concur in representing the number of dead and wounded in the edge of the cedars as very large. Many were lying side by side along the ledge in the position they assumed to await our approach, while others had fallen as they turned to retreat.[10]

Harker's brigade fell back to the vicinity of the Nashville Pike, rallied, and formed a defensive position. Part of the unit then counterattacked.

Report of Col. Charles G. Harker, USA—Continued

The command was now ordered to fall back and form on a rocky eminence covered with cedars, being a very strong position. The Thirteenth Michigan, from their position, opened upon the enemy with telling effect, and, having caused his ranks to waver, followed up the advantage with a charge, supported by the Fifty-first Illinois Volunteers, who had now come to our relief. They completely routed the enemy. The Thirteenth Michigan retook two pieces of artillery, abandoned by our battery, and captured 58 prisoners.[11]

Harker's counterattack caught Johnson's Brigade by surprise and repulsed it as other brigades from Cleburne's Division were falling back.

Report of Brig. Gen. Bushrod R. Johnson, CSA—Continued

The retreat was made without order. The lines were broken and men of different regiments, brigades, and divisions were scattered all over the fields. The movement was to me totally unexpected, and I have yet to learn that there existed a cause commensurate with the demoralization that ensued. At the moment in which I felt the utmost confidence in the success of our arms I was almost run over by our retreating troops. I contended with the tide step by step, but made no impression on the retreating columns until they had gained the woods, when, by calling on a number of color-bearers, I succeeded in planting the colors of several regiments, and the men then assembled upon them with ranks much thinned. I cannot but think that the whole ultimate fortunes of the field were lost by this backward movement. Our men were in sight of the Nashville pike; some have said they were on it. The enemy's right was doubled back upon their center. Had we held this position the line of communication of the enemy would have been cut. We could have flanked them and enfiladed their whole line, which was no doubt in disorder. It was unfortunate that our artillery was not promptly moved forward to support us. My battery was at this time in position, by order of General

Hardee. I do not think that our artillery was sufficiently used on our left. General Liddell's battery arrived on the ground, and he proceeded to put it in position for the work to be done, but did not succeed in time to open before the retreat commenced. Had we received re-enforcements we might have returned and regained the ground. But very soon the enemy planted a formidable battery on an eminence near the railroad, sweeping all the open fields and commanding even the woods in which our lines were formed. The enemy's infantry was also brought forward and posted in great strength, so as to be protected by the side slopes of the railroad and pike, and the trees and rocks in the cedar glade. It would then have been very hazardous to assail them with any force by our former approach.[12]

Although Beatty's, Fyffe's and Harker's brigades were pushed back to the vicinity of the Nashville Pike, they were able to slow Cleburne's advance. The Confederate attack was greatly reduced in strength by this time, and a counterattack drove them back.

This critical decision by Rosecrans shifted troops to his right in time to stop and repel what had been a successful attack by Cleburne's Division. McCown's two brigades' maneuvering off the axis of advance and Bragg's failure to add Breckinridge's Division to the main attack necessitated a pause along the Wilkinson Pike. This gave Rosecrans the time to send three brigades to the right flank. If Breckinridge's Division was not to be added to the attack, the failure to have it conduct a demonstration or a limited attack at McFadden's Ford removed any threat to the Union left, and it allowed Rosecrans to send reinforcement from there to his right.

If Rosecrans had not made the critical decisions to cancel his attack and reinforce his right, in all probability Cleburne's Division and part of McCown's Division would have reached the Nashville Pike in the rear of the Army of the Cumberland. That event would have given us a different history of the battle.

Return to your car for the drive to Stop 6.

Drive forward to the Asbury Road, turn left, and drive 0.7 mile to the Nashville Pike. Turn right on the Nashville Pike and drive southeast for 0.3 mile to the National Cemetery. Turn left into the parking area, park, leave your car, and walk to the cemetery wall that parallels the Nashville Pike. Stand where you can look southwest across the open field to the far tree line.

Stop 6—Thomas Orders the Artillery Repositioned

You are on the western edge of the National Cemetery, which was established in June 1864. The soldiers buried here are Union dead from the Battle of Stones River and the skirmishes before and after it. Of the 7,121 interred at the National Cemetery, 6,139 are Civil War veterans. The remaining soldiers are veterans of later wars. The cemetery was closed in January 1974 and is now maintained by the National Park Service.[13]

As you look southwest across the fields on the other side of the Nashville Pike you can see at a distance of six hundred yards a large cedar woods. Stop 4, near the Wilkinson Pike, is another 2,400 yards (1.4 miles) farther to the southwest. The Round Forest is 750 yards (0.4 mile) to your left. Stop 5 is 1,650 yards (0.9 mile) to your right front. Notice how the ground behind you rises to a fifteen-foot elevation and forms a seven-hundred-yard-long terrain feature. This terrain feature is between the railroad and the Nashville Pike. It dominates the open fields southwest of the pike, provides excellent observation and fields of fire, and was an ideal position for Civil War artillery.

When Johnson's and Davis's divisions of the Right Wing collapsed and were forced to retreat, Sheridan's division assumed its third defensive position along the Wilkinson Pike. To support Sheridan's right flank, Maj. Gen. Lovell H. Rousseau's First Division of Maj. Gen. George H. Thomas's Center Wing was ordered into the cedars. Rousseau's division was initially positioned just to the west of the Ashbury Road–Nashville Pike intersection. He had three of his four brigades and two of three artillery batteries. Ordered to support Sheridan, Rousseau marched his division south on a course parallel to and on the other side of the Nashville Pike. The troops would have passed in front of you from right to left. When the unit reached the open field, it turned right and deployed. Lieut. Col. Oliver L. Shepherd's Fourth Brigade was on the right, Col. John Beatty's Second Brigade was on the left, and Col. Benjamin F. Scribner's First Brigade was retained as the reserve. Lieut. Francis L. Gunther's Battery H, Fifth US Artillery and Lieut. George W. Van Pelt's Battery A, First Michigan Artillery accompanied the infantry.

Report of Maj. Gen. Lovell H. Rousseau, USA, Commanding First Division, Center Wing, Army of the Cumberland

At about 9 a.m. on the 31st, the report of artillery and heavy firing of small-arms on our right announced that the battle had begun, by an attack on the right wing, commanded by Major-General

McCook. It was not long before the direction from which the firing came indicated that General McCook's command had given way and was yielding ground to the enemy. His forces seemed to swing around toward our right and rear. At this time General Thomas ordered me to advance my division quickly to the front, to the assistance of General McCook.

We consulted and agreed as to where the line should be formed. This was in a dense cedar brake, through which my troops marched in double-quick time, to get into position before the enemy reached us. He was then but a few hundred yards to the front, sweeping up in immense numbers, driving everything before him. This ground was new and unknown to us all. The woods were almost impassable to infantry, and artillery was perfectly useless.

Our lines were hardly formed before a dropping fire of the enemy announced his approach. General McCook's troops, in a good deal of confusion, retired through our lines and around our right under a most terrific fire. The enemy, in pursuit, furiously assailed our front, and, greatly outflanking us, passed around to our right and rear.[14]

Major General Lovell H. Rousseau, USA, commanding division. National Archives.

Rousseau's division had made contact with McCown's. You last saw McCown's Division along the Wilkinson Pike in the vicinity of Stop 4. Once it had reorganized and resupplied ammunition, it continued its attack. At the Wilkinson Pike it had been on the left of Cleburne's Division. However, as Cleburne moved forward toward Stop 5 on the Ashbury Road, McCown made a more abrupt partial right turn and passed behind Cleburne. His division was then placed on Cleburne's right and on a line for the cedars, the open fields, and the rising terrain where the National Cemetery is located today.

The two artillery batteries attempted to accompany the deployed brigades into the cedars. Lieutenant Guenther tried to send his cannon with Shepherd's brigade. Seeing the difficulty the infantry was having in the cedars, and knowing the trees would create an impossible situation for artillery, Guenther went to Rousseau. Finding Rousseau and Thomas together, he informed them that positioning his guns in the heavy cedars would probably result in their loss. Thomas directed Rousseau to move his artillery out of the cedars to good firing positions. Moving east, Guenther's battery occupied a position in the open field in front of you. After firing several rounds at Confederates emerging from the woods, the battery moved across the Nashville Pike and assumed a firing position on the elevated terrain feature. Gunther's Battery H, Fifth US Artillery was located behind you where the artillery piece and flagpole are today.

At the same time, Rousseau found Lieut. George W. Van Pelt and relayed Thomas's order to move his battery away from the cedars to a better firing position. Van Pelt shifted his battery east, crossed the Nashville Pike, and went into a firing position to Guenther's right.

With a combined twelve guns, Guenther's Battery H (four Napoleons and two 10-pound Parrott Rifles) and Van Pelt's Battery (six 10-pound Parrott Rifles) provided an anchor point for the establishment of a final defensive line along the Nashville Pike. These batteries were soon joined on their right by Capt. James H. Stokes's Chicago Board of Trade Battery with six guns (two James Rifles and four 6-pound smoothbore guns) and the three battalions of the Pioneer Brigade. Lieut. Alanson J. Stevens then placed his Battery B, Pennsylvania Artillery with six guns (two James Rifles and four 6-pound smoothbore guns) between Van Pelt's and Stokes's batteries. To Stokes's right, the six guns (four 10-pound Parrott Rifles and two Napoleons) of Capt. George R. Swallow's Seventh Indiana Battery went into a firing position. To your left, Lieut. George Estep's Eighth Indiana Battery with six guns (two 12-pound howitzers and four 6-pound smoothbore guns) added its firepower to the defenses. These six batteries with a total of thirty-six guns occupied an eight-hundred-yard-wide position parallel to the Nashville Pike. They were supported by the Pioneer Brigade, the Second Ohio and Thirty-third Ohio, and other regiments from Rousseau's divisions as they rallied on the artillery.

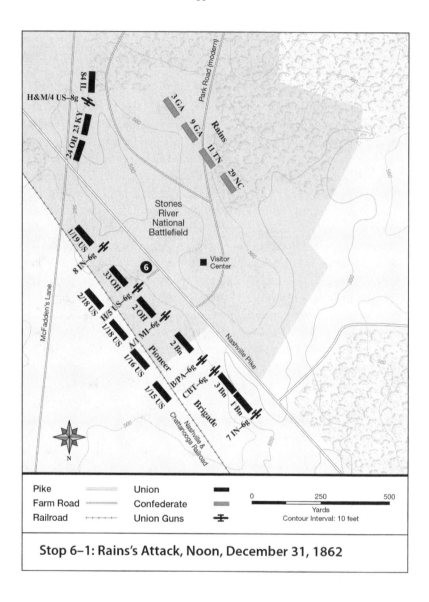

Stop 6–1: Rains's Attack, Noon, December 31, 1862

No sooner was this position formed than McCown's Division began to emerge from the cedars. The first attack was made by Rains's Brigade followed by Ector's and McNair's Brigades.

Lieut. Alfred Pirtle, the ordnance officer for Rousseau's division, was along the railroad tracks with the division's ordnance wagons. He came to the artillery's location so he could observe the fighting. After the war he provided a vivid account of what he saw.

Narrative of Lieut. Alfred Pirtle, USA, Ordnance Officer, First Division, Center Wing, Army of the Cumberland

The field in every direction had become covered with troops much demoralized and disorganized. Van Pelt had opened fire, drawing some reply from the rebel infantry in the edge of the cedars; another battery had been posted to his right and fired a few shots. The battery to Van Pelt's [left] was Battery H, Fifth U.S. Artillery. The regular brigade was supporting the two batteries, with the Second Ohio Infantry on their right.

On this nucleus General Rosecrans began to reform his line of battle, extending it northwardly.

I was standing near a gun rather to the rear of [Van Pelt's battery] looking towards the dark cedars, where I knew the enemy were, because none of our force remained beyond the front of these batteries and their supports. A small space of ground lay before us; then the turnpike, then a cotton patch about 300 yards wide. Near the right edge of the cotton patch was a clump of small trees, tall weeds, and deep grass.

As I looked on, an officer on foot, sword in hand sprang into view with a shout; in an instant the edge of the timber was alive with a mass of arms, heads, legs, guns, swords, gray coats, brown hats, shirt sleeves, and the enemy were upon us, yelling and running. Not a shot from them, then one or two paused to throw up their guns, fire and yell, and then run forward to try to gain the front. By no order that I heard, the whole of the guns of the batteries together fired, covering their front with a cloud of smoke, hiding all objects in it, and then as fast as they could load they fired into the cloud. They ceased, and as the curtain of vapor rolled up, not a moving object beneath it came into sight, but the dreadful effects of the cannonade were shown. The number of dead and wounded had been fearfully increased, and cries and groans reached our ears.

I felt the enemy would make another charge. Since the first attack at daybreak they had for miles swept up everything in their impetuous, unceasing rush, and now victory was within their grasp, since if this brief stand was carried, Rosecrans would be rolled away from the road to Nashville, perhaps routed.

The interval was used by our men in getting the guns depressed so as to rake the ground from the turnpike to the cedars; filling swab buckets, taking harness off dead horses, replacing sound instruments for damaged ones, and caring for the wounded.

All this time our army was being rapidly placed in position on the new line of battle, keeping the two batteries for the pivot, as I have mentioned, extending up the turnpike.

The advance of the enemy [again] was in several deep lines of battle. . . . These lines advanced very rapidly and completely deployed, at which instance our batteries opened on them a deafening, unceasing, deadly fire. I never saw guns served on drill as fast as those were now. Before the recoil was expended, the gunners grasp the spokes and threw the pieces into position; like lightning the sponge was run in, turned and withdrawn, the load sent home and the piece fired.

And the enemy! They were running, swarming across the field, firing and shouting. We kept our gaze fastened on the charge coming, coming on like the breakers of the sea, always nearer at each succeeding wave. But men were not yet born who could longer face that storm of iron sweeping death and distraction to all in its path. They broke and fled.[15]

To the right of your location the Pioneer Brigade supported the artillery batteries. Earlier that morning, the brigade had been doing improvement work on McFadden's Ford and the approach road. With the collapse of the Union right, Rosecrans had ordered them into this area. They arrived just in time to meet McCown's attack. As Lieutenant Pirtle described the artillery fight, Sgt. Henry V. Freeman described the actions of the Pioneers as they fulfilled their secondary role and fought as infantry.

Narrative of Sgt. Henry V. Freeman, USA, Second Battalion, Pioneer Brigade, Army of the Cumberland

Crossing the railroad to the open space between it and the Nashville Pike we filed to the right and formed line of battle. "Battalion, lie down!" was ordered, and the line lay prostrate, each man keenly peering into the thicket in front for the retreating "blue-coats" and "gray-backs" following hard after, of whom the approaching musketry told. On came the sounds of battle nearer and nearer. Then

Sergeant Henry V. Freeman, USA,
Pioneer Brigade. U.S. Army Military
History Institute.

at length the battle line of struggling blue slowly falling back came
into view through the trees. They were loading and firing as they
retired. But their ammunition was about exhausted, and they passed
over our prostrate line and laid down behind it. The order "Battalion, rise up!" came like an electric shock.

The brigade was by some mischance short of ammunition; some
companies had not more than twenty rounds [per man]. Morton, the
brigade commander . . . rode to the front saying: "Men, you haven't
got much ammunition, but give 'em what you have, and then wade
in on 'em with the bayonets." He then gave the order, "Fix bayonets!" "Confound it," said a lieutenant, "that will interfere with their
loading." It was a mistake at that time, but the order was obeyed
for the time being, though the men soon removed them as the firing began. The Confederates were near at hand. Suddenly their line
seemed to burst through the thicket just in front. "Commence firing!" and our volleys were fired into them. Men were dropping here
and there, and others filled the vacant places. . . . "Pour in the shot
boys! Give 'em hell!" were some of the exultant exclamations. The
immediate danger was over. The Confederates gave way rapidly, and
the line pressed forward after them. But it was not prudent to push
ahead too far.

A brief lull followed. Very soon the Board of Trade Battery again opened with renewed vigor. Then through the cedars came dense Confederate columns rolling forward to anticipated victory. "Battalion, rise up!" and again came the shock of battle. But the fire of the [batteries] demoralized them, and they did not stand long. "Forward!" came the command; and our line steadily advanced, but only for a short distance.[16]

Ector's Brigade was the left brigade in McCown's battle line. As you look at the field in front of you, the brigade attacked across its right side. The commander provided a description of his brigade's experience during this attack.

Report of Brig. Gen. Matthew D. Ector, CSA, Commanding Ector's Brigade, McCown's Division, Hardee's Corps, Army of Tennessee

We were ordered forward, and I was told to cause the left of my brigade to oblique to the right. We had marched about 1 mile in this direction. General Rains in the mean time was driving back the enemy, when unfortunately, he fell, mortally wounded. He had driven them through a dense cedar forest and into a field. Their left wing had either been routed or driven back upon their center; the right of their center had also been driven back some distance, and their forces were thus massed in a very formidable position in a field not far from the Nashville pike. General McNair's and my brigades entered the field near the southwest corner (just above it). About 200 yards from the west side of the fence, immediately before us, was a cedar brake. Near the head of this brake it widened out, where the ground was very rocky. I had thought for some time the left of my command was obliquing too much, and so informed the division commander. He sent me word that General Hardee, who was in command of that corps of our army, desired I should continue to move in this way. The enemy was in ambuscade in this cedar brake on the left of my command. They had a very formidable battery planted about 250 yards in a northeast direction from us; one nearly in a north direction about the same distance off, and the third one in a field a quarter of a mile northwest of us. All these batteries turned loose upon us. About the same time their infantry, whose position

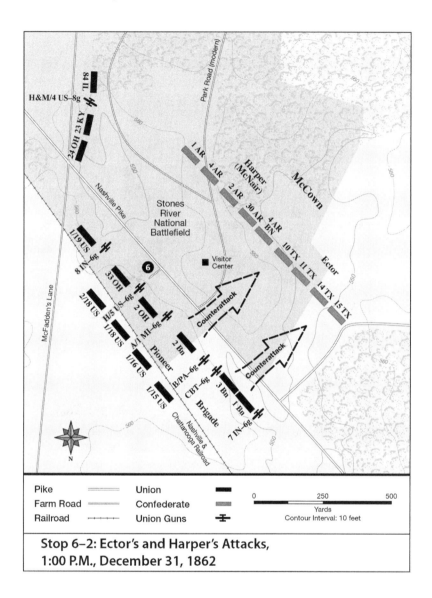

**Stop 6–2: Ector's and Harper's Attacks,
1:00 P.M., December 31, 1862**

had been ascertained by my skirmishers, unmasked themselves and opened fire. The Fourteenth and Fifteenth Texas Regiments were soon in a desperate struggle; the regiments on the right of them were equally exposed to their artillery. Immediately sent Major [F. M.] Spencer to Colonel Harper, who was in command of the brigade on my right (General McNair having become too unwell),

Brigadier General Matthew D. Ector, CSA,
commanding brigade. Library of Congress.

to move his brigade up to my assistance. I hastened to the left of my command. My men had driven back one line of their infantry upon the second line; still behind them was a third line. . . . The cedars were falling and being trimmed by bombs, canister, and iron hail, which seemed to fill the air. My men had not yielded an inch, but, sheltering themselves behind the rocks, would lie down and load, rise to their knees, fire into the closed blue line not over 60 yards from them. . . . Believing it to be impossible to bring my entire brigade to bear with full force, and that an attempt to do it would be attended with great sacrifice of life, I ordered them to fall back.[17]

If you would like to see the defense of this position from a different perspective, walk to the position of Lieut. George Estep's Eighth Indiana Battery.

Face to your left and walk beside the wall (either inside or outside) for 160 yards to the southeast edge of the cemetery and the position of Estep's battery. Do not walk on the road. Face so that you are again looking southwest across the fields to the cedar tree line.

The Eighth Indiana Battery had six guns (two 12-pound howitzers and four 6-pound smoothbore guns) at this location. This was the left flank battery of the key terrain defensive position along the Nashville Pike. Lieutenant Estep provided an account of his battery's combat.

Report of Lieut. George Estep, USA,
Commanding Eighth Indiana Battery, First Division,
Left Wing, Army of the Cumberland

I put my battery in position on Wednesday morning about 9 o'clock, by order of General Rosecrans, on the west side of the railroad, supported on the right by two batteries, and on the left by the Nineteenth Infantry (regulars); fired 114 rounds (at a range of 800 yards) at the enemy, who were driving back our infantry advance. I then advanced the battery 75 or 80 yards, supported, as in the first position, by the two batteries on my right and the Nineteenth Infantry on my left.

At this position the enemy in three lines made three desperate charges, and were as often repulsed by my battery. I expended 70 rounds of canister, and was compelled four or five times to double-charge the pieces in order to drive the enemy; this beginning at a range of 90 yards, and increasing as the enemy became confused and retired. I also fired from this position 106 rounds of shrapnel and solid shot, at a range of about 800 yards, at the lines of the enemy advancing on our right.[18]

Look south (your left front) across the fields. At a distance of 450 yards is the edge of a wood. The open area just before this wood was the position of Lieut. Charles C. Parsons's Batteries H and M, Fourth US Artillery armed with eight guns (four 12-pound howitzers and four 3-inch Ordnance Rifles). Parsons's guns were initially facing southeast. When the Confederate attack developed against this position, Parsons swung his guns around and fired into the Confederate brigades' right flank as they attacked across the fields.

The successful defense of this position and the Nashville Pike prevented the Confederates from severing the Union supply and communications lines to Nashville. Thomas's seemingly small but critical decision to reposition artillery set in motion a chain of events that transformed this area into a formidable defensive position.

Return to your car for the drive to Stop 7.

Depart the parking area, turn left onto the Nashville Pike, and drive southeast for 0.4 mile to the parking area on your left. Turn left into the parking area, leave your car, and stand so that you can look southeast down the pike. Be careful—do not get too close to the road's high-speed traffic. The railroad tracks to your left are an active rail line. Again, do not get too close.

Stop 7—Bragg and Polk Attack the Round Forest

You are on the edge of a small wood that was called the Round Forest in 1862. The forest extended from where you are to the other side of the railroad tracks to your left. A cornfield was on the left edge of the forest. The ground in front of you and to you right was a mixture of open fields and cotton fields. The overpass you see 275 yards in front of you is for today's Thompson Lane; it was not there in 1862. Just beyond the overpass is the site of the Cowan House. This house was burned, but its remains and outbuildings created an obstacle that divided any attack against this position.

Five hundred and fifty yards in front of you, Stones River makes an abrupt turn. Up to this turn the river flows northwest, and after the turn it flows north to McFadden's Ford. Before the turn, when it is flowing northwest, the river runs parallel and next to the Nashville Pike. This part of the river severely limits the area in which the right flank of any Confederate attack against this position can maneuver. Behind you, McFadden Lane crosses the Nashville Pike. The lane comes from McFadden Ford 1,600 yards (0.9 mile) to your left. It crosses the Nashville Pike behind you and continues south (to your right), through the trees, for 1,400 yards (0.8 mile) to the Wilkinson Pike.

You are at the left center of the Army of the Cumberland's position at dawn on December 31, 1862. The army's right flank, in the vicinity of Stop 3, was located 4,400 yards (2.5 miles) to your right (southwest). The left flank was stationed at McFadden's Ford, 1,600 yards (0.9 mile) to your left (north). The ground between McFadden's Ford and the Nashville Pike was occupied by Brig. Gen. Horatio P. Van Cleve's and Brig. Gen. Thomas J. Wood's divisions of Maj. Gen. Thomas L. Crittenden's Left Wing. Crittenden's third division, Brig. Gen. John M. Palmer's division, extended the position from the pike along McFadden's Lane for 500 yards, where it joined with Brig. Gen. James S. Negley's division of the Center Wing. From Negley's right, the three divisions of the Right Wing occupied the ground from the Wilkinson Pike to the vicinity of the Franklin Road-Gresham Lane intersection.

Rosecrans and Bragg both planned to envelop one another's right on December 31. Van Cleve's and Wood's divisions were to be Rosecrans's main

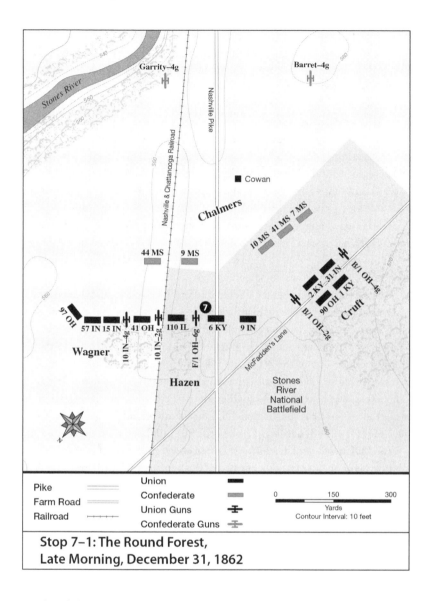

**Stop 7–1: The Round Forest,
Late Morning, December 31, 1862**

attack, while Palmer and Negley's units were the supporting attack. As Van Cleve's and Wood's forces were moving into position and crossing Stones River and Palmer's and Negley's divisions were beginning to move forward, Bragg's envelopment struck Rosecrans's right, and the supporting attack hit the Union center.

The result was a cancellation of Rosecrans's attack and a repositioning of units. Two of Van Cleve's and one of Wood's brigades were marched to the army's right. The remaining six brigades were shifted to defend the area from McFadden's Ford to the tree line along McFadden's Lane on your right. Col. Samuel W. Price's brigade was positioned at McFadden's Ford. Col. George Wagner defended the area north of where the river turns to the Round Forest's north edge. Your current location was the position of Col. William B. Hazen's brigade. Brig. Gen. Milo S. Hascall's brigade had been ordered to the army's right, but it could not get through because the roads were clogged with retreating and advancing units. Hascall initially positioned his brigade as a reserve behind Hazen and Wagner. As the fighting developed it came forward and reinforced the Round Forest position. To your right across the pike and along the tree line was Brig. Gen. Charles Cruft's brigade. Col. William Grose's brigade was positioned between but slightly behind Hazen's and Cruft's brigades. Grose's brigade reversed its orientation from southeast to northwest and assisted in defeating McCown's attack that went across the open field toward today's cemetery.

According to Bragg's plan, Withers's and Cheatham's Divisions would make a supporting attack against the center and left center of the Union position. These two divisions were deployed with Withers in the front line and Cheatham in the second line. Their attack positions stretched 3,300 yards (1.9 miles) southwest from the Nashville Pike, ending just north of the Franklin Road. The right flank brigade of Withers's Division, Brig. Gen. James R. Chalmers's, was next to the Nashville Pike and 1,000 yards (0.6 mile) in front of your location. Brig. Gen. Daniel S. Donelson's brigade, Cheatham's Division's right flank brigade, was 1,200 yards (0.7 mile) behind Chalmers.

As McCown's and Cleburne's Divisions commenced the envelopment (main attack) of Rosecrans's right flank, Withers's and Cheatham's Divisions began their supporting attacks. The first attack against the Union position where you are was made by Chalmers's five-regiment Brigade. As the attack approached the Round Forest, the burnt Cowan House and outbuildings divided the brigade into two segments. One segment attacked Cruft's position to your right. The other segment attacked Hazen's position. Both segments were repulsed with significant losses.

Donelson's five-regiment brigade made the next attack. As in the previous assault, the Cowan House ruins split the brigade into two sections. One section attacked Cruft's position; the other, Hazen's. Half of Donelson's brigade became casualties in this attack. Brigadier General Chalmers was wounded and did not write about his brigade's attack. However, Brigadier General Donelson documented his brigade's experiences, and his report is indicative of both units' attacks.

Report of Brig. Gen. Daniel S. Donelson, CSA, Commanding Donelson's Brigade, Cheatham's Division, Polk's Corps, Army of Tennessee

I moved my brigade forward at 10 o'clock Wednesday morning, December 31 (the right being the directing regiment and the railroad the line of direction), until it reached the front line, from which General Chalmers' brigade had started, where it was halted until orders should be received to advance to the support of General Chalmers. From the moment I moved from my first position in the morning until dark that night my brigade was constantly under the fire of shot and shell from the enemy's batteries.

The brigade had occupied its position along the front line (behind Chalmers' breastworks) only a few minutes, when, General Chalmers having received a severe wound, his brigade was broken and the greater part of it fell back in disorder and confusion. Under orders from Lieutenant-General Polk, I immediately advanced my brigade to its support, and, indeed, its relief, under a shower of shot and shell of almost every description. During this advance my horse was shot under me, from which, and another wound received at the Cowan house, he died during the day. In advancing upon and attacking the enemy under such a fire, my brigade found it impossible

Brigadier General Daniel S. Donelson, CSA, commanding brigade. Library of Congress.

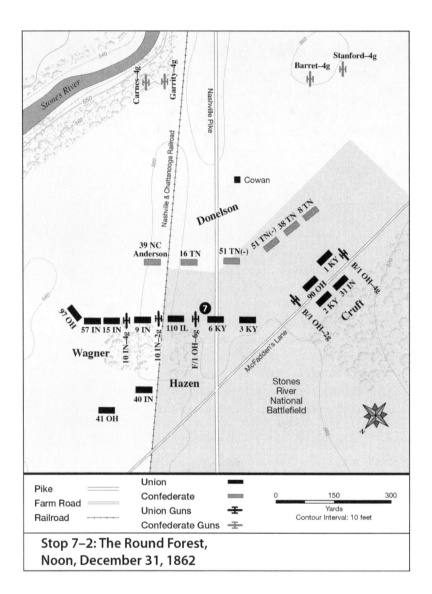

Stop 7–2: The Round Forest,
Noon, December 31, 1862

to preserve its alignment, because of the walls of the burnt house known as Cowan's and the yard and garden fence and picketing left standing around and about it; in consequence of which, Savage's [Sixteenth Tennessee] regiment, with three companies of Chester's [Fifty-first Tennessee] regiment, went to the right of the Cowan house, and advanced upon the enemy until they were checked by three batteries of the enemy, with a heavy infantry support, on the hill to the [left] of the railroad [the Round Forest], while the other two regiments (Carter's [Thirty-eighth Tennessee] and Moore's [Eighth Tennessee]), with seven companies of Chester's regiment, went to the left of that house through a most destructive cross-fire, both of artillery and small-arms . . . until they arrived at the open field beyond the cedar brake, in a northwest direction from the Cowan house, when, having exhausted their ammunition, they retired to the Wilkinson pike in order to reform their regiments and replenish their cartridge-boxes.

Colonel Savage's regiment, with three companies of Colonel Chester's, held, in my judgment, the critical position of that part of the field. Unable to advance, and determined not to retire, having received a message from Lieutenant-General Polk that I should in a short time be re-enforced and properly supported, I ordered Colonel Savage to hold his position at all hazards, and I felt it to be my duty to remain with that part of the brigade, holding so important and hazardous a position as that occupied by him. Colonel Savage, finding the line he had to defend entirely too long for the number of men under his command, and that there was danger of his being flanked, either to the right or left, as the one or the other wing presented the weaker front, finally threw out the greater part of his command as skirmishers, as well to deceive the enemy as to our strength in his rear as to protect his long line, and held his position, with characteristic and most commendable tenacity, for over three hours. At the expiration of that time Jackson's brigade came up to my support, but instead of going to the right of the Cowan house and to the support of Colonel Savage, it went to the left of the house and over the ground which the two left regiments and seven companies of my brigade had already gone over. After Jackson's, General Adams' brigade came up to the support of Colonel Savage, when, the latter withdrawing his regiment to make way for it, it attacked the enemy with spirit for a short time, but it was soon driven back in disorder and confusion, Colonel Savage's regiment retiring with it.[19]

There were eventually five brigades (Hazen's, Wagner's Hascall's, Grose's, and Schafer's) and regiments from other brigades defending the Round Forest. Colonel Hazen's report is typical of the fighting in defense of this position.

Report of Col. William B. Hazen, USA, Commanding, Second Brigade, Second Division, Left Wing, Army of the Cumberland

The enemy had by this time taken position about the burnt house, and the action became at my position terrific. The efforts of the enemy to force back my front and cross the cotton-field, out of which my troops had moved, were persistent, and were prevented only by the most unflinching determination upon the part of the Forty-first Ohio and One hundred and tenth Illinois Volunteers to hold their ground to the last. [See Map—Stop 7-1.]

Upon this point, as a pivot, the entire army oscillated from front to rear the entire day. The ammunition of the Forty-first Ohio Volunteers was by this time nearly exhausted, and my efforts to replenish were up to this time fruitless. I dispatched word to the rear that assistance must be given, or we must be sacrificed, as the position I held could not be given up, and gave orders to Lieutenant-Colonel Wiley to fix his bayonets and to Colonel Casey (without bayonets) to club his guns and hold the ground at all hazards, as it was the key of the whole left. The responses satisfied me that my orders would be obeyed so long as any of those regiments were left to obey them. I now brought over the Ninth Indiana from the right, and immediately posted it to relieve the Forty-first Ohio Volunteers. [See Map—Stop 7-2.]

Colonel William B. Hazen, USA, commanding brigade. National Archives.

A few discharges from the fresh regiments sufficed to check the foe, who drew out of our range, and . . . [a] lull and rest came acceptably to our troops upon the left, their advance upon the right having also been checked.[20]

It was after Donelson's attack that Bragg decided to move four brigades of Maj. Gen. John C. Breckinridge's division to this side of Stones River and attach them to Lieut. Gen. Leonidas Polk's corps. Two brigades were brought over the river initially, and then two more followed.

It was then that Polk, with Bragg's concurrence, made the critical decision as to where these reinforcements would be used. The first two brigades, Brig. Gens. Daniel W. Adams's and John K. Jackson's, attacked the Round Forest position. As you view it, Adam's brigade was on the left of the railroad, and Jackson's brigade was on the right.

Report of Brig. Gen. Daniel W. Adams, CSA, Commanding Adams's Brigade, Breckinridge's Division, Hardee's Corps, Army of Tennessee

My brigade . . . was ordered from the right of General Breckinridge's division, to which it belonged, to cross Stone's River, where I was directed to report to Lieutenant-General Polk. In obedience to this order, received from the commanding general, I crossed the river at the ford above the Nashville pike, and finding Lieutenant-General Polk, reported to him in person, and received from him an order to take a battery of the enemy, which was some [1,700] yards in advance of the ford where I had crossed the river, and on an eminence between the Nashville pike and the river. I immediately formed the infantry of my brigade in line of battle in the open plain near the river, and advanced until reaching a place known as Cowan's house, on the pike, where I found the burnt ruins of a large brick house, a close picket fence, and a deep cut in the railroad, which ran parallel with the pike, and the rough and broken ground on the river bank, presented such serious obstacles as prevented my continuing to advance in line of battle. I therefore moved Colonel Gibson's [Thirteenth and Twentieth Louisiana] by the right flank through a gateway in the direction of the river, and formed it in line of battle, with its right resting on the river. I then moved Colonel Fisk's [Sixteenth and Twenty-fifth Louisiana] in

Brigadier General Daniel W.
Adams, CSA, commanding brigade.
Library of Congress.

column of companies up the pike until clear of the obstacles, where I had it formed in line of battle, with its [left] resting on the railroad. The Thirty-second Alabama, having moved by the left flank so as to avoid the burnt buildings, was again formed in line on the left of Colonel Fisk's regiment. Line being again formed, I gave the command to charge the battery, which was promptly executed.

As the men approached the brow of the hill, they came fully in view and range of the enemy's guns, and were checked by a terrible fire from his artillery, posted on the second elevation, about 150 or 200 yards distant. At my repeated command, however, they continued to advance until the enemy opened with a battery from a cedar thicket on my left, and what appeared to be a brigade of infantry, and at the same time they commenced moving down the river in force, apparently to get in rear of my command. Under these circumstances, I continued the fight for a period of about one hour, in which my men fought most gallantly and nobly. Finding that I was overpowered in numbers, with a force of infantry on my front, on my right, and on my left, supporting [batteries] of some fifteen or twenty guns, strongly posted in the cedar thicket on the second eminence on my front, and that my men were being rapidly killed and wounded, and the effort to turn my right likely to prove successful, I had reluctantly to give the command to fall back. Owing to the obstacles before mentioned, some confusion and disorder was created in falling back, which caused some delay in reforming the brigade, much to my regret.

At one time during the engagement a portion of the enemy's line in my front faltered and gave way under the well-directed fire and continued advance of my brigade, and I had strong hopes of success, and pressed the command forward, but the enemy was promptly re-enforced; and, finding it wholly impracticable to take this battery, supported, as it was, on the right and left by heavy forces of infantry.[21]

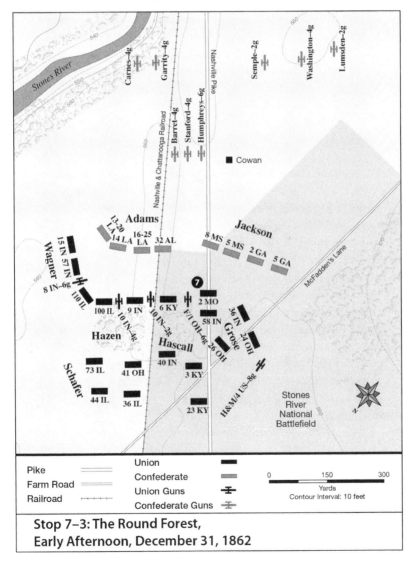

Stop 7–3: The Round Forest, Early Afternoon, December 31, 1862

Report of Col. William B. Hazen, USA—Continued

Another assault was made by the enemy, in several lines, furiously upon our front, succeeding in pushing a strong column past the burnt house, covered by the palisading, to the wood occupied by [Cruft's] brigade and the Sixth Kentucky. All of our troops occupying these woods now fell back, exposing my right flank, and threatening an assault from this point that would sweep away our entire left. General Palmer seeing this danger, and knowing the importance of this position, sent the Twenty-fourth Ohio Volunteers, Colonel Jones, and a fragment of the Thirty-sixth Indiana, under Captain Woodward, to my support. I posted these with the Forty-first Ohio Volunteers, with the left of the line resting upon the Ninth Indiana, and extending to the right and rear, so as to face the advancing column. It was a place of great danger, and our losses were here heavy, including the gallant Colonel Jones, of the Twenty-fourth Ohio Volunteers; but with the timely assistance of Parsons' battery [H and M, 4th US] the enemy was checked, and the [army's] left again preserved from what appeared certain annihilation.

The enemy now took cover in the wood, keeping up so destructive a fire as to make it necessary to retire behind the embankment of the railroad, which only necessitated the swinging to rear of my right, the left having been posted on it when the action commenced in the morning. A sharp fight was kept up from this position till about 2 p.m., when another assault in regular lines, supported by artillery, was made upon this position in force. This assault was resisted much more easily than the previous ones, there being now a large force of our artillery bearing upon this point. The enemy also extended his lines much farther to the left, causing something of a diversion of our troops in that direction. The One hundredth Illinois, Colonel Bartleson, was sent to me by the general commanding the army, which was posted with the One hundred and tenth Illinois and Ninth Indiana, in line to the front, with the right resting on the railroad.[22]

As they had done previously, defenders threw back the attacks by Adams's and Jackson's Brigades. One-third of the two brigades' soldiers fell in battle.

By this time, Cruft's brigade, which had been to your right across the field, had moved. As the Confederate attack through the cedars maneuvered behind his position, Cruft moved his brigade to this side of the Nashville Pike. Grose's unit fell back from its position and reformed to your right, where it helped defend the Round Forest. In addition, Hascall's brigade had moved forward and reinforced Hazen and Wagner. Wagner had previously brought his left flank forward so that it rested near the river and provided flanking fire against any Confederate attack.

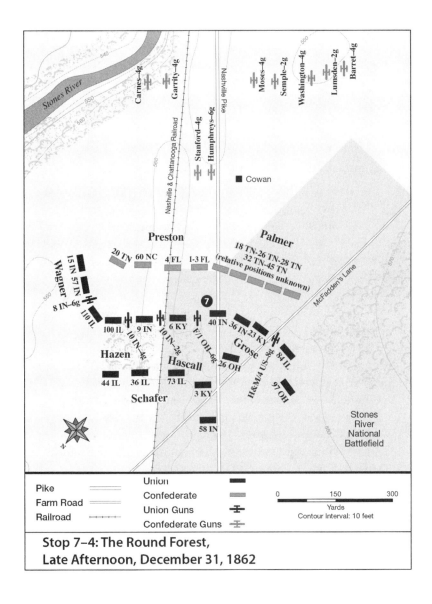

**Stop 7–4: The Round Forest,
Late Afternoon, December 31, 1862**

The longer the fight continued, the stronger this position became. Schafer's brigade and other regiments from Sheridan's division, which had rallied and resupplied ammunition, were added to the defenses. Moreover, that part of Rosecrans's defensive position behind you and parallel to the Nashville Pike had stabilized. As a result, the Union position resembled an inverted *L*. The Round Forest was the juncture of the two parts of the *L*. The short part extended from your location toward McFadden's Ford, and the long part extended northwest, parallel to the pike.

When the next two brigades from Breckinridge's Division, Col. Joseph B. Palmer's and Brig. Gen. William Preston's, crossed the river, they too were committed to another frontal attack against this position. These forces attacked with Preston's to the left of the road (as you view it) and Palmer's on the right.

Report of Brig. Gen. William E. Preston, CSA, Commanding Preston's Brigade, Breckinridge's Division, Hardee's Corps, Army of Tennessee

Not long after noon, we were ordered to cross the river at the ford, and, under the supervision of Major-General Breckinridge, my brigade, on the right, and that of Palmer on my left, were formed in line of battle on the ground originally occupied by Lieutenant-General Polk's command. The right of my brigade rested near the intersection of the Nashville Railroad and turnpike, and extended nearly at right angles westwardly, about half a mile south of Cowan's, or the burnt house.

These dispositions made, the order was given to advance in the direction of the burnt house toward a cedar forest beyond. Wide and open fields intervened, through which the command passed with great animation, in fine order. As we came near the farm-house, heavy batteries of the enemy, supported by strong lines of infantry near a railroad embankment, forming a strong defense, were visible obliquely to the right, on the northeast of the Nashville turnpike. The brigade advanced rapidly and steadily under a destructive fire from the artillery. The Twentieth Tennessee, passing to the right of the house, engaged the enemy with vigor on the right in some woods near the river, capturing some 25 prisoners and clearing the wood. The First and Third Florida, on the extreme left, pressed forward to the cedar forest with but little loss. The two central regi-

Brigadier General William Preston,
CSA, commanding brigade. From
Battles and Leaders of the Civil War,
volume 3.

ments (the Sixtieth North Carolina and Fourth Florida) found great difficulty in pressing through the ruins and strong inclosures of the farm-house, and, retarded by these obstacles and by a fire from the enemy's sharpshooters in front, and a very fierce cannonade, partially enfilading their lines, were for a moment thrown into confusion at the verge of the wood. They halted and commenced firing, but, being urged forward, they responded with loud shouts and gained the cedars. The enemy turned upon the wood a heavy fire from many pieces of artillery, across a field 400 or 500 yards distant, and, though we lost some valuable lives, the brigade maintained its position with firmness in the edge of the wood.

Having met Lieutenant-General Hardee, he ordered me, with Adams' brigade (under Colonel Gibson) added to my command, to hold the wood. We bivouacked for the night, establishing our pickets far in the field and very near the enemy.[23]

When brigade and regimental commanders saw the numbers of dead and wounded from previous offensives, they did not press their attacks against this position. Subsequently, they had far fewer casualties.

Report of Col. William B. Hazen, USA—Continued

At about 4 p.m. the enemy again advanced upon my front in two lines. The battle had hushed, and the dreadful splendor of this advance can only be conceived, as all description must fall vastly short. His right was even with my left, and his left was lost in the distance. He advanced steadily, and as it seemed, certainly to victory. I sent back all my remaining staff successively to ask for support, and braced up my own lines as perfectly as possible. The Sixth Kentucky had joined me from the other side some time previously, and was posted just over the embankment of the railroad. They were strengthened by such fragments of troops as I could pick up until a good line was formed along the track. A portion of Sheridan's division was also but a few hundred yards in rear, replenishing their boxes. A portion of General Hascall's troops was also on the right of the railroad.

The fire of the troops was held until the enemy's right flank came in close range, when a single fire from my men was sufficient to disperse this portion of his line, his left passing far around to our right.[24]

The attacks by Chalmers and then Donelson used a total of 3,400 troops, of which 1,199 were casualties. These assaults were necessary as part of the supporting attack, and they possibly held Union units in position that might have been committed elsewhere. When both of these attacks were repulsed with heavy losses, the futility of frontal assaults against the Round Forest position should have been evident to Polk and Bragg. Demonstrations or limited attacks from that point on would have held the Round Forest defenders in place.

Positioned across the river, Breckinridge's Division had five brigades with a strength of 7,927 soldiers. The effective strength of the four brigades that crossed the river was 6,034 men. This was a powerful combat force and might have made a significant difference if used properly.

Polk's fixation on attacking the Round Forest position and his decision as to the commitment of reserve brigades resulted in the unimaginative, piecemeal commitment of these units. Polk squandered their substantial combat power to no purpose.

A previous critical decision had created the situation that resulted in Polk's critical decision. Bragg's choice that left the main attack with insufficient combat power for unforeseen events has been discussed. Breckinridge's Division, or a significant part of it, would have been the only other force that could have been added to the main attack. If it had not been included, it could have been sent to demonstrate or conduct limited attacks in the vicinity of McFadden's Ford. Used in this way, Breckinridge's troops would have prevented Rosecrans from moving units from his left to the right. Either one of these decisions would have precluded a situation whereby Polk had any decision authority over Breckinridge's four brigades.

Polk's critical decision set the course of the fighting on this part of the battlefield and prevented a significant force from having an effect on a more important part of the battle.

Return to your car for the drive to Stop 8.

Return to the Nashville Pike, turn right, drive northwest on the pike for 1.2 miles to a parking area on the left. Turn into this area, park, leave your car, and walk to the marker for Rosecrans's headquarters.

Stop 8—Rosecrans Decides to Remain

This is the location of the Daniel Cabin, where Rosecrans had his headquarters during the battle. The cabin no longer exists, but a marker indicates the headquarters' location.

The placement of this headquarters provides insight into one of the command and control measures used before the radio came to the battlefield. Rosecrans's headquarters was located beside the Nashville Pike, which was the Army of the Cumberland's major route of supply and communication.

The Daniel Cabin beside Nashville Pike was Rosecrans's headquarters during the battle.

Any reinforcements or supply trains coming from Nashville would use the most direct route—this road. The commander of the reinforcements or supply train would send a member of his staff, or go himself, to the army headquarters for an update on the situation and instructions as to where to position his unit. A headquarters next to the major route into the army's rear area would be easy to find, and it would minimize confusion.

Rosecrans did not spend much time here during the fighting on December 31. He wanted to be close to the action to see what was happening and how best to redistribute his units. On the night after the first day of battle, Rosecrans met with his three wing commanders at the Daniel Cabin. Part of their discussion concerned whether to retreat or remain in position. To retreat would be to surrender the battlefield to Bragg and give the Confederates a victory. A Confederate victory so soon after the disastrous Union defeat at Fredericksburg and the forced withdrawal of Grant's first attempt to capture Vicksburg would create severe political repercussions for President Lincoln, at home and abroad.

The Army of the Cumberland's killed and wounded soldiers numbered 8,580. Some of these losses were offset by the arrival of two infantry brigades from Nashville. A third infantry brigade with a 303-wagon supply train would arrive on January 3. The reserve ammunition supply was ordered issued. The amount was enough to allow for one more day of combat.

Two of Rosecrans's wing commanders (Crittenden and Thomas) were for remaining in position, and one (McCook) was for retreating. Rosecrans's decision was to remain in position. Any other decision would have changed the history of the battle from that point on.

Return to your car for the drive to Stop 9.

Drive back to the Nashville Pike, turn right, and drive southeast for 1.4 miles to a road on your left. Turn left and follow the road back northwest for 0.2 mile to a parking area. Park and walk south from the edge of the parking area for 50 yards, then follow the trail to the left to the marker for Bragg's headquarters.

Stop 9—Bragg Decides to Attack Rosecrans's Left Flank

This was not Gen. Braxton Bragg's headquarters before the battle. His headquarters (main or rear command post) was located in a large house in Murfreesboro that no longer exists. This house would have been Bragg's headquarters from the time the Army of Tennessee arrived in this area until just before the battle, when he moved to this location.

Bragg's headquarters marker.

Today, Bragg's headquarters where you are would be called a forward or battle command post (CP). It was located next to the Nashville Pike and was easy for subordinate commanders and couriers to find. We don't know for sure, but in all probability several tents would have been erected to provide some protection from the winter rains and sleet. Just like Rosecrans, Bragg would not have spent all of his time here; he would have positioned himself where he could observe the fighting.

At this location, Bragg ordered four brigades of Breckinridge's Division to cross to this side of the river on December 31. Here, he made the critical decision to attack Rosecrans's left flank on January 2, 1863.

Bragg had expected that the Army of the Cumberland would evacuate during the night of December 31 / January 1. Wagons were reportedly moving in the Union rear area, and he believed they were doing so in preparation for Rosecrans's ordering a retreat. However, skirmishers sent forward in the morning discovered that the Union army was still in position. The wagons had been moving the wounded back north, not evacuating supplies, ammunition, and equipment prior to a retreat.

The Army of Tennessee's position on January 1 went from Wayne's Hill, 750 yards northeast of you, in a westerly direction for 3,500 yards (2 miles). Seven hundred yards northwest of you, the Confederate position intersected Stones River, the railroad, and the Nashville Pike. From there it continues west.

Rosecrans did not retreat on January 1, but he began making preliminary offensive deployments of units. The most significant deployment was sending Van Cleve's division across Stones River at McFadden's Ford (2,400 yards north) to occupy the high ground north of Wayne's Hill. Occupation of this area gave Rosecrans two advantages. It provided him a staging area east of the river where he could renew his original plan to envelop Bragg's right flank. This terrain also gave Rosecrans a position to place artillery that could dominate and enfilade the right of Bragg's position. Sufficient artillery on this terrain might have forced Bragg to withdraw and reposition most of his units from his center and his right, which could also cause a repositioning of the remaining units.

On Friday morning, January 2, Bragg received a report that a Union force had crossed to the east side of the river and occupied the key terrain north of Wayne's Hill. Doing nothing was not an option, so Bragg decided to attack this force. A successful offensive would drive the Union troops back across the river, give Bragg the key terrain where his artillery could dominate part of Rosecrans's position, and provide a staging area to continue attacks against the Union left.

On December 31 four of the five brigades under Maj. Gen. John C. Breckinridge had been brought to this side of the river and had unsuccessfully attacked the Round Forest position. That night, one of those brigades had recrossed the river to reinforce the remaining unit on Wayne's Hill. When Bragg decided to attack, he sent two more of Breckinridge's brigades back across the river. Breckinridge thus had a force of four brigades, five batteries and one section of his divisional artillery, and ten reinforcing guns from two more batteries for his assault.

Bragg's decision pushed the battle into a third day. Had he not launched this attack, the fighting may have ended in a stalemate on January 2, with each army waiting for the other to retreat or to resume some form of offensive action.

The attack commenced at 4:00 p.m., and Confederate forces enjoyed early success in driving the brigades of Van Cleve's division off the key terrain and back across the river. Breckinridge's brigades continued to press the attack to the river. What happened next was the most dramatic use of artillery in the Western Theater during the war.

Prior to going to Stop 10, follow these instructions if you want to see the ford that Breckinridge's brigades used to cross the river on December 31 and January 2. From the Bragg headquarters marker, walk east through the trees and brush for a short distance to the Stones River Greenway path. Turn right

Stones River ford used by Breckinridge's Division on December 31, 1862, and January 2, 1863.

on the path and walk 200 yards southeast. After 200 yards, turn left, then walk close to the riverbank so that you can see where the ford was.

Return to your car for the drive to Stop 10.

Drive back to the Nashville Pike, turn right, and drive 0.6 mile to the Thompson Lane overpass access road. Turn left and drive to Thompson Lane, then turn right, move to the left lane, and drive 0.2 mile to US 41 / NW Broad Street. Turn left at the US 41 / NW Broad Street intersection, move to the right lane, and drive 0.4 mile to Van Cleve Lane (in 1862 this was McFadden Lane). Turn right and drive 0.6 mile to the parking area and a tall monument. Park, leave your car, and stand beside the two guns next to the parking area. Face in the direction the guns are pointed (east).

Stop 10—Mendenhall Reinforces with Artillery

At the time of the battle this flat plateau, which extends north to south for 800 yards, was composed of cornfields and open ground. Any guns placed here had clear fields of fire to and across the river. The plateau had sufficient depth to allow guns to move forward, back, and laterally as required. The length of the position allowed many guns to be brought into action without overcrowding. All of these factors made this an ideal location to concentrate artillery.

Stones River and McFadden's Ford are 200 yards in front of you at the bottom of the plateau. The road to the ford is 100 yards to your right. Thompson Lane and the bridge over Stones River, neither of which was there in 1863, are 200 yards directly in front of you. The high ground that Breckinridge's attack captured is 900–1000 yards in front of you.

This is the area where Van Cleve's division, with Wood's division to his right at Harker's Ford, was to cross the river on December 31 and envelop Bragg's right flank. However, the immediate success of Bragg's envelopment cancelled this Union attack. Part of Wood's division remained near the Round Forest defensive position. Two of Van Cleve's brigades were ordered to reinforce the Union right. Col. Samuel W. Price's brigade and Lieut. Cortland Livingston's Third Wisconsin Battery were left in position here to guard the ford. On January 1 the rest of Van Cleve's division, under the command of Col. Samuel Beatty, returned to this position. When they were ordered onto the high ground across the river, Price's brigade and Third Wisconsin Battery went with them.

Your current location became a key position due to the initial success of Breckinridge's attack and the retreat of the Union forces back across the river. You are standing at the position of Capt. George R. Swallow's Seventh Indiana Battery (four 10-pound Parrott Rifles and two Napoleons). To Swallow's left were the surviving guns from the three batteries of Negley's division. In position from right to left were Lieut. Alexander Marshall's Battery G, First Ohio (a 12-pound howitzer and a 6-pound Wiard Rifle); Capt. Frederick Schultz's Battery M, First Ohio (three guns, type known; see end notes); and Lieut. Alban A Ellsworth's Battery B, First Kentucky (one 10-pound Parrott Rifle). To the left of Ellsworth's battery was Capt. William E. Standart's Battery B, First Ohio (three guns, type unknown; see end notes). This battery was the left of the artillery line.[25]

To the right of Swallow's Seventh Indiana Battery was Lieut. Cortland Livingston's Third Wisconsin Battery (four 10-pound Parrott Rifles and two 12-poundhowitzers). To this battery's right was Lieut. Charles C. Parsons's Batteries H and M, Fourth US (four 3-inch Ordnance Rifles and four 12-pound howitzers). Capt. James H. Stokes's Chicago Board of Trade Battery (two James Rifles and four 6-pound smoothbore guns) was positioned on Parsons's right. On Stokes's right was Lieut. Norval Osburn's Battery F, First Ohio (four guns, type unknown; see end notes). To Osburn's right, Lieut. George Estep's Eighth Indiana Battery (two 12-pound howitzers and four 6-pound smoothbore guns) was the right of the artillery position above McFadden's Ford.[26]

Two additional batteries were stationed farther to Estep's right. They were Lieut. Alanson J. Stevens's Twenty-sixth Pennsylvania Battery (two James

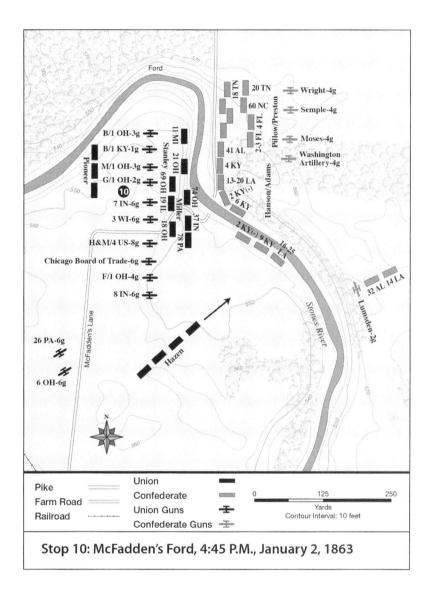

Stop 10: McFadden's Ford, 4:45 P.M., January 2, 1863

Rifles and four 6 pound smoothbore guns) and Capt. Cullen Bradley's Sixth Ohio Battery (four 10-pound Parrott Rifles and two Napoleons). These two batteries delivered oblique and enfilade fire into the left of the attacking Confederate infantry.

The ten batteries at the position above McFadden's Ford had a total of forty-five guns. The two batteries to the right had twelve guns. Captain

Mendenhall had positioned a total of fifty-seven guns to defend the area in the vicinity of McFadden's Ford. These twelve batteries came from the three divisions (Van Cleve's, Palmer's, and Wood's) of the Left Wing, one division (Negley's) of the Center Wing, and from the Pioneer Brigade.

At 4:00 p.m. Breckinridge's Division commenced its attack against Van Cleve's division on the key high ground on the other side of the river. Within thirty minutes the Union defenders had been driven off and were retreating to this side of the river. The area the Confederates had just captured had had several rolling depressions that could have been used to provide protection from Mendenhall's artillery. Flush with victory, instead of consolidating their gains, the Confederate infantry rushed forward in pursuit and into the kill zone of the defending artillery.

Report of Capt. John Mendenhall, USA, Chief of Artillery, Left Wing, Army of the Cumberland

About 4 p.m., while riding along the pike with General Crittenden, we heard heavy firing of artillery and musketry on the left. We at once rode briskly over, and, arriving upon the hill near the ford, saw our infantry retiring before the enemy. The general asked me if I could not do something to relieve Colonel Beatty [commanding Van Cleve's division] with my guns. Captain [George R.] Swallow [Seventh Indiana Battery] had already opened with his battery. I ordered Lieutenant [Charles C.] Parsons [Battery H and M, Fourth US Artillery] to move a little forward and open with his guns; then rode back to bring up Lieutenant [George] Estep, with his Eighth Indiana Battery. Meeting Captain [James St. C.] Morton, with his brigade of Pioneers, he asked for advice, and I told him to move briskly forward with his brigade, and send his battery [Chicago Board of Trade Battery] to the crest of the hill, near the batteries already engaged. The Eighth Indiana Battery took position to the right of Lieutenant Parsons.

I rode to Lieutenant [Alanson J.] Stevens [Twenty-sixth Pennsylvania Battery], and directed him to change front, to fire to the left and open fire; and then to Captain [William E.] Standart [Battery B, First Ohio Artillery], and directed him to move to the left with his pieces; and he took position covering the ford. I found that Captain [Cullen] Bradley [Sixth Ohio Battery] had anticipated my wishes, and had changed front to fire to the left, and opened upon the enemy; this battery was near the railroad. Lieutenant [Cortland] Livingston's

[Third Wisconsin] battery, which was across the river, opened upon the advancing enemy, and continued to fire until he thought he could no longer maintain his position, when he crossed over, one section at a time, and opened fire again. The firing ceased about dark.

During this terrible encounter of little more than an hour in duration, [forty-five] pieces of artillery, belonging to the left wing, the Board of Trade Battery of six guns, and the batteries of General Negley's division, about [six] guns, making a total of about fifty-seven pieces, opened fire upon the enemy. The enemy soon retired, our troops following; three batteries of the left wing crossed the river in pursuit.[27]

The six guns of Captain Swallow's Seventh Indiana Battery were positioned at this location. Swallow's graphic account of the combat at McFadden's Ford reveals the perspective of a battery commander.

Report of Capt. George R. Swallow, USA, Commanding Seventh Indiana Battery, Third Division, Left Wing, Army of the Cumberland

About 4 p.m. I received word that the enemy were advancing in force to attack the left of our wing. Their lines of infantry soon came in full view, and the batteries on my right and left, together with my own, opened a rapid and vigorous fire upon their advancing columns. They soon opened a galling artillery fire upon us from three different points. The battery on my left retired a short distance, and the one on my right commenced to fire, retiring. Seeing this, I ordered the battery to fix prolonge, to fire retiring. About this time the vent of my left piece became filled with friction primers, and was ordered to the rear for repair without my knowledge. The drivers of the other pieces, seeing this piece moving to the rear, supposed the order had been given to retire, and drove some 40 yards to the rear before they could be halted. The order was then given to advance, and one piece was moved by hand to its first position; the rest were limbered and moved to the position first occupied, except the gun that had been ordered to the rear, where all the ammunition was expended except a few rounds of canister. In this engagement we had 1 man killed and 2 wounded.[28]

Within a very short period of time, perhaps fifteen to twenty minutes, the fifty-seven Union guns had brought the Confederate advance to a halt.

Long after the war was over, Confederate veterans remembered being on the receiving end of this artillery. Edwin P. Thompson, a lieutenant in the Sixth Kentucky Infantry of Hanson's Brigade, wrote the best description of this Union cannonade.

Narrative of Lieut. Edwin P. Thompson, CSA, Sixth Kentucky Infantry, Hanson's Brigade, Breckinridge's Division, Hardee's Corps, Army of Tennessee

The main body of the Confederates were on the point of dashing wildly into the river, the very earth trembled as with an exploding mine, and a mass of iron hail was hurled upon them. The rushing host had been checked in mid-career, and now staggered back. The artillery bellowed forth such thunder that men were stunned and could not distinguish sounds. There were falling timbers, crashing arms, the whirring of missiles of every description, the bursting of the dreadful shell, the groans of the wounded, and the shouts of the officers, mingled in one horrid din that beggars description. To

Lieutenant Edwin Porter Thompson, CSA, Sixth Kentucky Infantry. From "Confederate Veteran," July 1889.

endeavor to press forward now was folly, to remain was madness, and the order was given to retreat. Some rushed back precipitately, while others walked away with deliberation, and some even slowly and doggedly, as though they scorned the danger or had become indifferent to life. . . . But they paid toll at every step back over that ground which they had just passed with the shout of victors. . . . The actual combat had lasted less than an hour. . . . It was stated by a participant that the time from giving of the command "Charge bayonets" til the Confederates had been driven back was forty-two minutes. . . . In the short space of time mentioned, and chiefly during the last fifteen minutes, Breckinridge's loss, as stated by himself, was seventeen hundred men—more than thirty-seven per cent.[29]

The sustained deadly fire from Mendenhall's guns stopped, broke up, and then drove back Breckinridge's infantry. Brigadier General Negley's two brigades (Stanley's and Miller's), which had been supporting the artillery, counterattacked and drove the Confederates back to the higher ground and beyond. As it became dark, the key terrain east of the river was again occupied by Union troops.

Though the commanders may not have realized it, the Battle of Stones River was over when the artillery and infantry weapons ceased firing in the early evening hours of January 2.

Time permitting, walk several hundred yards to the left or right of Swallow's battery, and you will be able to visualize where the other batteries were deployed. This will provide you with a greater appreciation for the strength of this position.

This completes your battlefield tour of the critical decisions. For an in-depth tour of the entire battle, see Matt Spruill and Lee Spruill's *Winter Lightning: A Guide to the Battle of Stones River.*

APPENDIX II

UNION ORDER OF BATTLE

ARMY OF THE CUMBERLAND
  Maj. Gen. William S. Rosecrans

RIGHT WING
  Maj. Gen. Alexander McD. McCook

FIRST DIVISION
  Brig. Gen. Jefferson C. Davis

FIRST BRIGADE
  Col. P. Sidney Post
  59th Illinois
  74th Illinois
  75th Illinois
  22d Indiana

SECOND BRIGADE
  Col. William P. Carlin
  21st Illinois
  38th Illinois
  101st Ohio
  15th Wisconsin

THIRD BRIGADE
Col. William E. Woodruff
25th Illinois
35th Illinois
81st Indiana

ARTILLERY
2d Minnesota Battery
5th Wisconsin Battery
8th Wisconsin Battery

SECOND DIVISION
Brig. Gen. Richard W. Johnson

FIRST BRIGADE
Brig. Gen. August Willich (c)
Col. William Wallace
Col. William H. Gibson
89th Illinois
32d Indiana
39th Indiana
15th Ohio
49th Ohio

SECOND BRIGADE
Brig. Gen. Edward N. Kirk (mw)
Col. Joseph B. Dodge
34th Illinois
79th Illinois
29th Indiana
30th Indiana
77th Pennsylvania

THIRD BRIGADE
Col. Philemon P. Baldwin
6th Indiana
5th Kentucky
1st Ohio
93d Ohio

ARTILLERY
5th Indiana Battery
1st Ohio, Battery A
1st Ohio, Battery E

CAVALRY
3d Indiana, Companies G, H, I, and K

THIRD DIVISION
Brig. Gen. Philip H. Sheridan

FIRST BRIGADE
Brig. Gen Joshua W. Sill (k)
Col. Nicholas Greusel
36th Illinois
88th Illinois
21st Michigan
24th Wisconsin

SECOND BRIGADE
Col. Frederick Schaefer (k)
Lieut. Col. Bernard Laiboldt
44th Illinois
73d Illinois
2d Missouri
15th Missouri

THIRD BRIGADE
Col. George W. Roberts (k)
Col. Luther P. Bradley
22d Illinois
27th Illinois
42d Illinois
51st Illinois

ARTILLERY
1st Illinois, Battery C
4th Indiana Battery
1st Missouri, Battery G

CENTER WING
  Maj. Gen. George H. Thomas

FIRST DIVISION
  Maj. Gen. Lovell H. Rousseau

FIRST BRIGADE
  Col. Benjamin F. Scribner
  38th Indiana
  2d Ohio
  33d Ohio
  94th Ohio
  10th Wisconsin

SECOND BRIGADE
  Col. John Beatty
  42d Indiana
  88th Indiana
  15th Kentucky
  3d Ohio

THIRD BRIGADE
  Col. John C. Starkweather (arrived evening December 31)
  24th Illinois
  79th Pennsylvania
  1st Wisconsin
  21st Wisconsin

FOURTH BRIGADE
  Lt. Col. Oliver L. Shepherd
  15th United States, 1st Battalion
  16th United States, 1st Battalion, and Company B, 2d Battalion
  18th United States, 1st Battalion, and Companies A and D, 3d Battalion
  18th United States, 2d Battalion, and Companies B, C, E, and F,
      3d Battalion
  19th United States, 1st Battalion

ARTILLERY
  Kentucky, Battery A
  1st Michigan, Battery A
  5th United States, Battery H

CAVALRY
2d Kentucky (six companies)

SECOND DIVISION
Brig. Gen. James S. Negley

FIRST BRIGADE
Brig. Gen. James G. Spears (arrived morning January 3)
1st Tennessee
2d Tennessee
3d Tennessee
5th Tennessee
6th Tennessee

SECOND BRIGADE
Col. Timothy R. Stanley
19th Illinois
11th Michigan
18th Ohio
69th Ohio

THIRD BRIGADE
Col. John F. Miller
37th Indiana
21st Ohio
74th Ohio
78th Pennsylvania

ARTILLERY
Kentucky, Battery B
1st Ohio, Battery G
1st Ohio, Battery M

THIRD DIVISION
Brig. Gen. Speed S. Fry

FIRST BRIGADE
Col. Moses B. Walker (arrived afternoon December 31)
82d Indiana
12th Kentucky
17th Ohio

31st Ohio
38th Ohio

SECOND BRIGADE (not at Stones River)
Col. John M. Harlan
10th Indiana
74th Indiana
4th Kentucky
10th Kentucky
14th Ohio

THIRD BRIGADE (not at Stones River)
Brig. Gen. James B. Steedman
87th Indiana
2d Minnesota
9th Ohio
35th Ohio

ARTILLERY
1st Michigan, Battery D (arrived afternoon December 31)
1st Ohio, Battery C (not at Stones River)
4th United States, Battery I (not at Stones River)

FOURTH DIVISION (not at Stones River)
Brig. Gen. Robert B. Mitchell

FIRST BRIGADE
Brig. Gen. James D. Morgan
10th Illinois
16th Illinois
60th Illinois
10th Michigan
14th Michigan

SECOND BRIGADE
Col. Daniel McCook
85th Illinois
86th Illinois
125th Illinois
52d Ohio

CAVALRY
2d Indiana, Company A
5th Kentucky
3d Tennessee

ARTILLERY
2d Illinois, Battery I
10th Wisconsin Battery (arrived morning of January 3)

FIFTH DIVISION (not at Stones River)
Brig. Gen. Joseph J. Reynolds

FIRST BRIGADE
Col. Albert S. Hall
80th Illinois
123d Illinois
101st Indiana
105th Ohio

SECOND BRIGADE
Col. Abram O. Miller
98th Illinois
17th Indiana
72d Indiana
75th Indiana

ARTILLERY
18th Indiana Battery
19th Indiana Battery

LEFT WING
Maj. Gen. Thomas L. Crittenden

FIRST DIVISION
Brig. Gen. Thomas J. Wood (w)
Brig. Gen. Milo S. Hascall

FIRST BRIGADE
Brig. Gen. Milo S. Hascall
Col. George P. Buell

100th Illinois
58th Indiana
3d Kentucky
26th Ohio

SECOND BRIGADE
Col. George D. Wagner
15th Indiana
40th Indiana
57th Indiana
97th Ohio

THIRD BRIGADE
Col. Charles G. Harker
51st Indiana
73d Indiana
13th Michigan
64th Ohio
65th Ohio

ARTILLERY
8th Indiana Battery
10th Indiana Battery
6th Ohio Battery

SECOND DIVISION
Brig. Gen. John M. Palmer

FIRST BRIGADE
Brig. Gen. Charles Cruft
31st Indiana
1st Kentucky
2d Kentucky
90th Ohio

SECOND BRIGADE
Col. William B. Hazen
110th Illinois
9th Indiana
6th Kentucky
41st Ohio

THIRD BRIGADE
  Col. William Grose
  84th Illinois
  36th Indiana
  23d Kentucky
  6th Ohio
  24th Ohio

ARTILLERY
  1st Ohio, Battery B
  1st Ohio, Battery F
  4th United States, Batteries H and M

THIRD DIVISION
  Brig. Gen. Horatio P. Van Cleve (w)
  Col. Samuel Beatty

FIRST BRIGADE
  Col. Samuel Beatty
  Col. Benjamin C. Grider
  79th Indiana
  9th Kentucky
  11th Kentucky
  19th Ohio

SECOND BRIGADE
  Col. James P. Fyffe
  44th Indiana
  86th Indiana
  13th Ohio
  59th Ohio

THIRD BRIGADE
  Col. Samuel W. Price
  35th Indiana
  8th Kentucky
  21st Kentucky
  51st Ohio
  99th Ohio

ARTILLERY
7th Indiana Battery
Pennsylvania, Battery B (26th)
3d Wisconsin Battery

CAVALRY
Brig. Gen. David S. Stanley

CAVALRY DIVISION
Col. John Kennett

FIRST BRIGADE
Col. Robert H. G. Minty
2d Indiana
3d Kentucky
4th Michigan
7th Pennsylvania

SECOND BRIGADE
Col. Lewis Zahm
1st Ohio
3d Ohio
4th Ohio

ARTILLERY
1st Ohio, Battery D (section)

RESERVE CAVALRY (under direct command of Brig. Gen. Stanley)
15th Pennsylvania
1st Middle (5th) Tennessee
2d Tennessee

UNATTACHED CAVALRY
4th U.S. Cavalry

PIONEER BRIGADE
Capt. James St. C. Morton
1st Battalion
2d Battalion

3d Battalion
Illinois Light Artillery, Chicago Board of Trade Battery

ENGINEERS AND MECHANICS
1st Michigan

(k) killed
(w) wounded
(mw) mortally wounded
(c) captured[1]

APPENDIX III

CONFEDERATE ORDER OF BATTLE

ARMY OF TENNESSEE
Gen. Braxton Bragg

POLK'S CORPS
Lieut. Gen. Leonidas Polk

FIRST DIVISION
Maj. Gen. Benjamin F. Cheatham

DONELSON'S BRIGADE
Brig. Gen. Daniel S. Donelson
8th Tennessee
16th Tennessee
38th Tennessee
51st Tennessee
84th Tennessee
Carnes's (Tennessee) Battery

STEWART'S BRIGADE
Brig. Gen. Alexander P. Stewart
4th Tennessee and 5th Tennessee
19th Tennessee
24th Tennessee

31st Tennessee and 33d Tennessee
Stanford's (Mississippi) Battery

MANEY'S BRIGADE
   Brig. Gen. George Maney
   1st Tennessee and 27th Tennessee
   4th Tennessee (Provisional Army)
   6th Tennessee and 9th Tennessee
   Tennessee Sharpshooters
   Smith's (Mississippi) Battery

SMITH'S (VAUGHAN'S) BRIGADE
   Col. Alfred J. Vaughan Jr.
   12th Tennessee
   13th Tennessee
   29th Tennessee
   47th Tennessee
   154th Tennessee
   9th Texas
   Allin's (Tennessee) Sharpshooters
   Scott's Tennessee Battery

WITHERS'S DIVISION
   Maj. Gen. Jones M. Withers

DEA'S (LOOMIS'S) BRIGADE
   Col. John Q. Loomis (w)
   Col. John G. Coltart
   19th Alabama
   22d Alabama
   25th Alabama
   26th Alabama
   39th Alabama
   17th Alabama Battalion Sharpshooters
   1st Louisiana (Regulars)
   Robertson's (Florida) Battery

CHALMERS'S BRIGADE
   Brig. Gen. James R. Chalmers (w)
   Col. Thomas W. White
   7th Mississippi

    9th Mississippi
    10th Mississippi
    41st Mississippi
    9th Mississippi Battalion
    Blythe's (44th Mississippi) Regiment
    Garrity's (Alabama) Battery

ANDERSON'S BRIGADE
    Brig. Gen. James P. Anderson
    45th Alabama
    24th Mississippi
    27th Mississippi
    29th Mississippi
    30th Mississippi
    39th North Carolina
    Barret's (Missouri) Battery

MANIGAULT'S BRIGADE
    Col. Arthur M. Manigault
    24th Alabama
    28th Alabama
    34th Alabama
    10th South Carolina
    19th South Carolina
    Waters's (Alabama) Battery

HARDEE'S CORPS
    Lieut. Gen. William J. Hardee

BRECKINRIDGE'S DIVISION
    Maj. Gen. John C. Breckinridge

ADAMS'S BRIGADE
    Brig. Gen. Daniel W. Adams (w)
    Col. Randall L. Gibson
    32d Alabama
    13th Louisiana and 20th Louisiana
    16th Louisiana and 25th Louisiana
    14th Louisiana Battalion
    Washington Artillery, 5th Battery

PALMER'S BRIGADE
Col. Joseph B. Palmer
Brig. Gen. Gideon J. Pillow
18th Tennessee
26th Tennessee
28th Tennessee
32d Tennessee
45th Tennessee
Moses's (Georgia) Battery

PRESTON'S BRIGADE
Brig. Gen. William Preston
1st Florida and 3d Florida
4th Florida
60th North Carolina
20th Tennessee
Wright's (Tennessee) Battery

HANSON'S BRIGADE
Brig. Gen. Roger Hanson (mw)
Col. Robert P. Trabue
41st Alabama
2d Kentucky
4th Kentucky
6th Kentucky,
9th Kentucky
Cobb's (Kentucky) Battery

JACKSON'S BRIGADE (attached to Breckinridge's Division)
Brig. Gen. John K. Jackson
5th Georgia
2d Georgia Battalion Sharpshooters
5th Mississippi
8th Mississippi
Pritchard's (Georgia) Battery
Lumsden's (Alabama) Battery

CLEBURNE'S DIVISION
Maj. Gen. Patrick R. Cleburne

POLK'S BRIGADE
Brig. Gen. Lucius E. Polk
1st Arkansas
13th Arkansas and 15th Arkansas
5th Confederate
2d Tennessee
5th Tennessee
Calvert's Helena (Arkansas) Battery

LIDDELL'S BRIGADE
Brig. Gen. St. John R. Liddell
2d Arkansas
5th Arkansas
6th Arkansas and 7th Arkansas
8th Arkansas
Swett's (Mississippi, Warren Artillery) Battery

JOHNSON'S BRIGADE
Brig. Gen. Bushrod R. Johnson
17th Tennessee
23d Tennessee
25th Tennessee
37th Tennessee
44th Tennessee
Darden's Jefferson (Mississippi) Battery

WOOD'S BRIGADE
Brig. Gen. Sterling A. M. Wood
16th Alabama
33d Alabama
3d Confederate
45th Mississippi
15th Mississippi Battalion, Shaprshooters
Semple's (Alabama) Battery

MCCOWN'S DIVISION
Maj. Gen. John P. McCown

ECTOR'S BRIGADE (Dismounted Cavalry)
Brig. Gen. Matthew D. Ector

10th Texas Cavalry
11th Texas Cavalry
14th Texas Cavalry
15th Texas Cavalry
Douglas's (Texas) Battery

RAINS'S BRIGADE
Brig. Gen. James E. Rains (k)
Col. Robert B. Vance
3d Georgia Battalion
9th Georgia Battalion
29th North Carolina
11th Tennessee
Eufaula (Alabama) Battery

MCNAIR'S BRIGADE
Brig. Gen. Evander McNair
Col. Robert W. Harper
1st Arkansas Mounted Rifles (dismounted)
2d Arkansas Mounted Rifles (dismounted)
4th Arkansas
30th Arkansas
4th Arkansas Battalion
Humphreys's (Arkansas) Battery

CAVALRY
Brig. Gen. Joseph Wheeler

WHEELER'S BRIGADE
Brig. Gen. Joseph Wheeler
1st Alabama
3d Alabama
51st Alabama
8th Confederate
1st Tennessee (attached from Pegram's Brigade)
___ Tennessee Battalion
___ Tennessee Battalion
Wiggins's (Arkansas) Battery

BUFORD'S BRIGADE
Brig. Gen. Abraham Buford
3d Kentucky
5th Kentucky
6th Kentucky

PEGRAM'S BRIGADE
Brig. Gen. John Pegram
1st Georgia
1st Louisiana
1st Tennessee (attached to Wheeler's Brigade)
2d Tennessee (attached to Wharton's Brigade)
12th Tennessee Battalion
Robinson's Howitzer Battery

WHARTON'S BRIGADE
Brig. Gen. John A. Wharton
14th Alabama Battalion
1st Confederate
3d Confederate
2d Georgia
3d Georgia (detachment)
2d Tennessee (attached from Pegram's Brigade)
4th Tennessee
Davis's Tennessee Battalion
8th Texas
Murray's (Tennessee) Regiment
White's (Tennessee) Battery

UNASSIGNED ARTILLERY
Baxter's (Tennessee) Battery
Byrne's (Kentucky) Battery
Gibson's (Georgia) Battery

(k) killed
(w) wounded
(mw) mortally wounded[1]

NOTES

Introduction

1. Stephen W. Sears, *To the Gates of Richmond: The Peninsula Campaign* (New York: Ticknor & Fields, 1992), 6, 106; Allan Nevins, *The War for the Union, Volume 2, War Becomes Revolution 1862–1863* (New York: Charles Scribner's Sons, 1960), 2, 90, 118, 131; US War Department, *The War of the Rebellion: A Compilation of the Official Records of the Union and Confederate Armies*, 70 volumes in 128 parts (Washington, DC: US Government Printing Office, 1880–1901), ser. 1, vol. 11, pt. 1:8–50. (Hereafter cited as *OR*, followed by the appropriate volume and part number. Unless otherwise noted, all citations are from series 1.)

2. *OR*, vol. 9:506–12, 530–35, 540–45, 551.

3. Mark M. Boatner III, *The Civil War Dictionary* (New York: David McKay, 1959), 932–35, 627–28; Herman Hattaway and Archer Jones, *How the North Won: A Military History of the Civil War* (Urbana: University of Illinois Press, 1983), 52.

4. Boatner, *Civil War Dictionary*, 394–97, 591–92, 752–57.

5. *OR*, vol. 11, pt. 2:489–98; *OR*, vol. 12, pt. 2:5–8, 176–79, 551–59.

6. *OR*, vol. 19, pt. 1:144–45; *OR*, vol. 19, pt. 2:590–92, 593–94, 596, 600; D. Scott Hartwig, *To Antietam Creek: The Maryland Campaign of September 1862* (Baltimore: Johns Hopkins University Press, 2012), 50–51.

7. *OR*, vol. 19, pt. 1:149–51; *OR*, vol 19, pt. 2:626–27; Boatner, *Civil War Dictionary*, 310–13.

8. Boatner, *Civil War Dictionary*, 871. Hattaway and Jones, *How the North Won*, 311–14.

9. *OR*, vol. 16, pt. 1:1088–94; *OR*, vol. 20, pt. 1:184–85, 188–200, 663–72.

10. Ibid.

11. Thomas L. Connelly, *Army of the Heartland: The Army of Tennessee, 1861–1862* (Baton Rouge: Louisiana State University Press, 1967), 3.

12. Ibid.

13. Ibid.; Thomas E. Griess, ed., *Atlas for the American Civil War* (Wayne, NJ: Avery, 1987), 1.

14. Griess, *Atlas for the American Civil War*, 3–4.

15. Matt Spruill and Lee Spruill, *Winter Lightning: A Guide to the Battle of Stones River*, 2nd ed. (Knoxville: University of Tennessee Press, 2015), 10–11.

16. Ibid.

17. *OR*, vol. 20, pt. 1:674; James Lee McDonough, *Stones River: Bloody Winter in Tennessee* (Knoxville: University of Tennessee Press, 1980), 69.

18. Boatner, *Civil War Dictionary*, 605–6.

19. *OR*, vol. 20, pt. 1:196.

20. Peter Cozzens, *No Better Place to Die: The Battle of Stones River* (Urbana: University of Illinois Press, 1990), 40, 47, 55; McDonough, *Stones River*, 37, 74; Larry J. Daniel, *Days of Glory: The Army of the Cumberland, 1861–1865* (Baton Rouge: Louisiana State University Press, 2004), 199; John Fitch, *Annals of the Army of the Cumberland* (Philadelphia, 1864; repr., Mechanicsburg, PA: Stackpole Books, 2003), 382; Thomas L. Connelly, *Autumn of Glory: The Army of Tennessee, 1862–1865* (Baton Rouge: Louisiana State University Press, 1971), 42.

21. *OR*, vol. 20, pt. 1:843; Cozzens, *No Better Place to Die*, 41, 48, 50, 52, 64, 71–72, 81, 83; McDonough, *Stones River*, 69, 78, 81.

22. The ten bloodiest battles (killed, wounded, and captured in order are: Gettysburg (51,112), Chickamauga (34,624), Chancellorsville (30,039), Spotsylvania (27,399), Antietam (26,134), Wilderness (25,416), Second Manassas (25,251), Stones River (24,645), Shiloh (23,741), and Fort Donelson (19,455).

Chapter 1

1. Connelly, *Army of the Heartland*, 222. Kenneth A. Hafendorfer, *Battle of Richmond Kentucky, August 30, 1862* (Louisville: KH Press, 2006), 6, 8, 10–13; "The Opposing Forces at Perryville, KY," in *Battles and Leaders of the Civil War: Being for the Most Part Contributions by Union and Confederate Authors,* ed. Robert U. Johnson and Clarence C. Buel (New York, 1884–89; repr., Secaucus, NJ: Castle Books, 1982), 3:30; Kenneth W. Noe, *Perryville: This Grand Havoc of Battle* (Lexington: University Press of Kentucky, 2001), 369–73, 381–82; Joseph Wheeler, "Bragg's Invasion of Kentucky," *Battles and Leaders of the Civil War*, 3:7.

2. Connelly, *Autumn of Glory*, 14–15; Cozzens, *No Better Place to Die*, 8, 29–30; Stanley F. Horn, *The Army of Tennessee* (Indianapolis: Bobbs-Merrill, 1941; repr., Wilmington, NC: Broadfoot, 1987), 188–89.

3. *OR*, vol. 20, pt. 2:386.

4. Ibid., 411–12.

5. Ibid., 413, 418–20; Grady McWhiney, *Braxton Bragg and Confederate Defeat, Volume 1: Field Command* (New York: Columbia University Press, 1969), 344.

6. *OR*, vol. 20, pt. 2:453.

7. Ibid., 461, 458; Ezra J. Warner, *Generals in Gray: Lives of the Confederate Commanders* (Baton Rouge: Louisiana State University Press, 1959), 280; *OR*, vol. 20, pt. 1:658–61.

8. *OR*, vol. 20, pt. 1, 658–61; *OR*, vol. 20, pt. 2:413, 418–20, 447–48.

9. Warner, *Generals in Gray*, 30–31; Connelly, *Autumn of Glory*, 19.

10. Warner, *Generals in Gray*, 242–43; Boatner, *Civil War Dictionary*, 657–58.

11. Warner, *Generals in Gray*, 124–25; Boatner, *Civil War Dictionary*, 374; Steven E. Woodworth, *Jefferson Davis and His Generals: The Failure of Confederate Command in the West* (Lawrence: University Press of Kansas, 1990), 162, 165–66.

12. *OR*, vol. 20, pt. 2:420; Connelly, *Autumn of Glory*, 27.

13. *OR*, vol. 20, pt. 1:661.

14. Warner, *Generals in Gray*, 332–33.

15. Warren E. Grabau, *Ninety-Eight Days: A Geographer's View of the Vicksburg Campaign* (Knoxville: University of Tennessee Press, 2000), 5–6.

16. Ibid.; Hattaway and Jones, *How the North Won*, 311; Steven E. Woodworth, *Nothing But Victory: The Army of the Tennessee, 1861–1865* (New York: Alfred A. Knopf, 2005), 253, 260.

17. Boatner, *Civil War Dictionary*, 232–33; Grabau, *Ninety-Eight Days*, 6; Woodworth, *Nothing But Victory*, 253; Woodworth, *Jefferson Davis and His Generals*, 169.

18. Woodworth, *Jefferson Davis and His Generals*, 179–83; Connelly, *Autumn of Glory*, 38–40; *OR*, vol. 20, pt. 2:449–50.

19. Woodworth, *Jefferson Davis and His Generals*, 183; Horn, *Army of Tennessee*, 192; Connelly, *Autumn of Glory*, 40–41; *OR*, vol. 17, pt. 2:800; *OR*, vol. 20, pt. 2:441, 493; McWhiney, *Braxton Bragg*, 344–45; Edwin C. Bearss, *The Campaign for Vicksburg* (Dayton: Morningside, 1985), 1:145; Bragg's and Johnston's estimates were very close; on December 20, 1862, Rosecrans's strength was 90,441 men (*OR* vol. 20, pt. 2:213).

20. *OR*, vol. 20, pt. 2:413; *OR*, vol. 20, pt. 1:660.

21. John E. Clark Jr., *Railroads in the Civil War: The Impact of Management on Victory and Defeat* (Baton Rouge: Louisiana State University Press, 2001), 20; Vincent J. Esposito, ed., *The West Point Atlas of American Wars* (New York: Praeger, 1959), 1:17; Griess, *Atlas for the American Civil War*, 2; Bearss, *Campaign for Vicksburg*, 1:209; Richard M. McMurry, *Two Great Rebel Armies: An Essay in Confederate Military History* (Chapel Hill: University of North Carolina Press, 1989), 62–63; Connelly, *Autumn of Glory*, 41.

22. Hattaway and Jones, *How the North Won*, 311–14; Woodworth, *Jefferson Davis and His Generals*, 184; Grabau, *Ninety-Eight Days*, 5–6; Woodworth, *Nothing But Victory*, 265.

23. The strength of Stevenson's Division was approximately 7,500 to 10,000 soldiers. In his December 15, 1862, letter to James A. Seddon, Davis uses the number 8,000 (*OR*, vol. 20, pt. 2:449–50). Johnston's December 20, 1862, letter to Davis estimates troop strength at 8,000 or 10,000 (*OR*, vol. 20, pt. 2:459–60). In a postwar article for *Century Magazine*, Johnston uses the number 10,000 (Joseph E. Johnston, "Jefferson Davis and the Mississippi Campaign," in *Battles and Leaders of the Civil War*, 3:474). Kirby Smith states in a December report to Johnston that Stevenson's Division, which had been in Smith's corps, departed with four brigades totaling nine thousand troops. As one of these brigades came from Eastern Tennessee and not Bragg's army, the number subtracted from Bragg could have been 7,500 (*OR*, vol. 20, pt. 2:462–63). Woodworth gives the number as 9,000 (*Jefferson Davis and His Generals*,

183), and Horn uses 10,000 (*Army of Tennessee*, 193); Stevenson submitted a report on January 10, 1863, indicating that his division's strength was 7,693 (*OR*, vol. 17, pt. 2:831; *OR*, vol. 20, pt. 2:258; Bearss, *Campaign for Vicksburg*, 1:172, 187).

24. *OR*, vol. 20, pt. 2:458; *OR*, vol. 20, pt. 1:658–61; *OR*, vol. 20, pt. 2:413, 418–20, 447–48; Horn, *Army of Tennessee*, 196; McDonough, *Stones River*, 64.

25. *OR*, vol. 20, pt. 2:420; Connelly, *Autumn of Glory*, 27; Brian S. Wills, *A Battle from the Start: The Life of Nathan Bedford Forrest* (New York: HarperCollins, 1992), 83; Civil War Trust, Parker's Crossroads, Confederate Order of Battle, http://www.Civilwar.org/battlefields/parkers crossroads.html "The Christmas Raid: December 21, 1862–January 5, 1863," Lexington Rifles: 1862, last modified June 14, 2015, www .lexingtonrifles.com/1862.htm.

26. *OR*, vol. 20, pt. 2:59; Cozzen, *No Better Place to Die*, 45; *OR*, vol. 17, pt. 1:592.

27. *OR*, vol. 17, pt. 1:592.

28. Warner, *Generals in Gray*, 92–93.

29. Wills, *Battle from the Start*, 85–96; *OR*, vol. 17, pt. 1:546–47, 593–97; Horn, *Army of Tennessee*, 194–95.

30. *OR*, vol. 20, pt. 1:154; George B. Davis, Leslie J. Perry, Joseph W. Kirkley, and Calvin D. Cowles, *Atlas to Accompany the Official Records of the Union and Confederate Armies* (Washington, DC, 1891–95; repr., New York: Fairfax, 1983), plate 150.

31. Warner, *Generals in Gray*, 220–21.

32. *OR*, vol. 20, pt. 1:153–58; Horn, *Army of Tennessee*, 195.

33. *OR*, vol. 17, pt. 1:477, 481; Ulysses S. Grant, *Personal Memoirs of U. S. Grant* (New York, 1885; repr., De Capo, 1986), 225.

34. *OR*, vol. 20, pt. 1:189; *OR*, vol. 20, pt. 2:2, 35, 102, 218; William M. Lamers, *The Edge of Glory: A Biography of General William S. Rosecrans, U.S.A.* (New York: Harcourt, Brace, & World, 1961; repr., Baton Rouge: Louisiana State University Press, 1999), 192, 194.

35. *Field Manual 17-95 Cavalry Operations* (Washington, DC: Department of the Army, 1996), chapters 3, 4, and 5.

36. Esposito, *West Point Atlas*, map 76.

37. Daniel, *Days of Glory*, 172; Noe, *Perryville*, 340.

38. Daniel, *Days of Glory*, 172.

39. Earl J. Hess, *Banners to the Breeze: The Kentucky Campaign, Corinth, and Stones River* (Lincoln: University of Nebraska Press, 2000), 117–18.

40. Noe, *Perryville*, 341–42; *OR*, vol. 16, pt. 2:621–22, 626–27, 640–41, 654–55; *OR*, vol. 20, pt. 2:11.

41. Ezra J. Warner, *Generals in Blue: Lives of the Union Commanders* (Baton Rouge: Louisiana State University Press, 1964), 410–11; Lamers, *Edge of Glory*, 16–18.

42. *OR*, vol. 16, pt. 2:640–41; *OR*, vol. 20, pt. 2:19, 22.

43. Daniel, *Days of Glory*, 183; Benjamin F. Cooling, *Fort Donelson's Legacy: War and Society in Kentucky and Tennessee, 1862–1863* (Knoxville: University of Tennessee Press, 1997), 149–50; Thomas B. Van Horne, *History of the Army of the Cumberland: Its Organization, Campaigns, and Battles,* (Cincinnati, 1875; repr., Wilmington, NC: Broadfoot, 1988), 207–9; *OR*, vol. 20, pt. 2:3, 12, 35–36, 58.

44. *OR*, vol. 16, pt. 2:641; *OR*, vol. 20, pt. 2:35, 93, 102.

45. *OR*, vol. 20, pt. 2, 117–18.

46. Ibid., 118.

47. *OR*, vol. 20, pt. 2:123–24; Stephen E. Ambrose, *Halleck: Lincoln's Chief of Staff* (Baton Rouge: Louisiana State University Press, 1962), 107; Cooling, *Fort Donelson's Legacy*, 172–73.

48. Daniel, *Days of Glory*, 184; Henry M. Cist, *The Army of the Cumberland* (New York, 1882; repr., Wilmington, NC: Broadfoot, 1989), 81; *OR*, vol. 20, pt. 1:189; *OR*, vol. 20, pt. 2:9; Davis, Perry, Kirkley, and Cowles, *Atlas to Accompany the Official Records of the Union and Confederate Armies*, plates 24–3, 30–2; Fitch, *Annals of the Army of the Cumberland*, 382.

49. Woodworth, *Jefferson Davis and His Generals*, 187; Horn, *Army of Tennessee*, 196; Cozzens, *No Better Place to Die*, 45; Daniel, *Days of Glory*, 199; *OR*, vol. 20, pt. 2:59, 258; *OR*, vol. 20, pt. 1:189; Cist, *Army of the Cumberland*, 81; Van Horne, *History of the Army of the Cumberland*, 217–18; Fitch, *Annals of the Army of the Cumberland*, 382; Connelly, *Autumn of Glory*, 43, 45.

50. *OR*, vol. 20, pt. 1:663, 772.

51. Connelly, *Autumn of Glory*, 24.

52. *OR*, vol. 23, pt. 2:688–89, 695.

53. McWhiney, *Braxton Bragg*, 345; Archer Jones, *Civil War Command and Strategy: The Process of Victory and Defeat,* (New York: Free Press, 1992), 143, 221; Connelly, *Autumn of Glory*, 38.

54. *OR*, vol. 20, pt. 1:672–73.

55. *OR*, vol. 20, pt. 2:422.

56. *OR*, vol. 20, pt. 1:663, 772–73; Edwin C. Bearss, Nightfall December 28, 1862, Evening, Positions About 10:00 P.M., December 29, 1862, and December 30, 1862, Stones River Troop Movement Maps, 1959.

57. *OR*, vol. 20, pt. 1:201.

58. Ibid., 189–91.

59. *Field Manual 30-0* (Washington, DC: Department of the Army, 2011), ch. 3.

60. *OR*, vol. 20, pt. 1:663–64, 672–73; Edwin C. Bearss, Map: Nightfall, December 28, 1862, Stones River Troop Movement Maps, 1959.

61. Bearss, Map: Positions About 10 P.M., December 29, 1862, Stones River Troop Movement Maps, 1959. Van Horne, *History of the Army of the Cumberland*, 223; Sources provide several names for this road: Nashville Pike (or Turnpike), Murfreesboro Pike, and Nashville-Murfreesboro Pike. Throughout this book it will be called the *Nashville Pike* or just *pike*.

62. *OR*, vol. 20, pt. 1:190–91, 448, 463–64; Cozzens, *No Better Place to Die*, 65–66; Spruill and Spruill, *Winter Lightning*, 18.

63. Bearss, Map: Positions About 10 P.M., December 29, 1862, Stones River Troop Movement Maps, 1959.

64. *OR*, vol. 20, pt. 1:501; Bearss, Map: Positions About 10 P.M., December 29, 1862, Stones River Troop Movement Maps, 1959.

65. Warner, *Generals in Blue*, 207.

66. US Department of the Interior Geological Survey, Map: Murfreesboro, Tennessee, 1:24000.

67. Bearss, Map: Positions About 10 P.M., December 29, 1862, Stones River Troop Movement Maps, 1959; *OR* vol. 20, pt. 1:663, 911.

68. Bears, Map: Positions About 10 P.M., December 29, 1862, Stones River Troop Movement Maps, 1959; Warner, *Generals in Gray*, 123–24.

69. *OR*, vol. 20, pt. 1:825, 829, 835, 837.

70. Ibid., 501, 506–7, 509–10, 511, 512, 514–15; Seventh-third Indiana Infantry File, Regimental Files, Stones River National Battlefield Archives, Murfreesboro, TN.

71. US Department of the Interior Geological Survey, Map: Murfreesboro, Tennessee, 1:24000. Key terrain provides an advantage to the forces occupying or controlling it. To control key terrain it is not necessary to

occupy it physically, but only to prevent the enemy from occupying or controlling it.

72. *OR*, vol. 20, pt. 1:501, 506–7, 509–10, 511, 512, 514–15, 823, 829–30; Cozzens, *No Better Place to Die*, 67.

73. *OR*, vol. 20, pt. 1:191, 448–49, 501, 507; Cozzens, *No Better Place to Die*, 67.

74. Data for December 29, 1862, Murfreesboro, TN, Astronomical Applications Department of the US Naval Observatory website, last modified December 19, 2011, http://aa.usno.navy.mil/index.php.

75. Bearss, Map: Positions About 10 P.M., December 29, 1862, Stones River Troop Movement Maps, 1959.

Chapter 2

1. Bearss, Map: Evening, December 30, 1862, Stones River Troop Movement Maps, 1959.

2. Matt Spruill, *Storming the Heights: A Guide to the Battle of Chattanooga* (Knoxville: University of Tennessee Press, 2003), 185–86.

3. *OR*, vol. 20, pt. 1:92; Cozzens, *No Better Place to Die*, 76–77; Spruill and Spruill, *Winter Lightning*, 22.

4. *OR*, vol. 20, pt. 1:663–64, 773.

5. Ibid., 664; Cozzens, *No Better Place to Die*, 76.

6. *OR*, vol. 20, pt. 1:664.

7. Ibid., 663–64, 773; Spruill and Spruill, *Winter Lightning*, 24–25.

8. *OR*, vol. 20, pt. 1:663–64, 773; Spruill and Spruill, *Winter Lightning*, 29; Bearss, Map: 6:00 A.M., December 31, 1862, Stones River Troop Movement Maps, 1959

9. *OR*, vol. 20, pt. 1:664, 668; Spruill and Spruill, *Winter Lightning*, 29; Bearss, Map: 6:00 A.M., December 31, 1862, Stones River Troop Movement Maps, 1959; Larry J. Daniel, *Battle of Stones River: The Forgotten Conflict Between the Confederate Army of Tennessee and the Union Army of the Cumberland* (Baton Rouge Louisiana State University Press, 2012), 64.

10. *OR*, vol. 20, pt. 1:664, 782; Daniel, *Stones River*, 48–49.

11. *OR*, vol. 20, pt. 1:773, 958–59, 966, 970.

12. Spruill, *Storming the Heights*, 185–86; OR, vol. 20, pt. 1:664.

13. *OR*, vol. 20, pt. 1:674–75.

14. Edwin C. Bearss, *Cavalry Operations—Battle of Stones River* (Washington, DC: National Park Service, 1959), 56–57; *Field Manual 17-95,* chapters 3, 4, and 5.

15. Bearss, Map: 6:00 A.M., December 31, 1862, Stones River Troop Movement Maps, 1959; Spruill and Spruill, *Winter Lightning,* 60.

16. Bearss, Map: 6:00 A.M., December 31, 1862, Stones River Troop Movement Maps, 1959.

17. Bearss, Map: 6:00 A.M., December 31, 1862, Stones River Troop Movement Maps, 1959; *OR,* vol. 20, pt. 1:773, 660, 911–12.

18. Warner, *Generals in Gray,* 199–200.

19. Bearss, Map: 6:00 A.M., December 31, 1862, Stones River Troop Movement Maps, 1959; *OR,* vol. 20, pt. 1:844, 660.

20. Warner, *Generals in Gray,* 53–54.

21. Bearss, Map: 6:00 A.M., December 31, 1862, Stones River Troop Movement Maps, 1959; *OR,* vol. 20, pt. 1:255, 295, 348, 175–77; Spruill and Spruill, *Winter Lightning,* 31.

22. Sun and Moon data for December 31, 1862, Astronomical Applications Department of the US Naval Observatory website, last modified December 19, 2011, http://aa.usno.navy.mil/index.php; Bearss, Maps: 6:00 A.M., December 31, 1862, 7:00 A.M. to 8:00 A.M., December 31, 1862, Stones River Troop Movement Maps, 1959; *OR,* vol. 20, pt. 1:912; Cozzens, *No Better Place to Die,* 83–88.

23. Bearss, Map: 7:00 A.M. to 8:00 A.M., December 31, 1862, Stones River Troop Movement Maps, 1959; Cozzens, *No Better Place to Die,* 89–90.

24. Cozzens, *No Better Place to Die,* 90–91; *OR,* vol. 20, pt. 1:844; Spruill and Spruill, *Winter Lightning,* 45.

25. Bearss, Maps: 9:00 A.M., December 31, 1862, 10:00 A.M. to 11:00 A.M., December 31, 1862, Stones River Troop Movement Maps, 1959; *OR,* vol. 20, pt. 1:845.

26. Bearss, Maps: 9:00 A.M., December 31, 1862, 10:00 A.M. to 11:00 A.M., December 31, 1862, Stones River Troop Movement Maps, 1959.

27. *OR,* vol. 20, pt. 1:912.

28. Spruill and Spruill, *Winter Lightning,* 60; Daniel, *Battle of Stones River,* 95.

29. Spruill and Spruill, *Winter Lightning,* 74; Daniel, *Battle of Stones River,* 151–52.

30. Spruill and Spruill, *Winter Lightning,* 131–32, 145.

31. *OR*, vol. 20, pt. 1:192, 243; Spruill and Spruill, *Winter Lightning*, 22.

32. *OR*, vol. 20, pt. 1:192; Cozzens, *No Better Place to Die*, 76–77; William D. Bickham, *Rosecrans' Campaign with the Fourteenth Army Corps, or, the Army of the Cumberland* (Cincinnati, 1863), 199.

33. *OR*, vol. 20, pt. 1:192; Cozzens, *No Better Place to Die*, 77.

34. *OR*, vol. 20, pt. 1:192; Cozzens, *No Better Place to Die*, 77.

35. *OR*, vol. 20, pt. 1:449, 460, 574; Bearss, Maps: 6:00 A.M., 7:00 A.M. to 8:00 A.M., December 31, 1862, Stones River Troop Movement Maps, 1959; Van Horne, *History of the Army of the Cumberland*, 235–36.

36. *OR*, vol. 20, pt. 1:193.

37. Bickham, *Rosecrans' Campaign*, 209–10; *OR*, vol. 20, pt. 1:93.

38. *OR*, vol. 20, pt. 1:193.

39. Bearss, Maps: 6:00 A.M., 9:00 A.M. 10:00 A.M. to 11:00 A.M., December 31, 1862, Stones River Troop Movement Maps, 1959.

40. *Ibid.*, 193, 377–78; Jim Lewis, "Lincoln's Hard Earned Victory," *Blue and Gray Magazine*, September 2012, 25.

41. *OR*, vol. 20, pt. 1:193, 574.

42. *OR*, vol. 20, pt. 1:193, 449, 460, 574; Daniels, *Battle of Stones River*, 146–52; Cozzens, *No Better Place to Die*, 130–31.

43. *OR*, vol. 20, pt. 1:193, 243.

44. *Ibid.*, 193, 349, 377; Lewis, "Lincoln's Hard Earned Victory," 25; Spruill and Spruill, *Winter Lightning*, 99–100.

45. Warner, *Generals in Blue*, 413; *OR*, vol. 20, pt. 1:177, 378.

46. *OR*, vol. 20, pt. 1:378; Daniel, *Battle of Stones River*, 134.

47. Warner, *Generals in Blue*, 500–501.

48. *OR*, vol. 20, pt. 1:238, 382; John C. Tidball, *The Artillery Service in the War of the Rebellion, 1861–65*, ed. Lawrence M. Kaplan (Yardley, PA: Westholme, 2011), 252; Mark W. Johnson, *That Body of Brave Men: The U.S. Regular Infantry and the Civil War in the West, 1861–1865* (Cambridge, MA: Da Capo, 2003), 274–76; "Union Artillery at the Battle of Stones River," Stones River National Battlefield Archives, Murfreesboro, TN.

49. *OR*, vol. 20, pt. 1:238; Johnson, *That Body of Brave Men*, 276; Alfred Pirtle, "Stones River Sketches," in *Sketches of War History, 1861–1865: Papers Read before the Ohio Commandery of the Military Order of the Loyal Legion of the United States* (Cincinnati: Monfort, 1908), 6:99–100; "Union

Artillery at the Battle of Stones River," Stones River National Battle-field Archives.

50. *OR*, vol. 20, pt. 1:251, 382, 476, 579, 550; Bearss, Maps: 10:00 A.M. to 11:00 A.M., Noon, 1:00 P.M., 2:30 P.M., December 31, 1862, Stones River Troop Movement Maps, 1959; Edwin C. Bearss, *Union Artillery and Breckinridge's Attack—Battle of Stones River* (Washington, DC: National Park Service, 1959), 125; Spruill and Spruill, *Winter Lightning*, 140–48; "Union Artillery at the Battle of Stones River," Stones River National Battlefield Archives; Bickham, *Rosecrans' Campaign*, 258.

51. *OR*, vol. 20, pt. 1:476, 927–28, 939, 947.

52. Lewis, "Lincoln's Hard Earned Victory," 14; Cozzens, *No Better Place to Die*, 151.

53. Bearss, Map: 7:00 A.M. to 8:00 A.M., December 31, 1862, Stones River Troop Movement Maps, 1959; Lewis, "Lincoln's Hard Earned Victory," 15.

54. *OR*, vol. 20, pt. 1:192–93, 460, 516–17, 574.

55. Ibid., 493; Lewis, "Lincoln's Hard Earned Victory," 54.

56. *OR*, vol. 20, pt. 1:543–44; Lewis, "Lincoln's Hard Earned Victory," 54.

57. Spruill and Spruill, *Winter Lightning*, 164–65; Lewis, "Lincoln's Hard Earned Victory," 56.

58. *OR*, vol. 20, pt. 1:658, 664, 705, 753.

59. *Ibid.*, 658, 677, 803, 837, 842, 908–9; Daniel, *Battle of Stones River*, 153, 158; Bearss, Map: 10:00 A.M. to 11:00 A.M., December 31, 1862, Stones River Troop Movement Maps, 1959; Jack D. Welsh, *Medical Histories of Confederate Generals* (Kent, OH: Kent State University Press, 1995), 35.

60. *OR*, vol. 20, pt. 1:676, 710–11, 713–20; Lewis, "Lincoln's Hard Earned Victory," 55.

61. *OR*, vol. 20, pt. 1:407–8, 527–28; Bickham, *Rosecrans' Campaign*, 265.

62. *OR*, vol. 20, pt. 1:664, 674–75, 782; Bearss, Map: 10:00 A.M. to 11:00 A.M., December 31, 1862, Stones River Troop Movement Maps, 1959.

63. Bearss, Map: Noon, December 31, 1862, Stones River Troop Movement Maps, 1959.

64. *OR*, vol. 20, pt. 1:665–66, 690, 783.

65. Ibid., 690, 793.

66. OR, vol. 20, pt. 1:675, 678, 793–94; Daniel, *Battle of Stones River*, 163–65; Cozzens, *No Better Place to Die*, 162–64; Welsh, *Medical Histories of Confederate Generals*, 1.

67. *OR*, vol. 20, pt. 1:674, 838–39, 840.

68. *OR*, vol. 20, pt. 1, 721, 732, 768, 803, 836–37, 842–43, 908–9, 956; Lewis, "Lincoln's Hard Earned Victory," 56; Larry J. Daniel, *Cannoneers in Gray: The Field Artillery of the Army of the Tennessee*, rev. ed. (Tuscaloosa: University of Alabama Press, 2005), 61–62.

69. *OR*, vol. 20, pt. 1:349–50, 467–69, 493–94, 561; Spruill and Spruill, *Winter Lightning*, 172; Lewis, "Lincoln's Hard Earned Victory," 56.

70. *OR*, vol. 20, pt. 1:675, 783–84, 804–5, 811–12; Bearss, Maps: 2:30 P.M., 3:30 P.M., December 31, 1862, Stones River Troop Movement Maps, 1959.

71. Cozzens, *No Better Place to Die*, 164–66.

72. Lewis, "Lincoln's Hard Earned Victory," 57.

73. Matt Spruill, *Guide to the Battle of Chickamauga* (Lawrence: University Press of Kansas, 1993), 113, 118–20.

74. Data for December 31, 1862, Murfreesboro, TN, Astronomical Applications Department of the US Naval Observatory website, last modified December 19, 2011, http://aa.usno.navy.mil/index.php; Bearss, Map: Nightfall, December 31, 1862, Stones River Troop Movement Maps, 1959.

75. *OR*, vol. 20, pt. 1:675, 676–81, 769, 956; "Confederate Artillery at the Battle of Stones River," Stones River National Battlefield Archives.

76. Bearss, Map: Nightfall, December 31, 1862, Stones River Troop Movement Maps, 1959.

77. *OR*, vol. 20, pt. 1:200–201, 393, 416, 442.

78. *OR*, vol. 20, pt. 1:235–42; "Union Artillery at the Battle of Stones River," Stones River National Battlefield Archives. If 6 horses were assigned to pull the limber cart and gun, 557 horses could move 92 guns, or 62 percent of Rosecrans's artillery before the first day's fighting. If the six horses required to pull the second limber and caisson are factored in then 46 guns could be moved.

79. *OR*, vol. 20, pt. 1:242; Bearss, *Union Artillery and Breckinridge's Attack*, 125–26. The table on page 242 of *OR* vol. 20, pt. 1 indicates that the Union artillery fired 20,307 rounds during the battle. Extrapolating from the data provided in *Union Artillery and Breckinridge's Attack*, approximately 2,272 artillery rounds were fired at McFadden's Ford on January 2, 1863. Therefore, approximately 18,000 rounds were fired on December 31, 1862, and January 1, 1863.

80. *OR,* vol. 20, pt. 1:226–29; Bearss, *Cavalry Operations—Battle of Stones River,* 93n13.

81. Gates P. Thruston, "Personal Recollections of the Battle in the Rear at Stones River, Tennessee," in *Sketches of War History, 1861–1865: Papers Read before the Ohio Commandery of the Military Order of the Loyal Legion of the United States* (Cincinnati: Monfort, 1908), 6:227, 229–30; Thomas L. Crittenden, "The Union Left at Stones River", in Johnson and Buel, *Battles and Leaders of the Civil War,* 3:633; *OR,* vol. 20, pt. 1:520.

82. *OR,* vol. 20, pt. 1:242, 667.

83. *OR,* vol. 20, pt. 1:667; David Urquhart, "Bragg's Advance and Retreat," in Johnson and Buel, *Battles and Leaders of the Civil War,* 3:607; Gilbert C. Kniffen, "The Battle of Stones River," in Johnson and Buel, *Battles and Leaders of the Civil War,* 3:630; Connelly, *Autumn of Glory,* 61; Fitch, *Annals of the Army of the Cumberland,* 677.

84. Cozzens, *No Better Place to Die,* 172–73; Lamers, *Edge of Glory,* 235–36; Daniel, *Days of Glory,* 218; Crittenden, "Union Left at Stones River," 3:633–34; John L. Yaryan, "Stones River," in *War Papers: Read before the Indiana Commandery, Military Order of the Loyal Legion of the United States* (Indianapolis, 1898), 1:172–73, 174–75.

85. Lamers, *Edge of Glory,* 235; Cozzens, *No Better Place to Die,* 174; Crittenden, "Union Left at Stones River," 3:634.

86. Cozzens, *No Better Place to Die,* 174; Fitch, *Annals of the Army of the Cumberland,* 677.

Chapter 3

1. Spruill and Spruill, *Winter Lightning,* 182; Bearss, Map: Nightfall January 1, 1863, Stones River Troop Movement Maps, 1959.

2. Spruill and Spruill, *Winter Lightning,* 182; Bearss, Map: Nightfall January 1, 1863, Stones River Troop Movement Maps, 1959; *OR,* vol. 20, pt. 1:667.

3. Cozzens, *No Better Place to Die,* 174.

4. *OR,* vol. 20, pt. 1:455, 471, 476, 504, 508, 722, 742, 751, 756; Spruill and Spruill, *Winter Lightning,* 188.

5. *OR,* vol. 20, pt. 1:575–76; Horn, *Army of Tennessee,* 206; Bearss, *Union Artillery and Breckinridge's Attack,* 12, 180.

6. *OR*, vol. 20, pt. 1:667–68.

7. Ibid., 662.

8. Bearss, *Union Artillery and Breckinridge's Attack*, 13.

9. *OR*, vol. 20, pt. 1:668, 758, 759, 784–85, 797–98, 803, 808, 812, 824, 826, 837; Spruill and Spruill, *Winter Lightning*, 193; "Confederate Artillery at the Battle of Stones River," Stones River National Battlefield Archives. Breckinridge's division's artillery consisted of Lieut. William C. D. Vaught's Washington Artillery Battery (six guns), Lieut. Ruel W. Anderson's Moses's (Georgia) Battery (four guns), Capt. Eldridge E. Wright's Tennessee Battery (four guns), Capt. Robert Cobb's Kentucky Battery (four guns), Capt. Edward P. Byrnes's Kentucky Battery (four guns), and a section (two guns) of Lieut. Harvey H. Cribbs's Lumsden's (Alabama) Battery, bringing the total number guns to twenty-four. Robertson's Florida Battery (six guns) and two sections of Semple's Alabama Battery (four guns) brought ten additional guns to the fight.

10. *OR*, vol. 20, pt. 1:574, 575–76.

11. Ibid., 518, 528–29, 561.

12. *OR*, vol. 20, pt. 1:408, 433; Lanny K. Smith, *The Stones River Campaign, 26 December 1862—5 January 1863: The Union Army* (Jasper, TX: published by the author, 2008), 539.

13. OR, vol. 20, pt. 1:785–86, 796, 808, 812, 826; Spruill and Spruill, *Winter Lightning*, 193–94.

14. *OR*, vol. 20, pt. 1:786; Cozzens, *No Better Place to Die*, 185–86; Daniel, *Battle of Stones River*, 186–87.

15. *OR*, vol. 20, pt. 1:577, 827; Cozzens, *No Better Place to Die*, 185–86; Daniel, *Battle of Stones River*, 186–87.

16. *OR*, vol. 20, pt. 1:599, 798, 808, 812–13, 823; Cozzens, *No Better Place to Die*, 187; Daniel, *Battle of Stones River*, 186–87.

17. *OR*, vol. 20, pt. 1:577; Daniel, *Battle of Stones River*, 187.

18. *OR*, vol. 20, pt. 1:450.

19. Francis B. Heitman, *Historical Register and Dictionary of the United States Army, From Its Organization, September 29, 1789 to March 2, 1903*, 2 vols. (Urbana: University of Illinois Press, 1963).

20. Ibid., 412, 415; Bearss, *Union Artillery and Breckinridge's Attack*, 19–20. Battery M, First Ohio Artillery began the battle with two 12-pound howitzers, one 10-pound Parrott Rifle, and one James Rifle.

21. *OR*, vol. 20, pt. 1:523, 525; Bearss, *Union Artillery and Breckinridge's Attack*, 19–20. Battery F, First Ohio Artillery began the battle with four James Rifles and two 12-pound howitzers.

22. Bearss, Maps 4:00 P.M. and 4:45 P.M., January 2, 1863, Stones River Troop Movement Maps, 1959; Astronomical Applications Department of the US Naval Observatory website, last modified December 19, 2011, http://aa.usno.navy.mil/index.php.

23. Bearss, Map, 4:45 P.M., January 2, 1863, Stones River Troop Movement Maps, 1959.

24. *OR*, vol. 20, pt. 1:251, 476, 521, 582–83; Bearss, *Union Artillery and Breckinridge's Attack*, 58–59, 67, 68–69. Battery B, First Ohio Artillery began the battle with four James Rifles and two 6-pound smoothbore guns.

25. Bearss, *Union Artillery and Breckinridge's Attack*, 21–22, 59.

26. Edwin P. Thompson, *History of the Orphan Brigade* (Louisville, 1898), 180–81.

27. *OR*, vol. 20, pt. 1:408, 424, 434.

28. Ibid., 662.

29. OR, vol.20 pt.1, 674; Spruill and Spruill, *Winter Lightning*, 213.

30. *OR*, vol. 20, pt. 1:700.

31. *Ibid.*, 185. Concerned with the rising water on the night of January 3, Rosecrans brought his units on the high ground back to the west side of the river so that they would not be isolated if attacked.

32. *FM 3-90-1*, Offense and Defense, (Washington, DC: Department of the Army, 2013), 6-1.

33. *OR*, vol. 20, pt. 1:669, 683; Connelly, *Autumn of Glory*, 67.

34. *OR*, vol. 20, pt. 1:177–78, 200, 372, 375, 393, 416, 442–43.

35. *OR*, vol. 20, pt. 1:178–79, 371, 372; McDonough, *Stones River*, 65.

36. *OR*, vol. 20, pt. 1:669.

37. Ibid., 669, 959.

38. David A. Powell and David A. Friedrichs, *The Maps of Chickamauga: An Atlas of the Chickamauga Campaign, Including the Tullahoma Operations, June 22—September 23, 1863* (El Dorado Hills, CA: Savas Beatie, 2009), 2–5.

Chapter 4

1. *OR,* vol. 20, pt. 1, 668–69, 778.

2. Ibid., 692, 778, 959, 969.

3. Cozzens, *No Better Place to Die,* 202; Daniel, *Battle of Stones River,* 203.

4. Powell and Friedrichs, *Maps of Chickamauga,* 2.

5. *OR,* vol. 20, pt. 1, 244, 247, 408.

6. Ibid., 408–9, 618, 638; *OR,* vol. 20, pt. 2, 300.

7. The General Assemblies of Ohio and Indiana both sent resolutions of thanks to Rosecrans and his army (*OR,* vol. 20, pt. 1:187, 188).

8. Ibid., 197, 215, 228, 242; Daniel, *Days of Glory,* 229.

9. OR, vol. 20, pt. 1:185; *OR,* vol. 23, pt. 2:21, 59.

10. *OR,* vol. 20, pt. 2:35, 93.

11. Daniel, *Battle of Stones River,* 203; *OR,* vol. 23, pt. 2:688.

12. Spruill and Spruill, *Winter Lightning,* xv; *OR,* vol. 23, pt. 1:58; Daniel, *Battle of Stones River,* 198.

13. *OR,* vol. 23, pt. 2:757–61.

14. *OR,* vol. 20, pt. 2:311; *OR,* vol. 23, pt. 2:37.

15. *OR,* vol. 23, pt. 2:41, 298; *OR,* vol. 23, pt. 1:410.

16. *OR,* vol. 20, pt. 1:154, 201, 674; Wills, *Battle from the Start,* 87.

17. *OR,* vol. 23, pt. 2:74, 298; Richard A. Baumgartner, *Blue Lightning: Wilder's Mounted Infantry in the Battle of Chickamauga* (Huntington, WVA: Blue Acorn, 2007), 65.

18. Bearss, *Union Artillery and Breckinridge's Attack; OR,* vol. 20, pt. 1:416, 441–42; Tidball, *Artillery Service,* 276.

19. *OR,* vol. 23, pt. 2:21, 59.

20. *A Fortress Like No Other* (Stones River National Battlefield brochure); Lewis, "Lincoln's Hard Earned Victory," 49.

21. Spruill and Spruill, *Winter Lightning,* 217–18; Lewis, "Lincoln's Hard Earned Victory," 7; Abraham Lincoln to William S. Rosecrans, *The Collected Works of Abraham Lincoln,* ed. Roy P. Basler (New Brunswick, NJ: Rutgers University Press, 1953), 6:424.

22. Spruill and Spruill, *Winter Lightning,* 217–18.

Appendix I

1. *OR*, vol. 20, pt. 1:501.

2. Milton T. Russell, "A Charge in Water and Darkness", in *Deeds of Valor from the Records in the Archives of the United States Government: How American Heroes Won the Medal of Honor* . . . , ed. W. F. Beyer and O. F. Keydel (Detroit: Perrien-Keydel Company, 1907) 1:123–24. Some sources spell *Russell* as *Russel*.

3. *OR*, vol. 20, pt. 1:506–7.

4. Ibid., 501.

5. Ibid., 774.

6. Ibid., 912.

7. Ibid., 844–45.

8. Ibid., 192–93.

9. Ibid., 502–3.

10. Ibid., 879. The captured guns were from the Sixth Ohio Battery and were retaken in a counterattack by the Thirteenth Michigan.

11. Ibid., 503.

12. Ibid., 879–80.

13. Daniel A. Brown, *Marked for Future Generations* (Denver, CO: National Park Service Technical Information Center, 1985).

14. *OR*, vol. 20, pt. 1:377–78.

15. Pirtle, "Stones River Sketches," 100–3.

16. Henry V. Freeman, "Some Battle Recollections of Stone's River," in *Military Essays and Recollections: Papers Read before the Commandery of the State of Illinois, MOLLUS* (Chicago, 1894; repr., Wilmington, NC: Broadfoot, 1992), 3:234–37.

17. *OR*, vol. 20, pt. 1:927–28.

18. Ibid., 475–76.

19. Ibid., 710–12.

20. Ibid., 544.

21. Ibid., 793–94.

22. Ibid., 544–45.

23. Ibid., 811–12.

24. Ibid., 545.

25. Battery B, First Ohio began the battle with four James Rifles and two 6-pound smoothbore guns; Battery M, First Ohio began the battle with two 12-pound howitzers, one 10-pound Parrott Rifle, and one James Rifle.

26. Battery F, First Ohio began the battle with four James Rifles and two 12-pound howitzers.

27. *OR*, vol. 20, pt. 1:455–56.

28. Ibid., 579.

29. Edwin P. Thompson, *History of the Orphan Brigade* (Louisville, 1898), 181–82.

Appendix II

1. *OR*, vol. 20, pt. 1:174–82.

Appendix III

1. *OR*, vol. 20, pt. 1:658–61.

BIBLIOGRAPHY

Ambrose, Stephen E. *Halleck: Lincoln's Chief of Staff.* Baton Rouge: Louisiana State University Press, 1962.

Astronomical Applications Department of the US Naval Observatory website. Last modified December 19, 2011. http://aa.usno.navy.mil/index.php.

Baumgartner, Richard A. *Blue Lightning: Wilder's Mounted Infantry in the Battle of Chickamauga.* Huntington, WV: Blue Acorn, 2007.

Bearss, Edwin C. *The Campaign for Vicksburg.* 3 vols. Dayton: Morningside, 1985.

———. *Cavalry Operations—Battle of Stones River.* Washington, DC: National Park Service, 1959.

———. Stones River Troop Movement Maps. Washington, DC: National Park Service, 1959.

———. *Union Artillery and Breckinridge's Attack—Battle of Stones River.* Washington, DC: National Park Service, 1959.

Bickham, William D. *Rosecrans' Campaign with the Fourteenth Army Corps, or, the Army of the Cumberland.* Cincinnati, 1863.

Boatner, Mark M., III. *The Civil War Dictionary.* New York: David McKay, 1959.

Brown, Daniel A. *Marked for Future Generations.* Denver: National Park Service Technical Information Center, 1985.

"Christmas Raid, The: December 21, 1862–January 5, 1863." Lexington Rifles: 1862. Last modified June 14, 2015. www.lexingtonrifles.com /1862.htm.

Cist, Henry M. *The Army of the Cumberland*. New York, 1882. Reprint, Wilmington, NC: Broadfoot, 1989.

Clark, John E., Jr. *Railroads in the Civil War: The Impact of Management on Victory and Defeat*. Baton Rouge: Louisiana State University Press, 2001.

"Confederate Artillery at the Battle of Stones River." Stones River National Battlefield Archives, Murfreesboro, TN.

Connelly, Thomas L. *Army of the Heartland: The Army of Tennessee, 1861–1862*. Baton Rouge: Louisiana State University Press, 1967.

———. *Autumn of Glory: The Army of Tennessee, 1862–1865*. Baton Rouge: Louisiana State University Press, 1971.

Cooling, Benjamin F. *Fort Donelson's Legacy: War and Society in Kentucky and Tennessee, 1862–1863*. Knoxville: University of Tennessee Press, 1997.

Cozzens, Peter. *No Better Place to Die: The Battle of Stones River*. Urbana: University of Illinois Press, 1990.

Crittenden, Thomas L. "The Union Left at Stones River." In Johnson and Buel, *Battles and Leaders of the Civil War*, 3–607.

Daniel, Larry J. *Battle of Stones River: The Forgotten Conflict Between the Confederate Army of Tennessee and the Union Army of the Cumberland*. Baton Rouge: Louisiana State University Press, 2012.

———. *Cannoneers in Gray: The Field Artillery of the Army of the Tennessee*. rev. ed. Tuscaloosa: University of Alabama Press, 2005.

———. *Days of Glory: The Army of the Cumberland, 1861–1865*. Baton Rouge: Louisiana State University Press, 2004.

Davis, George B., Leslie J. Perry, Joseph W. Kirkley, and Calvin D. Cowles. *Atlas to Accompany the Official Records of the Union and Confederate Armies*. Washington, DC, 1891–95. Reprint, New York: Fairfax, 1983.

Esposito, Vincent J., ed. *The West Point Atlas of American Wars*. 2 vols. New York: Praeger, 1959.

Field Manual 3-0 Operations. Washington, DC: Department of the Army, 2008.

Field Manual 3-90-1, Offense and Defense. Washington, DC: Department of the Army, 2013.

Field Manual 17-95 Cavalry Operations. Washington, DC: Department of the Army, 1996.

Fitch, John. *Annals of the Army of the Cumberland.* Philadelphia, 1864. Reprint, Mechanicsburg, PA: Stackpole Books, 2003.

Fortress Like No Other, A. (Stones River National Battlefield brochure)

Freeman, Henry V. "Some Battle Recollections of Stone's River." In *Military Essays and Recollections: Papers Read before the Commandery of the State of Illinois, MOLLUS.* Vol. 3. Chicago, 1894. Reprint, Wilmington, NC: Broadfoot, 1992.

Grabau, Warren E. *Ninety-Eight Days: A Geographer's View of the Vicksburg Campaign.* Knoxville: University of Tennessee Press, 2000.

Grant, Ulysses S. *Personal Memoirs of U. S. Grant.* New York, 1885. Reprint, Da Capo, 1986.

Griess, Thomas E, ed. *West Point Atlas for the American Civil War.* Wayne, NJ: Avery, 1987.

Hafendorfer, Kenneth A. *Battle of Richmond Kentucky, August 30, 1862.* Louisville: KH Press, 2006.

Hartwig, D. Scott. *To Antietam Creek: The Maryland Campaign of September 1862.* Baltimore: Johns Hopkins University Press, 2012.

Hattaway, Herman, and Archer Jones. *How the North Won: A Military History of the Civil War.* Urbana: University of Illinois Press, 1983.

Heitman, Francis B. *Historical Register and Dictionary of the United States Army, From Its Organization, September 29, 1789 to March 2, 1903.* 2 vols. Urbana: University of Illinois Press, 1963.

Hess, Earl J. *Banners to the Breeze: The Kentucky Campaign, Corinth, and Stones River.* Lincoln: University of Nebraska Press, 2000.

Horn, Stanley F. *The Army of Tennessee.* Indianapolis: Bobbs-Merrill, 1941. Reprint, Wilmington, NC: Broadfoot, 1987.

Johnson, Mark W. *That Body of Brave Men: The U.S. Regular Infantry and the Civil War in the West, 1861–1865.* Cambridge, MA: Da Capo, 2003.

Johnson, Robert U., and Clarence C. Buel, eds. *Battles and Leaders of the Civil War: Being for the Most Part Contributions by Union and Confederate Officers.* Vol. 3. New York, 1884–89. Reprint, Secaucus, NJ: Castle Books, 1982.

Johnston, Joseph E. "Jefferson Davis and the Mississippi Campaign." In Johnson and Buel, *Battles and Leaders of the Civil War,* 3–474.

Jones, Archer. *Civil War Command and Strategy: The Process of Victory and Defeat.* New York: Free Press, 1992.

Kniffen, Gilbert C. "The Battle of Stones River." In Johnson and Buel, *Battles and Leaders of the Civil War.*

Lamers, William M. *The Edge of Glory: A Biography of General William S. Rosecrans, U.S.A.* New York: Harcourt, Brace & World, 1961. Reprint, Baton Rouge: Louisiana State University Press, 1999.

Lewis, Jim. "Lincoln's Hard Earned Victory." *Blue and Gray Magazine,* September 2012.

Lincoln, Abraham. *The Collected Works of Abraham Lincoln.* Edited by Roy P. Basler. 8 vols. New Brunswick, NJ: Rutgers University Press, 1953–55.

McDonough, James Lee. *Stones River—Bloody Winter in Tennessee.* Knoxville: University of Tennessee Press, 1980.

McMurry, Richard M. *Two Great Rebel Armies: An Essay in Confederate Military History.* Chapel Hill: University of North Carolina Press, 1989.

McWhiney, Grady. *Braxton Bragg and Confederate Defeat, Volume 1: Field Command.* New York: Columbia University Press, 1969.

Nevins, Allan. *The War for the Union, Volume 2, War Becomes Revolution 1862–1863.* New York: Charles Scribner's Sons, 1960.

Noe, Kenneth W. *Perryville: This Grand Havoc of Battle.* Lexington: University Press of Kentucky, 2001.

"Parker's Cross Roads." Civil War Trust website. http://www.civilwar.org/battlefields/parker-s-cross-roads.html.

Pirtle, Alfred. "Stones River Sketches." In *Sketches of War History, 1861–1865: Papers Read before the Ohio Commandery of the Military Order of the Loyal Legion of the United States.* Vol. 6. Cincinnati: Monfort, 1908.

Powell, David A., and David A. Friedrichs. *The Maps of Chickamauga: An Atlas of the Chickamauga Campaign, Including the Tullahoma Operations, June 22—September 23, 1863.* El Dorado Hills, CA: Savas Beatie, 2009.

Russell, Milton T. "A Charge in Water and Darkness." In *Deeds of Valor from Records in the Archives of the United States Government: How American Heroes Won the Medal of Honor. . . . ,* edited by W. F. Beyer and O. F. Keydel. 2 vols. Detroit: Perrien-Keydel, 1907.

Sears, Stephen W. *To the Gates of Richmond: The Peninsula Campaign.* New York: Ticknor & Fields, 1992.

Seventy-third Indiana Infantry file. Regimental Files. Stones River National Battlefield Archives, Murfreesboro, TN.

Smith, Lanny K. *The Stones River Campaign, 26 December 1862—5 January 1863: The Union Army.* Jasper, TX: published by author, 2008.

Spruill, Matt, and Lee Spruill. *Winter Lightning: A Guide to the Battle of Stones River.* 2nd ed. Knoxville: University of Tennessee Press, 2015.

Spruill, Matt. *Guide to the Battle of Chickamauga.* Lawrence: University Press of Kansas, 1993.

———. *Storming the Heights: A Guide to the Battle of Chattanooga.* Knoxville: University of Tennessee Press, 2003.

Thompson, Edwin P. *History of the Orphan Brigade.* Louisville, 1898.

Thruston, Gates P. "Personal Recollections of the Battle in the Rear at Stones River, Tennessee." In *Sketches of War History, 1861–1865: Papers Read before the Ohio Commandery of the Military Order of the Loyal Legion of the United States.* Vol. 6. Cincinnati: Monfort, 1908.

Tidball, John C. *The Artillery Service in the War of the Rebellion, 1861–65.* Edited by Lawrence M. Kaplan. Yardley, PA: Westholme, 2011.

"Union Artillery at the Battle of Stones River." Stones River National Battlefield Archives, Murfreesboro, TN.

Urquhart, David. "Bragg's Advance and Retreat." In Johnson and Buel, *Battles and Leaders of the Civil War.*

US Department of the Interior Geological Survey. Map: Murfreesboro, Tennessee. 1:24000.

US War Department. *The War of the Rebellion: A Compilation of the Official Records of the Union and Confederate Armies.* 128 vols. Washington, DC, 1880–1901.

Van Horne, Thomas B. *History of the Army of the Cumberland: Its Organization, Campaigns, and Battles. . .* 2 vols. Cincinnati, 1875. Reprint, Wilmington, NC: Broadfoot, 1988.

Warner, Ezra J. *Generals in Blue: Lives of the Union Commanders.* Baton Rouge: Louisiana State University Press, 1964.

———. *Generals in Gray: Lives of the Confederate Commanders.* Baton Rouge: Louisiana State University Press, 1959.

Welsh, Jack D. *Medical Histories of Confederate Generals.* Kent, OH: Kent State University Press, 1995.

Wills, Brian S. *A Battle from the Start: The Life of Nathan Bedford Forrest.* New York: HarperCollins, 1992.

Woodworth, Steven E. *Jefferson Davis and His Generals: The Failure of Confederate Command in the West.* Lawrence: University Press of Kansas, 1990.

————. *Nothing But Victory: The Army of the Tennessee, 1861–1865.* New York: Alfred A. Knopf, 2005.

Yaryan, John L. "Stones River." In *War Papers: Read before the Indiana Commandery, Military Order of the Loyal Legion of the United States.* Indianapolis, 1898.

INDEX

186–87, 189; headquarters location, 188–89; invades Kentucky, 3, 9; letter to Davis, 39; orders army to retreat, 118, 125; personal history, 14; phases of attack, 60; plan for December 31, 54, 57, 83–84, 152, 174; position of army, 100; retreat from Kentucky, 10; telegram to Cooper, 10, 102, 114

Braxton Bragg Drive, 151

Breckinridge, John C., Maj. Gen., CSA (Div Cmdr), 91, 104 115; attacks Round Forest, 88–91, 124, 179–85; attacks vicinity of McFadden's Ford, 102, 105, 108, 110, 125, 194; crosses Stones River, 88, 179, 189; deployment for attack on January 2, 104–5; division of, 12, 13, 45, 50, 54, 56, 58, 59, 67, 86, 122, 138; misuse of division, 186; re-crosses Stones River, 103, 190; repulsed at McFadden's Ford, 110, 112

Breckinridge's Ford, 190

Buckner, Simon B., Maj. Gen., CSA (Div Cmdr), division of, 12

Buell, Don Carlos, Maj. Gen., USA (Army Cmdr), 6, 31, 37; army of, 10; relieved of command, 6, 32; telegram from Halleck, 32

Buford, Abraham, Brig. Gen., CSA (Bde Cmdr), 17; brigade of, 17

Burnside, Ambrose E., Maj. Gen., USA, 1, 2, 34

Carnes, William W. Capt. CSA (Carnes's TN Btry), battery of, 86, 100

Carter, John C., Col., CSA (38th TN), regiment of, 177

Casey, Thomas S., Col., USA (110th IL), 178

Cason Lane, 144

cavalry missions, 29–30, 59

Chalmers, James R., Brig. Gen., CSA (Bde Cmdr): attacks Round Forest, 84, 91, 124, 174; brigade of, 174

Chattanooga (TN), 6, 7, 10, 37, 115, 117, 129; importance of, 4

Cheatham, Benjamin F., Maj. Gen., CSA (Div Cmdr), 115; division of, 12, 146; supporting attack, 56, 57, 59, 174

Chester, John, Col., CSA (51st TN), regiment of, 176, 177

Chickamauga, Battle of, 7, 92

Chickasaw Bluffs, Battle of, 2, 21

Church, Josiah W, Capt., USA (Btry D, 1st MI Arty), battery of, 177

Clairmont Drive, 151

Cleburne, Patrick R., Maj. Gen., CSA, (Div Cmdr): attack repulsed, 66, 174, 180; deployment for attack, 62, 144; division of, 13, 45, 50, 54, 59, 72, 122; main attack, 56, 57, 59, 60, 63, 65, 68, 74, 150, 174; personal history, 62; reaches Nashville Pike, 66; report of, 150–51

Clifton (TN), 25

Cobb, Robert, Capt., CSA (Cobb's KY Btry), battery of, 46, 47, 89, 138, 143

Columbia (KY), 27

Columbia (TN), 25

Cooper, Samuel, Gen., CSA (Adjutant General), 10; telegram from Bragg, 10, 102, 114

Corinth (MS), 6, 19, 33; importance of, 4

Cowan House, 84, 174, 175, 179

Crab Orchard (KY), 31

Critical decision: criterion, xiii-xiv; hierarchy of, xiii-xiv; how presented, xvi; importance of, xiii-xiv; list of, xiv-xv; types, xiv, 119

Crittenden, Thomas L., Maj. Gen., USA (Wing Cmdr), 43, 47, 48, 96, 129, 188; advance from Nashville, 42, 43, 138; critical decision, 40–50, 121, 144; deployment of wing, 138; Left Wing of, 51, 52, 138

Cruft, Charles, Brig. Gen., USA (Bde Cmdr): brigade of, 83; defends Round Forest, 84, 86, 182, 183; retreat of, 86

Cumberland Gap (TN), 4, 10, 31

Cumberland River, 2, 4, 27, 29; as a supply line, 36, 38, 135